P9-DIG-773

THE SCHOOL
I DESERVE

THE SCHOOL
I DESERVE

*Six Young Refugees
and Their Fight for
Equality in America*

....

JO NAPOLITANO

BEACON PRESS, BOSTON

BEACON PRESS
Boston, Massachusetts
www.beacon.org

Beacon Press books
are published under the auspices of
the Unitarian Universalist Association of Congregations.

24 23 22 21   8 7 6 5 4 3 2 1

This book is printed on acid-free paper that meets the uncoated paper
ANSI/NISO specifications for permanence as revised in 1992.

Text design and composition by Kim Arney

Library of Congress Cataloging-in-Publication Data
Name: Napolitano, Jo, author.
Title: The school I deserve : six young refugees and their fight for
equality in America / Jo Napolitano.
Description: Boston : Beacon Press, [2021] | Includes bibliographical references.
Identifiers: LCCN 2020057066 (print) | LCCN 2020057067 (ebook) |
ISBN 9780807024980 (hardcover) | ISBN 9780807024997 (ebook)
Subjects: LCSH: American Civil Liberties Union. | Refugee
children—Education—Pennsylvania—Lancaster. | Refugee children—Civil
rights—Pennsylvania—Lancaster. | Right to education—United States. |
Discrimination in education—Law and legislation—United States.
Classification: LCC LC3733.L36 N36 2021 (print) | LCC LC3733.L36 (ebook) |
DDC 371.826/9140974815—dc23
LC record available at https://lccn.loc.gov/2020057066
LC ebook record available at https://lccn.loc.gov/2020057067

*This book is dedicated to all the children
from foreign lands who call America home*

CONTENTS

FROM COLOMBIA TO COLUMBIA
IN FORTY SHORT YEARS

O F ALL I LEARNED IN THE COURSE OF REPORTING THIS BOOK, ONE statistic made me gasp: it would take a child born into poverty in Colombia at least three hundred years, or eleven generations, to earn the country's average income.

There it stood, dead last, a tiny Colombian flag on the bottom of a chart compiled in 2018, looking almost crushed under the weight of the twenty-nine nations that came before it, including China, India, Brazil, and South Africa. The message was clear: to be born destitute in Colombia is to be nearly condemned, the advancement so minuscule in the course of one person's lifetime, that it could hardly be detected, according to the Organisation for Economic Co-Operation and Development, or OECD.[1]

I was born in Bogota, Colombia's capital, in 1976, and abandoned by my birthmother at a bus stop a day later. Placed in an orphanage where I was barely fed, I weighed just five pounds at three and a half months old. I likely would have died had I not been adopted by a blue-collar couple from New York.

I'd love for the story to stop there. But my father abandoned our family roughly five years later, taking every penny of our savings with him and leaving us deeply indebted. I was raised by a single parent with no college education. Child-support payments were few and medical care an unfathomable luxury in my youth.

Despite these obstacles, I had a far better chance of success in life in America. I had a hard-working and determined mother who fully expected me to live up to my academic ability, no matter our circumstances. But upward mobility would remain a challenge. It would take five generations for a child born into a low-income family in the United States to earn the country's average income.

The OECD found that many children born into poverty around the world are trapped on the lowest rung of the social ladder. They have "less chance to move up and improve their occupational status and earnings" as compared to previous generations of their family. Equally troubling, their parents' income "will be one of the main factors, or the main factor, in explaining their own earnings."

Only one in ten people born to low-educated parents in the countries the OECD examined go on to college, compared to two-thirds of children with highly educated parents. Likewise, about a third of those born to manual workers will become manual workers themselves.

The organization said that upward mobility tended to be better for people born between 1955 and 1975, the year before I came to be. The cure? Education, at least in part.

The organization found that countries that devoted more money to quality education and that targeted those resources to disadvantaged groups had higher rates of what they called "education mobility." The same held true for healthcare.

"There is nothing inevitable about socio-economic advantage or disadvantage being passed from one generation to another, or floors or ceilings remaining persistently sticky," the report read. Policies can be designed to allow people to move up, especially for those at the lowest rung.

Those born to wealth or at least stability might be tempted to greet the OECD's findings with a shrug. We've long known that poor people stay poor and rich people stay rich. But the organization found that a lack of social mobility has a long-lasting and widespread impact on entire nations. Not only can it hurt their overall economic growth, but it means that many talents are missed out on or remain underdeveloped for those at the lowest levels.

And, it must be said, no one chooses the country to which they are born, or whether that nation is embroiled in civil war, is plagued with persistent poverty, or ravaged by crime.

Education catapulted me, in just one generation, from one of the lowest castes in the world to the middle class. I attended a solid public school on Long Island—it offered numerous college-level courses, reasonable class sizes, qualified teachers, and well-maintained facilities—and was more than prepared for college. I won a nearly full ride to Medill at Northwestern University and, in 2016, was named a Spencer Education Fellow at Columbia Journalism School, paid a generous stipend so I could research this book.

I doubt anyone at the orphanage recognized my potential during my stay, given my condition. But that doesn't mean it wasn't there the whole time.

The same, I believe, is true of the impoverished children who arrive in America as refugees, undocumented immigrants, and unaccompanied minors. While they might arrive in the States penniless or nearly so, they are not worthless. They have all the potential one might hope for. All they need is a chance.

THE SCHOOL
I DESERVE

CHAPTER 1

THE LONGEST GOODBYES

K HADIDJA ISSA SPENT THE EARLY MORNING HOURS OF AUGUST 16, 2016, consumed with worry. By the time her lawyer pulled up to her family's modest apartment at 7:00 a.m. to retrieve her, she was wide awake, just as she had been all night. The eighteen-year-old Sudanese refugee, who had moved to Lancaster, Pennsylvania, in the fall of 2015, had no idea what the day would bring. Never before had she seen the inside of a courtroom— not in America and not in her home country. But there she was on that cloudless summer morning, about to embark on a ninety-minute journey to Easton, Pennsylvania, to tell a federal judge why she was suing her local school district just ten months after arriving in the States.

The sinewy teen was too fidgety to eat, but, dutiful as she was, she scrambled eight eggs for her mother and five younger siblings and set the meal aside in a chipped ceramic bowl so that breakfast would be ready when they woke a half hour later. The task complete, she headed back upstairs to smooth her hair and dress for the occasion. Eager to impress the court, she picked out her finest clothes: a pair of dark blue jeans faded at the thigh, a crisp, white long-sleeved shirt a touch too big for her narrow frame, and, to the amusement of her attorneys, a spotless pair of gold-colored high-top sneakers. She tucked her pale blue headscarf behind both ears and headed for the door, trying to remember what her mother, Mariam, had been telling her all week: "Just listen to the lawyers. They'll know what to do."

The day had just begun but already had broken a dozen years of tradition. As the eldest daughter in a Sudanese family, Khadidja was tasked with caring for her younger brothers and sisters and had spent every morning for the past twelve years waking them from sleep and corralling them for breakfast. As soon as she was able, she took to carrying the smallest among them in a sling on her back. By the time the family arrived in Lancaster, only baby Howa was young enough to be secured this way, her legs straddling Khadidja's slender waist as she swept the floor or washed dishes. From the front, it often looked as though the teen had sprouted two tiny feet from her sides.

Though she enjoyed her place in the family hierarchy—a sideways glance from Khadidja could stop a fight in an instant—she aspired to be more than a caretaker. She dreamt of becoming a teacher or a nurse, and she learned from the adult refugees and volunteers who visited her family during their initial months in the States that such a journey could begin in only one place: her local public high school. Khadidja had no doubt she would be admitted. All three of her school-aged siblings were accepted with ease. One by one, they filled out the required paperwork, winced through their immunization shots, and tried their best to pull together the necessary school supplies.

But Khadidja wasn't given that chance. When she met with school officials inside the district's administrative offices in the fall of 2015, they told her through an interpreter she was too old to enroll and should instead look for work. "But I do not want to get a job," she pleaded in Arabic, her voice a high-pitched chirp. "Why would I work if I don't get an education?"

Sure, a low-wage job would allow her to more immediately bridge the gap between her mother's meager wages, the family's welfare benefits, and their ever-growing pile of bills. But Khadidja knew the only way to truly lift her family from poverty was to complete high school and then college, to qualify for a position that would bring home several times the income she would earn on a grimy factory floor.

Even more than that, she wanted to finally take control of her life. Ever since she was a little girl, Khadidja had lived on other people's terms. But there was nothing she could do. School officials refused to back down, hoping to wait her out as they had a hundred other refugees in recent years. One by one, they came from the most troubled hot spots around the globe, hoping for a fresh start in America. And one by one, they were told they had aged out of their high school education, a lie that would cost them their future.

Khadidja, careful to maintain her dignity despite her exasperation, left the building in silent defeat and cried for days about her exclusion. "Why is this happening?" she would ask her mother. "Why won't they let me go to school like everyone else?" Mariam, equally as perplexed as her daughter, had no answers.

Every morning for the next four months, Khadidja watched from the window of her family's apartment as her younger brothers and sisters took off for school, and every afternoon, she waited for them to burst through the front door with new knowledge. She was proud of their achievements, but their success only highlighted her failure. After just a few months in the classroom, they had begun to unravel the complexities of conversational English, so much so that they were losing their mother tongues of Fur (spoken in Darfur, Sudan) and Arabic. Their minds, overstuffed with the language and culture of a new nation, could retain only a finite amount of information before the older files had to be purged.

At first, Mariam held on to the hope that her children would have room in their heads for both, but the notion was shattered when one of her sons, Djalale, sitting down to dinner with a fork in hand, asked his mother what the utensil would be called in Fur. "Oh, my God!" she said through a burst of nervous laughter, in awe of how much her children had already lost.

Within two years, Djalale would change his name to Jalal because it was easier for his American teachers and fellow students to read and pronounce. For him, it was less important to hold on to the past than to be understood in the present.

While her younger brothers and sisters were beginning to change in ways large and small, this was far less true of Khadidja, who held on to every word from her childhood. After living almost half a year in America, she remained linguistically crippled, unable to answer even the simplest of questions in English.

Her native languages were of little use outside her home, leaving her increasingly isolated, but not alone. Khadidja didn't know it, but she wasn't the only refugee who had been barred from the district that year. Mahamed Hassan, a seventeen-year-old from Somalia, also was turned away, alongside several others. Many of the would-be students didn't know that every school-age child in America—no matter where they come from or how they arrive—is entitled by state and federal law to a public education in the community in which they live.

Each state determines its own cutoff age. For some, it's as low as nineteen. For others, it stretches until twenty-six. Students in Pennsylvania can remain in school through the semester in which they turn twenty-one.

But the on-the-ground reality often deviates from the law because older students who struggle with English are not a desirable demographic. They are less likely to graduate high school within four years as compared to their peers, making them a hot potato for schools already struggling to serve their general population. Some administrators will do almost anything to curb their enrollment, routing them to online programs, adult education courses, or job training. What they fail to understand or intentionally ignore is that students who have not yet mastered English have the same educational rights as all others. Black, Hispanic, poor, and differently abled students also lag in high school graduation rates, and none can be refused admission because of their race, ethnicity, economic status, or academic ability.[1] But with few advocates inside and outside the classroom, schools can easily cast non-English-speaking students as outsiders. When this happens, their education morphs from a right to a privilege, one that can be rescinded at will. Suddenly, schools are deemed generous—as opposed to merely law-abiding—for allowing them in.

Of course, the cost of denying a child's education is enormous for both the individual student and their community. Those who are refused admission or who drop out before they can obtain a high school diploma will face dire outcomes: not only will they earn more than $1 million less during the course of their lifetimes as compared to their college-educated peers, but they also will be twice as likely to live in poverty and face triple the unemployment rate.[2]

They also are far more likely to be arrested and to battle a serious chronic illness.[3] But perhaps the most troubling and surprising statistic involves mortality rates: those who fail to earn a high school diploma die, on average, ten years earlier than students who completed college.[4] Outcomes are likely worse for those who also must battle a language barrier.

Khadidja refused to resign herself to such a fate. If she wanted to die early, she reasoned, she would have stayed in Sudan.

Some of the refugees who were turned down by the Lancaster school district dropped the matter and searched for low-wage work; regional poultry plants might be empty without them. But others, including Khadidja and Mahamed, continued to press for admission with the help of their refugee resettlement caseworkers and translators.

After months of cajoling, the district finally agreed to enroll them, though the offer wasn't what they expected. The refugees assumed they would be sent to the district's main high school, McCaskey. The school was divided into two equally impressive buildings, and its pristine campuses had an International School for students just like them who needed help learning English. Khadidja's younger sister, Nouracham, was thriving there. But the district had other plans for older students, whom administrators believed had a slim chance of graduating.

Khadidja, Mahamed, and the other refugees ages seventeen and older were instead assigned to a high-discipline "alternative" school called Phoenix Academy. Housed inside a low-slung black-and-white building that some say better resembled a jail than a school, it was billed as a behavior modification program, one designed to rehabilitate troubled youth. While it was technically part of the school district, Phoenix had been outsourced to a private company called Camelot Education and operated under a far stricter set of rules as compared to McCaskey or most other American high schools.

Phoenix didn't aim to merely educate it students but rather to transform them into something else. According to its 2015–2016 student handbook, the academy pledged to change students' behavior from "anti-social" to "pro-social" and to help them develop the life skills needed to sustain the switch.[5]

Mahamed, handsome and charming with a wavy tuft of hair like a dollop of whipped cream atop his head, had heard about Phoenix through the refugees he met in Lancaster, each of whom had been in the country a year or so longer than he had. Those assigned to the campus or whose siblings had been made to attend couldn't wait to get out. "It's a school for bad kids," they would tell him, meaning chronic truants who were dangerously close to flunking out or students who had gotten into so many fights at McCaskey that they could no longer be trusted at the mainstream campus. Mahamed wondered what he did to warrant such a placement.

Phoenix's attendees, who were made to adhere to a strict dress code, were also closely monitored, subject to daily pat-downs. They were required to remove their shoes upon entry and to bang them together to prove they were free from contraband, including drugs and weapons. Backpacks were banned and students were not permitted to take books home. As a result, they had no homework, hampering their ability to improve their English once the school day ended.

But Phoenix's most controversial practice by far was its Handle With Care protocol, a physical restraint technique that would land students against a wall or on the ground with their hands pulled behind their backs within seconds, even for minor infractions. The procedure was supposed to be a last resort, but teachers and staff were said to have used it without proper cause. Camelot ran nearly forty campuses nationwide, all for so-called at-risk youth, and had been dogged by allegations of abuse in several cities, including nearby Reading, Pennsylvania, where cameras caught a staff member swinging a student into a wall headfirst.

. . . .

The United States District Court in Easton, Pennsylvania, was the last place Khadidja could ever have imagined herself. It was only a year earlier that she was living in a squalid refugee camp halfway around the world.

Born in Darfur, Sudan, in 1998, Khadidja spent her early years trying to outrun a notorious militia hell-bent on exterminating her entire ethnic group. She fled the country at the age of five to escape the tyrannical leadership of President Omar al-Bashir, who, through the militia, had orchestrated the murder, torture, and rape of hundreds of thousands of civilians. Among those he targeted was the Fur ethnic group to which Khadidja and her family belonged.

The violence that pushed Khadidja from her home was not new: civil wars had killed or displaced millions since the mid-1950s. The conflicts, fought on multiple fronts and made worse by drought, reached back generations and had shaped Khadidja's entire life path, even before she was born.

Her mother, Mariam Abdelaziz, had moved with her parents several times in her youth to avoid the bloodshed. Born in 1981, Mariam was accustomed to the constant uprooting. She was forced to abandon her education in the sixth grade after the Janjaweed, or "devils on horseback," leveled her school and surrounding village. With few other options, she married at age fourteen and had Khadidja four years later.

Khadidja was a fussy baby and a chronic crier. As a toddler, she barely ever listened to her mother. Mariam and her husband, Adam Issa, had their second child, Nouracham, two years later. The girls were well loved: a cry from either of the sisters could summon any one of a dozen aunts, uncles, or cousins, all of whom took part in raising them. But their joy would not last. Twenty-five of Mariam's relatives would die in the war, which burst forth with apocalyptic vigor at the start of 2003. The scorched-earth tactics of the Janjaweed left entire communities slaughtered, their belongings looted, their animals killed, and their water supplies contaminated with the bodies of the dead.

With no other viable option, Khadidja and her family abandoned their home, cast aside nearly all of their belongings, and joined thousands of others in a harrowing march out of Sudan to the neighboring country of Chad. "We walked until our feet swelled," Mariam recalled. "If we didn't turn away, we would have been killed. All of us."

When the refugees finally arrived at the Chadian border, they came upon an unexpected obstacle—a valley that, to their surprise, was filled with water. The Darfurians, who could not swim, lined the river in a panic, with the Janjaweed not far behind. Mariam was sure they would be shot or would drown trying to escape. What happened next, she said, was all but biblical. The Chadians who saw the refugees frozen at the water's edge jumped in to save them, carrying each rail-thin Darfurian to the shoreline on their backs. Mariam was amazed when the entire group made it across alive.

After their rescue, the Darfurians, including Khadidja and her family, waited inside Chad for months as the United Nations Human Rights Council processed their paperwork. It was during this time that Mariam realized the benefit of an education: educated refugees were hired by the UN to help build and run the camps. Able to earn a decent paycheck, they were far better off than Mariam and Adam, who had no choice but to beg local villagers to hire them for low-wage manual labor so they could feed their girls. Worse yet, the couple had to leave Khadidja and Nouracham, ages five and three, alone for eight hours a day with little food and water and zero supervision. "I was worried, but I didn't have a solution," Mariam said. "When we came home, everything was happening—crying, fighting. All of the kids were in bad shape at that time because there was nobody there to care for them."

Eventually, the family was admitted to the Goz Amer refugee camp, a fragile, flammable site that would grow to hold twenty thousand people. Plagued with fires and occasionally penetrated by militia groups, the overcrowded camp was one of the most difficult to keep safe. But the bare-bones site was the family's best option, though it could not erase the trauma they had already endured.

The journey had aged Khadidja nearly overnight, transforming her from a petulant little girl to an obedient and precocious child, one who regularly asked her mother the toughest of questions: "Why do we have to go through this? Why did we have to leave our country? When can we go back home?" Mariam, too exhausted to sugarcoat things, told her daughter the truth. "There is no home to go to," she said. "Those who stayed behind were shot dead."

But Khadidja endured, growing more and more accustomed to the camp with each passing week. Her early memories of Goz Amer are hazy, but she recalls caring for her siblings, playing with the other refugees, and watching her father at prayer.

Mariam gave birth to two sons in their first few years at the camp. Bolstered by his strong Muslim faith, Adam was determined to care for his growing family as best he could. He replaced their sweltering UN-issued tent with a far cooler straw hut and eventually found work picking tomatoes and watermelons at a nearby farm, using the money to supplement the family's modest allowances of oil and flour.

The work was grueling and the commute even worse: the farm was an hour away on foot, and to get there, Adam had to cross an unpredictable river. The water level was usually low, reaching only his knees, but it could change in an instant during the rainy season.

In the end, its volatility proved deadly: on August 5, 2007, Adam drowned as he was attempting to return home from work. "He thought he could walk it, but it was up to his neck," Mariam said.

The young widow searched for her husband for eight days. His body was never recovered, though she eventually found his clothes and shoes downstream. "I don't even have a single photo of him," she said. "But if I want to see his face, all I have to do is look at my oldest boy, Ibrahim."

Adam was the only man Mariam had ever loved, and though she was heartsick, her grief quickly morphed into worry as she wondered how she could provide for her family in his absence. With no other choice, she decided to replace Adam on the farm—and to bring her four children with her.

Mariam strapped baby Ibrahim to her back while nine-year-old Khadidja carried her infant brother, Djalale. Nouracham, who was seven at the time, walked alone. The family's workday started at dawn and ended at dusk, bookended by a one-hour walk each way, plus the time it took to cross the river—all for $5 per day. The money was enough to buy a handful of onions, a fistful of meat, and maybe a vegetable or two, but nothing else. The children, who attended school only in the summer when the farm was not in operation, had just three changes of used clothes each, purchased every two years with their maternal grandparents' help. They had little time or opportunity for entertainment.

A refugee who somehow obtained an old television set charged his neighbors five cents apiece to watch it, but at such a high price, Mariam's family caught only a few glimpses. It was where they saw their first images of America, a few flickering pictures of its streets and cities in a show they can no longer remember.

Khadidja, who at first could only babysit her younger brothers and sisters, soon was able to help with the manual labor, spending her youth hunched over in the punishing Chadian sun, sweat pouring down her back as she thrashed wheat alongside her mother. She rarely complained about her circumstance: teenage tantrums are a luxury of the rich.

Though their homeland was in shambles, factions of Mariam's extended family—including her mother—had moved back to Darfur, hoping to resume the life they once had. Mariam and her children joined her mother for nearly two years when Khadidja was in her mid-teens but ultimately returned to the camps. Her mother's home was intact, but much of their village was destroyed and there was no school for her children to attend. Despite these challenges, life moved on: Mariam remarried and had another child, a boisterous daughter named Rania. But she and her husband could not agree on whether to remain at the camp or return to Darfur and the couple soon divorced. Years later, Mariam married for the third time. Her husband, Alsadiq, looked after her children like they were his own. Finally, she had a tender confidant to share in the joys and burdens of parenthood.

In 2012, nine years after they first fled their home in Sudan, Mariam learned that she and her family were going to be relocated to the United States. It took another three years for their paperwork to be processed. When it came time to leave, the family was reluctant, not celebratory: the move meant they would leave behind their aunts, uncles, cousins, and grandparents—and it was unlikely they would ever be reunited.

Mariam also would have to part with Alsadiq—there was a problem with his paperwork—with whom she was pregnant with her sixth child. She considered forgoing the trip, but her parents told her it was unthinkable to turn down the opportunity to live in America. "If you stay here, your children will have no future," Mariam's mother told her. "You must give them a chance."

Unable to bring even a single suitcase on the journey, the family left the camp with nothing. Mariam gave their clothes, furniture, bedsheets, and kitchen supplies to one of her sisters and boarded a plane for America in October 2015 without a single dollar in her pocket.

· · · · · · · · · ·

When the family landed in New York City, they were immediately shuttled 170 miles west to Lancaster, where volunteers had already set up their spartan living quarters inside a plain, three-story red brick building in the worst section of town. Mariam was touched by the care and dedication of the resettlement staff and also by the willingness of complete strangers to prepare her new home, no matter how run-down.

The apartment's walls were cracked and scuffed. Holes in the drywall that had been patched years earlier had never been properly painted and remained an uneven mix of ivory, ecru, and the softest of grays. The kitchen linoleum, worn and split, curled at the edges, and the room had little ventilation: the apartment's entire first floor would fill with smoke each time the family cooked traditional Sudanese dishes, like Nouracham's beloved goat stew. The paint along the downstairs windowsills, applied in several thick layers, was chipped and flaking. Mariam's youngest daughter, Howa, born shortly after the family moved to Pennsylvania, would gnaw on it when no one was looking.

Khadidja, her mother, and her five siblings shared just one bathroom, leaving the children to pound their fists on the door whenever it was in use for too long. The less serious the need—the girls were particularly chided for using it to fix their hair—the louder their name would be screamed until they vacated it.

Everyone shared their bedroom with at least one other person, except for Khadidja, who slept each night in an upstairs hallway with no privacy at all. Her full-sized bed, covered in mismatched but immaculate sherbet-green sheets, was wedged between a worn hand-me-down dresser and a wonky air-conditioning unit that spewed cold air onto the crown of her head. Khadidja never complained about the bed's location. In the States, she and her family were free from persecution. Everything else was aesthetic.

As for her mother, Mariam was required to immediately begin unpaid labor in exchange for all America had given her. She started cleaning a local resettlement office and was later hired as a maid at a nearby hotel, earning $9 an hour. By some measures, the job was a good one. Her boss was flexible and understanding when she needed to tend to a sick child. But he would send her home hours early and without pay if the hotel had too many vacant rooms, so her earnings never met the family's needs.

Mariam did not want her children to be similarly hamstrung. She wanted them enrolled in school as quickly as possible and for Khadidja to set an example as the first to go to college. But the school district's decision to turn her away put their dreams on hold. When they arrived in the States, Khadidja had only a sixth-grade education, just like her mother. And it looked as though she would go no further.

CHAPTER 2

A NEW WORLD

B Y THE TIME KHADIDJA, MAHAMED, AND THEIR FAMILIES REACHED the United States in 2015, they were but a tiny fraction of the 65.3 million people across the globe forcibly displaced from their homes by war or persecution.[1] The number was unprecedented, marking what had been dubbed the greatest humanitarian crisis since World War II. About a third were refugees—more than half were children—and nearly forty-one million were internally displaced, meaning they were on the run within their own countries.

The figure represented one in every 113 people on the planet.[2] If the group, as a whole, formed its own nation, it would be more populous than the United Kingdom.

Those seeking to flee violence and oppression in their homelands often travel to nearby countries for help. Khadidja and her family left Sudan for Chad not only because it was relatively close but also because they hoped to return to Darfur. They couldn't fathom moving to another continent, until it happened.

America has taken in roughly three million refugees since 1980, accepting more than two hundred thousand newcomers that year alone.[3] The number has fluctuated dramatically ever since, pushed up or down in response to global crises and bent by the country's own political will.

The United States admitted 122,000 refugees in 1990 and 85,000 in 1999, but the trend didn't last.[4] The figure dropped to 27,000 after the terrorist attacks of September 11, 2001.[5] And while the number ticked up in the ensuing years—it hit nearly 70,000 the year Khadidja arrived and almost 85,000 in 2016—it never reached the heights of decades past despite the tremendous needs of refugees fleeing conflict, crime, and poverty.[6] Even Syria's well-documented civil war, which began in 2011 and left hundreds of thousands dead, including many children, didn't much prompt the nation to further open its doors.

In response to the crisis, President Barack Obama announced in September 2015 that the United States would admit at least ten thousand Syrian refugees in the fiscal year beginning in October, up from fewer than two thousand the previous year.[7] But his decision was met with tremendous pushback from critics troubled by terror attacks linked to immigrants in Paris, Belgium, and San Bernardino. Twenty-nine Republican governors objected to the notion, as did one Democratic governor, New Hampshire's Maggie Hassan.[8] Texas tried to block the Syrian refugees' resettlement in the state by suing the federal government in late 2015 but a federal judge ultimately dismissed the lawsuit.[9]

At the same time that it was begrudgingly admitting tens of thousands of refugees, the US also was grappling with a massive uptick in unaccompanied minors arriving at the nation's southern border. From 2013 through 2018, nearly three hundred thousand such children had landed inside the country from Guatemala, Honduras, El Salvador, and Mexico. Many left their homelands to escape drug- and gang-related violence, a type of mayhem it was impossible to avoid. Some had been forced to work as lookouts for drug traffickers. Others were made to join gangs against their wishes—and had to kill under threat of death.[10]

Homicide rates in Honduras, El Salvador, and Guatemala were the first, fourth, and fifth highest in the world in 2013.[11] Jacqueline Bhabha, professor of the Practice of Health and Human Rights at Harvard, wrote in July 2014 that living conditions for poor children in drug-infested neighborhoods in Central America "have become as dangerous as those for children trapped in Baghdad, Homs or Aleppo."[12] Those who survive violence or war in their homelands often miss years of education.

More than twenty-five million children were out of school in conflict zones around the world in 2017, UNICEF found. At the elementary school level, South Sudan had the highest rate of out-of-school children, at nearly 72 percent. Next in line was Chad, where half of all eligible children were kept from the classroom.[13] Khadidja had lived in both countries and exemplified this most disturbing trend.

And while 91 percent of children worldwide attended elementary school that year, only 61 percent of refugees had such an opportunity.[14] For low-income countries, the figure was less than 50 percent. The gap continued to widen for older children: just 23 percent of refugee adolescents worldwide attended middle and high school compared to a global average of 84 percent. The figure is even more abysmal in low-income countries, at 9 percent.[15]

Twelve-year-old Cesia Merary Mejia Bachez of El Salvador, who was attending a makeshift school in a crowded encampment in Matamoros, Mexico, in the summer of 2020, wanted to minimize the gap in her learning. A gifted student, she, along with her parents, hoped an American education would help her live up to her potential. "I know there are a lot more opportunities there," Cesia said in Spanish. "Expectations are also greater, but I know I'm up for the challenge."[16] Experts say children who miss years of schooling are often unable to make up for all that is lost. "At no time is education more important than in times of war," said UNICEF Chief of Education Josephine Bourne. "Without education, how will children reach their full potential and contribute to the future and stability of their families, communities and economies?"[17]

. . . .

It was danger that kept Mahamed Hassan indoors as a child growing up in Somalia. The streets of Mogadishu were too unsafe in the early 2000s for him to walk to school. Born in 1998, Mahamed knew only turmoil in his home country, which by the year of his birth had been embroiled in an internal conflict for seven years, ever since President Siad Barre was forced from power in 1991. Feuding clans and their myriad militias tore through the country with abandon, leaving hundreds of thousands dead in the ensuing decades. Famine, which killed more than a quarter million people between October 2010 and April 2012, including 133,000 children under age five, threatened millions more.[18]

Mahamed's mother, Faisa Abdulla, born in 1973, recalls a different Somalia, one that was safe for children to walk the streets of its ancient port-city capital. She remembers when Mogadishu, once referred to as the White Pearl of the Indian Ocean, would draw thousands of tourists each year, with each one eager to wade in its clear turquoise waters. Faisa recalls walking to the cinema with her friends as a teen, filling the movie house with laughter as Hong Kong martial artist Jackie Chan delighted the crowd with slapstick stunts and one-liners. She missed Mogadishu's open-air markets, where butchers would slaughter camels, goats, and lambs each day. "They didn't have refrigerators, so everything was fresh," she said.

But life was not without heartache for Faisa, who was just seven years old when her mother and father died within a month of each other. "They had problems with blood sugar," Faisa recalled. "In Somalia, if you don't have money, you can't go to hospital. No one helps you if you're poor." The second youngest of nine siblings, Faisa saw her academic ambitions die with her parents. She remained enrolled in school only through the fifth grade, though she continued in Madrasa, learning Arabic and studying the Quran for another year. She married at fourteen, her husband five years her senior.

Just like Khadidja's mother, Mariam, Faisa considered herself blessed: her husband, Mahamed, was attentive and kind. Running parallel to her happy marriage was a relatively stable period in Mogadishu's history. In her youth, Faisa was free to dress how she pleased and recalled that the clothing of the era was similar to what would be found in America today. It wasn't until the early '90s, when the country plunged into civil war, that stricter limitations were imposed. Suddenly, Mogadishu was under siege. "I used to see people killed in the street," she said. "I was scared to even go to the market. I was home all of the time." Despite the conflict, the couple had their first child, a girl, in 1992. By 2003, Faisa had eight children in total, though one boy died shortly after birth.

Her husband, a tailor who applied decorative lettering to T-shirts, continued to work through the conflict, despite the bloodshed just beyond his doorstep. Faisa prayed each day that her family wouldn't garner the attention of the Al-Qaeda–linked militant group Al-Shabaab, but the terror organization was already eying the couple's children. Local leaders demanded that her husband hand over their eldest daughter so she could be married to a militant and that their eldest son join in the fighting. "They asked many times and he always said no," Faisa said, smiling proudly.

Finally, after one too many refusals, her husband was shot dead in the street in 2010 in the village where his family lived. "I saw his body after he died," Faisa said. "The neighbors said there was someone killed there. I didn't know who it was. I went to look and saw my husband."

Faisa knew she and her children were in danger. As a single woman with no one to protect her family, she wanted to leave the country immediately, but she didn't have enough money for such a trip. She decided within days of her husband's killing to sell the family's only asset, their modest two-bedroom home.

Panic-stricken, she began locking her children indoors until she could find a buyer. Mahamed, age twelve and already despondent because of his father's death, grew increasingly restless under lockdown. "I just wanted to be able to go outside and hang out with friends," he said. "I wanted to be a kid."

A year passed before his mother unloaded the house for a price she can no longer remember, only that it was enough to pay for eight plane tickets to Cairo where she and her children were registered as refugees. Unlike Khadidja's family who lived in a camp, the Hassans resided in UN-issued housing inside the city proper. Faisa found work as a cook for a local family and earned $150 per month, not nearly enough to feed her children. Meals were regularly skipped. If the family ate breakfast, they would not eat dinner.

Faisa hoped that the move to Cairo would finally allow her children access to an education, but public school cost money, she said, and her family barely had enough to survive. She instead hired a tutor to teach her children Arabic and to study the Quran, but it wasn't enough to satisfy a curious Mahamed. He wanted to run through the hallways of his neighborhood junior high school, chase his friends from one classroom to the next, and smile at the pretty girls who would no doubt be smitten by the handsome boy with the curly brown hair.

When the family learned they would be resettled to the United States, Mahamed believed he would finally have the education he deserved, but he was wrong. A contentious registration meeting with Lancaster school officials in late 2015 ended his high school career before it began. Administrator Jacques Blackman, the school district's de facto enrollment gatekeeper known for refusing older immigrants, told Mahamed he could not be admitted because he did not speak English. Blackman instead referred the teen to a local literacy center.

Mahamed and Blackman differ in their account of the meeting: the teen said the administrator was rude and dismissive while Blackman considered Mahamed willful and disinterested. But no matter how they describe the tenor of the gathering, the outcome was clear: Mahamed was not enrolled.

Back at home, the teen cried to his mother, asking why he'd been unable to attend school in every place he'd ever lived. All he wanted, he told her, was to see the inside of a classroom for the first time. Just like Khadidja, each of his school-aged siblings was admitted to the district without issue. "So why not me?" he asked. Just like Mariam, Faisa had no answers.

Unbeknownst to the Lancaster refugees, immigrant children in other parts of the country were facing similar struggles. Just six months earlier, in April 2015, the New York Civil Liberties Union and Legal Services of Central New York sued the Utica City School District on behalf of six refugee students who had been excluded from the mainstream high school. The federal class action lawsuit claimed that since 2007, Utica, a longtime hub for refugees, had diverted refugees age seventeen and older to alternative programs that were academic dead ends, "despite the fact that New York law guarantees a free public education to youth younger than 21 who have not earned a diploma."[19] State Attorney General Eric T. Schneiderman doubled down on the claims in November 2015, filing a civil rights lawsuit against the school system for discriminating against young immigrants.[20]

Utica school officials cited a lack of funding for their enrollment decisions. "We want to be able to provide the sound basic education, which is guaranteed under the state constitution to all students, including our refugee population," school superintendent Bruce Karam said in an interview with a local radio station after the district was taken to court. "But in order to do this, the funding formula has got to be fixed, and Utica needs to get its fair share."[21]

While the Utica case made the national news, no one took note of what was happening to refugees in Lancaster. Only a year earlier, in September 2014, the school district's superintendent, Pedro Rivera, was honored by the Obama White House as a Latino Educator Champion of Change, in part for increasing graduation rates. "Education's hard work," Rivera said, speaking on a panel at the executive mansion. "Ultimately, at the end of the day, you can't phone it in. You have to be there and be present."[22]

Few on the outside thought Lancaster was discriminating against its own students. Rivera's star was on the rise. Just four months after his visit to the White House, he was nominated by Governor Tom Wolf to serve as Pennsylvania's secretary of education. His selection meant the refugees would have one fewer ally in their fight for equality: how could they or their advocates appeal to the state for help when the man who was responsible for Lancaster's admissions policies had just been named to the highest educational office in Pennsylvania?

CHAPTER 3

BEYOND THE HORSES
AND BUGGIES

M ORE THAN EIGHT MILLION TOURISTS FLOCK TO LANCASTER
County each year, spending well more than $2 billion annually.[1]
Week after week, no matter the season, they pour from their cars to pack
downtown markets before fanning out to Amish Country, treating themselves to nut-covered sweet breads and butter-coated pretzels.

Those who plan ahead often take in a show at the Fulton Theatre, a
stately Victorian playhouse built in 1852 and restored several times over.
The venue draws crowds almost every night of the week. Few visitors know
that it rests on the site of an infamous pre-Revolutionary jail—or that its
grounds were once soaked in blood.

Those who pass through Lancaster for a day or two might also be unaware
of its rich cultural history, especially as it relates to new arrivals. Thousands
of Puerto Ricans immigrated to the area in the 1940s and '50s to work on local farms before branching out to factory and service work.[2] Their numbers
saw a resurgence in the 1980s when New York City's Department of Human
Services paid some of its poorer residents to leave, covering their moving
expenses and bus fare to Pennsylvania.[3] Suddenly, the circumspect Pennsylvania Dutch had brash new neighbors, the self-proclaimed Dutchiricans.

Though the transplants were mostly eager to escape New York's toughest boroughs—many were able to buy their first homes in affordable cities

like Allentown—not everyone was met with a warm embrace: Some Puerto Rican children said their teachers would give up on them the moment they learned of their heritage.[4]

Time, exposure, assimilation, and, eventually, intermarriage at least partially thawed the chill between the two groups.[5] Two-thirds of Pennsylvania's population growth from 1970 to 2010 was made up of Latinos, and the state has absorbed myriad newcomers since then. Lancaster is an internationally recognized hub for refugees in part because of its reasonable housing costs and demand for low-wage labor.

Recent arrivals have relocated from Somalia, Sudan, Burma (or Myanmar), and Syria, among many other countries—and most report a pleasant welcome. The city's annual Race Against Racism is flush with participants, and its refugee fundraisers, sometimes held in the form of raucous benefit concerts, bring in thousands of dollars each year to help defray the costs of resettlement.

Longtime mayor and former hippie Rick Gray, who came to Lancaster in 1972 when he was twenty-seven years old, boasts about its open-mindedness. An early home to the Amish, Huguenots, Quakers, and Mennonites, the city has always accepted newcomers, he said; people of color account for nearly half its population of 59,000 souls.

But while Gray bragged about Lancaster's progressivism, he shied away from taking a stand on important civil rights issues, to the ire of Lancaster residents who wanted the city to move further left. He declined to join the anti-deportation sanctuary city movement that swept across the country in response to Donald Trump's hardline immigration policies. "I don't know what the term 'sanctuary city' actually means," Gray told a local news outlet weeks after Trump's election. "But I can tell you we have no plans to do anything differently than we are already doing."[6]

And Gray never announced his position on the refugees' lawsuit against the local school district, saying in December 2016 that he knew little about it.[7]

Like many liberal hubs around the nation, the city of Lancaster rests inside a staunchly conservative county. A Trump/Pence campaign sign sprang from nearly every exurban lawn in the summer of 2016. In the lead-up to the election, local immigrants, including Muslim refugees who had lived happily in the city for many years, felt the weight of suspicion for the first time since September 11, 2001. And unlike the aftermath of the September 11 attacks, when President George W. Bush made an impassioned plea for tolerance, Trump's rhetoric and tacit support for far-right ideology left racists emboldened and minorities exposed.

Hate crimes rose nationally, with neo-Nazis marching in numbers throughout the country. Perhaps one of their most sinister gatherings was held just forty-five miles away from Lancaster in Harrisburg, Pennsylvania, when some thirty white supremacists gathered on the steps of the state capitol on November 5, 2016, to show their might.

Assembly leaders, flanked by flags adorned with KKK, Confederate, and Nazi symbols, hoped the event would turn deadly: law enforcement agents who infiltrated the group said members of the so-called Aryan Strikeforce considered detonating a suicide bomb to kill some of the hundreds of counterprotesters they believed would be drawn to the gathering.[8] A terminally ill member volunteered to conceal the explosive in his oxygen tank. But for unknown reasons, the plan was never carried out. Several of the men were later indicted on weapons and drug charges.[9]

The incident made the local news. But there was another problem brewing in the city that had gone unreported. The Harrisburg School District had found a way to deny the admission of child refugees by setting up an arbitrary cutoff date for their enrollment. The district would not accept students under age eight after the first ten days of the start of the school year.

Of course, there were exceptions. Students who transferred from schools the Harrisburg district deemed compatible with its own were exempted from the rule. But the policy created an insurmountable barrier for immigrants, whose educational programs could not be vetted.[10]

. . . .

In the lead-up to the 2016 presidential election, anti-immigrant sentiment spewed like poison gas from televisions, radios, computers, and mobile phones throughout the country. Like the nation itself, students across America—including those in Lancaster—fell into two camps. Some became preoccupied with worry for their immigrant friends or for themselves. Others began threatening their peers with deportation, with some calling their Muslim classmates terrorists. Lancaster residents feared that if they did not take action, the hostility would escalate. They knew that contrary to what the mayor espoused, the city had long ago allowed scapegoatism to claim the lives of its most peaceful residents.

Lancaster was the site of one of the most notorious acts of barbarism against native people in American history: Two sets of murders carried out by a group of local Scots-Irish militiamen against the Conestogas in 1763 served as a shameful reminder of what prejudice and complacency could do. And while the slayings took place more than 250 years earlier and the death toll was relatively low, the murders sparked national outrage because the victims were defenseless and had lived peacefully alongside their white neighbors for years.

The Conestogas, made up of several different tribes of native peoples cast out from different parts of the country, felt relatively safe in the area in the years leading up to their slaughter.[11] They had abandoned their native clothing and built cabins of wood plank and bark. Some had converted to Christianity and many spoke English. Their transformation is not unlike that of modern-day refugees who, in their relocation to the States, often adopt a new lifestyle, losing a bit of their original culture.

No matter how cordial the Conestogas' relationship with local whites, the so-called Paxton Rangers had decided, during Pontiac's Rebellion, that all Indians were a threat. In the early morning of December 14, 1763, some fifty Paxton Rangers murdered the Conestogas as they slept. They might have killed more, but the others were sleeping at a nearby farmer's home and at an ironworks to avoid a snowstorm.

Their absence was only a temporary setback: Lancaster County's leadership moved the fourteen survivors—half of them children—to a newly constructed workhouse adjacent to its jail, allegedly for the Conestogas' protection. On December 27, the Paxton Rangers broke into the workhouse, pushed the unarmed men, women, and children into a snow-covered yard, and hacked them to death. Among the Conestogas' possessions were copies of several treaties meant to ensure their safety.

Millions of indigenous people were killed throughout North America in a genocide that spanned hundreds of years, but the slaughter of the Conestogas remains one of the most infamous attacks. The case stands out for several reasons, according to Jack Brubaker, a longtime Lancaster journalist and author of a book on the topic. The Conestogas were supposed to be protected by two layers of government—the commonwealth and the county—but neither stopped the killings or prosecuted those involved, which was unusual for the time, Brubaker said.

"This had not been the case with murders of peaceful Indians previously by white settlers; some were sentenced to jail," he said. "The killing of twenty defenseless Indians, mainly women and small children, in a cold and snowy December, at their village and in Pennsylvania's second-most-prominent town, created a brutal and savage image of Europeans that fair-minded observers recognized at the time—and still mourn today."[12]

The incident receded from memory in the ensuing decades but was resurrected in 2013 by historians on the 250th anniversary of the killings. It was then that prominent civic leaders, including Mayor Gray, met with local native peoples in an academic symposium to discuss the slayings. Two years later, around the same time that Khadidja and Mahamed had arrived in Pennsylvania, a plaque was unveiled at the site of the massacre, where the Fulton Theatre stands today.

On that afternoon, Gray apologized for the city's failure to protect the tribe. "On behalf of my predecessors in Lancaster government, I ask for forgiveness for those things we have done, and those things we should have done," Gray said. "We admit we were wrong."[13]

So prominent was the topic in the minds of local residents in the ensuing years that it was brought up during the city's April 2017 mayoral debates. Lancaster, one candidate said, should consider its history when shaping a new way forward in terms of its treatment of new immigrants. Like the rest of the nation, the city was at a crossroads. It could either take a step forward and bring together its diverse communities or it could shrink back in fear, allowing itself to grow further divided.[14]

. . . .

Roughly three thousand refugees were relocated to Pennsylvania in 2015. The volunteers from local churches who prepared their apartments and filled their cupboards upon arrival told them they were honored to help those in need. And even those Lancaster residents who were not intimately involved in resettlement efforts bristled at the vitriol leveled against the refugees on the national stage. Many erected signs on their front lawns reading, "No matter where you're from, we're glad you're our neighbor," with the message delivered in English, Spanish, and Arabic.

Refugees who were moved by the gesture showed their thanks by leaving candies at their doorsteps. But no amount of goodwill in the city's progressive center could counter the conservatism that surrounded it: when voters hit the polls in November 2016, Trump took Lancaster County by a whopping 20 percent margin. Local immigrants—including new transplants like Khadidja and Mahamed—were on notice.

So too was Sheila Mastropietro, director of the Lancaster office of Church World Service, one of the nation's oldest resettlement agencies. Church World Service, founded in 1946 in the aftermath of World War II, has resettled nearly half a million refugees since its inception. It has offices around the country; Lancaster's opened in 1987.

Back then, the city's refugee population was so small Mastropietro could serve all thirty cases—most of the new arrivals were Hmong or Vietnamese—from a one-woman office inside her home. It wasn't until two years later that she hired an additional caseworker to help with the scores of Jews and Soviet Christians who poured in from the former Soviet Union. Suddenly, the refugee population exploded. By the late 1980s and early '90s, Mastropietro's office was resettling some four hundred refugees per year, with many coming from Russia, Ukraine, and Belarus.

Croats, Bosnians, Albanians, and Kosovars came a few years later, along with Ethiopians, Liberians, and Eritreans. The early 2000s brought the so-called Lost Boys of Sudan along with Meskhetian Turks, originally from Georgia. Burmese and Bhutanese refugees made up a bulk of those who were resettled by her office between 2007 and 2014, and since then, she has seen a dramatic uptick in Somalis and Congolese.

Lancaster's Church World Service had resettled more than six thousand people since it opened, developing intimate relationships with exhausted refugees who needed help with everything from turning on the stove to reading the mail. As the numbers grew, so did Mastropietro's office. By the summer of 2016, the Lancaster office employed thirty-eight people, its staffing tied directly to the number of refugees it was to resettle in a given year.

Like all of the nation's nine major resettlement agencies, including Hebrew Immigrant Aid Society and the International Rescue Committee, Church World Service follows strict guidelines established by the federal government to help refugees become self-sufficient. Caseworkers assist with everything from employment services to housing and school enrollment. The agency's first task is to find each refugee an apartment and to furnish it.

Next, it must supply every newcomer with food and clothing for ninety days. Within that time, the refugees must find jobs, register their children in school, apply for Social Security cards, submit to a medical exam, attend follow-up doctor's appointments if needed, and register for English language classes. The government's goal was for the newcomers to stand on their own.

"It used to be all about self-sufficiency," Mastropietro said in the summer of 2016. "But in the past five years, it's become more than that and I like where it's headed."[15]

Prior to Trump taking office, federal officials wanted families not only to survive in the United States but also to thrive, she said. They wanted refugees to pursue pathways to higher education, including college and trade school, so they could pull themselves up.

One of the most important markers of success, federal officials believed, was for a family to move from their initial apartment to a better one. And nobody wanted this more than Khadidja's mother, Mariam. Though she was grateful for their apartment, it didn't take long for her to realize that she and her children lived in one of the most dangerous neighborhoods in the city.

The 500 block of Green Street was notorious for gang and drug activity. Local residents took to banging on the family's doors and windows at all hours for no discernable reason. The police once demanded entry to the apartment in the middle of the night, convinced that a fugitive sought refuge there. Worse yet, less than a year after their arrival, a young man pulled a knife on Khadidja as she walked home one afternoon. Shortly after, she and her youngest sister, Nouracham, watched ambulances respond to a shooting down the block. Months later, one of their brothers would be robbed of his bicycle by a teen who appeared to flash a gun. Mariam was incensed by all three incidents but was frantic about the holdup. No matter how she tried, she couldn't understand how ordinary American citizens could own firearms in what was supposed to be a safe and developed nation. "Why do they have guns?" she asked. "America is not at war!"

Fearful for her children's safety, moving became Mariam's top priority. She was concerned about the amount of time her young sons spent outside. Her daughters mostly stayed at home helping her, but the boys were gone for hours after school each day. Their mother worried that they could be hurt or coerced into joining the wrong crowd. A new home could change everything. Mariam knew exactly what the family needed: a clean, spacious apartment with a decent backyard and maybe even a second bathroom—but for far less money. Her caseworker told her it was impossible, but Mariam was a believer in miracles and slowly started to ask around.

CHAPTER 4

THE UNINVITED

A MERICA'S REPUTATION AS A LAND OF OPPORTUNITY HAS PERsisted for centuries, no matter the reality on the ground. Neither Khadidja nor Mahamed can remember the first time they were told about it, but it's been cemented in their brains since childhood. Hard work inevitably leads to success, they had come to believe. Race- and class-based disparities could be erased through perseverance.

"In America, everybody has a chance, no matter where they come from," Mahamed said.

Khadidja felt the same. Neither knew much about the nation's bloody history, its slaughter of native peoples, its yearslong fight to uphold slavery, its unequal treatment of women, its fraught relationship with minority groups, or its persistent demonization of immigrants. What they saw was a country that had twice elected a Black president, one whose father hailed from Kenya.

Barack Obama was a symbol of pride for many Africans, including Khadidja and Mahamed. And his election was more than the triumph of just one man. It proved that America was a welcoming, hopeful, and progressive country, one in which a self-proclaimed "skinny kid with a funny name" could rise to the nation's highest office.[1] Khadidja, who might have described herself in much the same way, drew inspiration from Obama's historic ascent. A year after she arrived, when she could finally afford a smartphone, she Photoshopped herself into a framed picture that Obama appeared to be admiring in a museum. In her mind, they were equals: both had the opportunity to catapult themselves above their original station through the sort of opportunities only America would allow.

Khadidja and Mahamed knew little about the country's contentious relationship through the years with its small but growing Muslim population. They were unaware of early immigration policies that prevented Muslims from entering the country in numbers and of the extensive monitoring of Muslims in post-9/11 America.[2]

They didn't know that from 2010 to 2018, more than 200 anti-Sharia bills had been introduced in forty-three states and enacted in more than a dozen.[3] Or that such legislation, often pushed by ultra-right wing groups, has only served to further alienate the followers of Islam and scare the public with misinformation about the faith.[4]

And, like much of the rest of the nation, the young refugees had no idea what was coming next. Insulated from American Islamophobia because of the language barrier, they didn't know the word *Muslim* had become a slur. They couldn't grasp that their faith was something to fear, fight against, or be forced to publicly denounce: They never knew that when Obama's detractors tried to discredit him or cast him as un-American, they called him a Muslim.

The America Khadidja and Mahamed knew was far gentler. And measured by rhetoric alone, they were right. President George W. Bush, in a defining speech delivered at the Islamic Center of Washington, DC, just days after the September 11 attacks, told a shaken nation that Muslims throughout the country shared in what was a collective grief.

"These acts of violence against innocents violate the fundamental tenets of the Islamic faith," he said. "Islam is peace."

The president, who had removed his shoes upon entering the mosque's prayer room out of respect for his hosts, tried hard in these most critical remarks to disentangle the religion from the attacks, saying, "When we think of Islam, we think of a faith that brings comfort to a billion people around the world."

In an effort to remind the public about the tremendous contribution of its Muslim citizenry, he said followers of Islam count themselves among the nation's "doctors, lawyers, law professors, members of the military, entrepreneurs, shopkeepers, moms and dads."

He implored non-Muslims to quell their rage, to honor rather than intimidate this small but highly visible segment of the population. "In our

anger and emotion, our fellow Americans must treat each other with respect," he said. "Those who feel like they can intimidate our fellow citizens
to take out their anger don't represent the best of America, they represent the worst of humankind, and they should be ashamed of that kind of
behavior."[5]

Academics noted a drop in anti-Muslim hate crimes after the president's
remarks.[6] But while Bush's words were kind, many have come to blame his
administration for exaggerating military intelligence about weapons of
mass destruction in Iraq in an effort to push the nation into battle.[7]

By the summer of 2015, when Trump announced his candidacy for president, the United States had been at war for decades—many of the conflicts
involving Muslim nations—and was embracing a loudly vocal, open-air
xenophobia.

Trump, eager to stoke public fear for his own benefit, offered his supporters in late September of that same year the first of many scapegoats,
doubling down on the nation's Islamophobia in a stunning speech in New
Hampshire. "And now I hear we want to take in 200,000 Syrians, right?"
Trump said. "And they could be—listen, they could be ISIS."[8]

Candidate Trump went on to describe Syrian refugees, who had survived
unspeakable atrocities in a country gripped by civil war, as a "200,000-man
army," a Trojan horse that could attack the country from within.[9] He
pledged their swift return home if he were elected. "I'm putting the people
on notice that are coming here from Syria as part of this mass migration,
that if I win, if I win, they're going back," he said, his comments meeting
with an explosion of applause.[10]

Khadidja's plane touched down in New York City the following day.
While Trump might have been talking specifically about Syrians, his
speech could easily be seen as an indictment of all Muslims. To a public
that was largely unfamiliar with the religion—Muslims made up only about
1 percent of the total US population at that time—and with the varied
people who practice the faith across the globe, the rhetoric was diffuse.[11]

Two months later, on December 2, 2015, two homegrown extremists,
a married Muslim couple, killed fourteen people and severely wounded
twenty-two others in a mass shooting in San Bernardino, California. Five
days after the tragedy, Trump called for a "total and complete shutdown
of Muslims entering the United States," erasing the demarcation between
Syrians and all other followers of Islam.[12] If his wishes had become policy

before Khadidja and her family boarded their flight, they might never have made it to the States.

Professor Brian Levin, director of the nonpartisan Center for the Study of Hate and Extremism at California State University, San Bernardino, found that after Trump's speech, anti-Muslim hate crimes rose 87.5 percent above already elevated levels.[13] The causes were unclear, Levin found, but might have included heated political rhetoric around several controversial issues, such as the shuttering of mosques, the creation of a Muslims registry, the promotion of waterboarding, increased surveillance of Muslims, and the proposed use of a religious test for refugees—all of which Trump supported.[14]

It was in this climate of fear and hatred that Khadidja, a dark-skinned African transplant who never left home without a headscarf, was made to fight for her most basic civil right: the right to attend school.

There will always be a close connection between immigration and education. For most years between 2002 and 2017, between 40 and 50 percent of all refugees entering the United States were twenty years old or younger, meaning they were eligible to attend the nation's public schools.[15]

Likewise, the number of children with at least one immigrant parent more than doubled between 1990 and 2019, when it reached nearly 18 million.[16] Reflecting this trend, the number of English language learners in the nation's public schools increased from approximately 3.8 million in 2000 to 5 million in 2017.[17]

For some, the change came far too quickly.

· · · · · · · · · ·

In June of 2015, when Trump announced he was joining the presidential race, he assailed Mexican immigrants in a speech that in another era would have made him unelectable. "When Mexico sends its people, they're not sending their best," he said. "They're sending people who have lots of problems and they're bringing those problems with us. They're bringing drugs. They're bringing crime. They're rapists. And some, I assume, are good people."[18]

Trump's comments left Hispanics standing in an unwanted spotlight. The remarkable uptick in unaccompanied minors to the nation's southern border (the number increased 90 percent between 2013 and 2014 reaching nearly seventy thousand) made them only more visible.[19] News coverage further complicated their plight as images of haggard brown-skinned migrants making their way across the border and in and out of the federal court system drove Americans into two camps: those who felt compassion for their struggle, and those who eyed the newcomers as a threat to public safety, education, security, jobs, and health.

And nowhere was the newcomers' presence more evident than inside the nation's public schools, where in 2014, children of color outnumbered white students for the first time. This was an unwelcome change for those who wanted America to return to an earlier time—though it's unclear what time period in the nation's history excluded immigrants.

Nevertheless, white anxiety was on the rise. It's unsurprising that this was the same year that dozens of area residents in Southern California managed to successfully block three busloads of undocumented immigrants from heading to a local processing center. Many of the newcomers were young children.

The migrants, who had arrived by a chartered flight from Texas, were met in Murrieta, California, with chants of "We don't want you!," "USA! USA!," and "Go back home!" The few law enforcement officials who responded to the scene did nothing to clear a path for them, and the buses were ultimately diverted to San Diego. The incident made national news.[20]

Mayor Alan William Long encouraged residents to make their voices heard in opposing the newcomers.[21] "We have droves of immigrants coming and nothing in place to really prevent that," he said. "What's happening now is that they are basically dispersing them to many different backyards and I think there are people and residents here in Murrieta who are ready to take a stand against that."[22]

But no amount of public protestation could stop the flow of migration from Mexico, Central America, or any other part of the globe. School administrators and politicians from one end of the country to the other called the newcomers a burden. Parents were equally flummoxed, speaking out at local school board meetings across the nation, calling for the children to be "sent home." For them, America's public education system was a zero-sum game: if foreign-born students had a greater slice of the pie, their own children would receive less. But not all communities felt this way.

Some strove to answer the call amid unimaginably difficult circumstances. The Paradise Valley Unified School District in Phoenix, Arizona, treated new arrivals like ambassadors. The district, one of the largest in the state, serves more than thirty thousand children across dozens of campuses.

More than a third receive free or reduced lunch, a key indicator of poverty. More than 30 percent of the overall student population is Hispanic.[23]

Paradise Valley had been reevaluating its programs for years in an effort to ensure all children had access to a high-quality education, no matter their zip code. In addition to numerous other measures, it quietly moved teachers and other resources from its wealthier campuses to those schools in greater need, giving low-income students a better chance to succeed.

It won national praise for its efforts to identify gifted ESL students by using a nonverbal assessment tool to place them in honors programs if they qualified, removing language as a barrier to their success. Its push toward equity and inclusion, which began roughly a decade ago, was tantamount to a miracle considering the district's location: Paradise Valley is in the heart of Sheriff Joe Arpaio's Maricopa County.

Arpaio's reign of terror began in 1993 and continued for twenty-four years. He made headlines soon after taking office when he opened Tent City, an outdoor jail that subjected inmates to 140-degree heat. Soon after winning office, he mobilized a 2,200-member civilian volunteer force—800 of whom were armed.[24] Much of the group's unpaid "work" involved immigration enforcement.

Anti-immigrant fervor left the sheriff and his supporters feeling emboldened, especially after the passage of Arizona Senate Bill 1070, considered one of the strictest anti-immigration measures in the country. The controversial bill required police to determine the immigration status of anyone they suspected was not in the States legally.[25]

Latinos and their advocates worried that it was tantamount to state-sanctioned harassment. "A lot of U.S. citizens are going to be swept up in the application of this law for something as simple as having an accent and leaving their wallet at home," said Alessandra Soler Meetze, president of the American Civil Liberties Union of Arizona.[26]

Despite these concerns, the bill became a model for others. Alabama—which saw its Hispanic population grow by 145 percent in ten years, rising to 185,600 by 2010—took the idea to a shocking extreme a year later with the passage of HB 56, intended to make the state unlivable for undocumented families. The bill, which proposed to protect its citizenry from the "economic hardship and lawlessness" caused by illegal immigration, encouraged police to demand proof of citizenship from anyone believed to be in the country unlawfully, even during routine traffic stops or roadblocks.[27]

It made it illegal for landlords to knowingly rent apartments to the undocumented, and it invalidated any contract knowingly entered with an undocumented person, including rental agreements. The law made it a misdemeanor for undocumented residents to seek employment and criminalized the harboring, transporting, or hiding of anyone without papers, with the ACLU calling it "a shocking throwback to the days of de jure segregation."[28] Even utility companies questioned whether they would be cited for serving the undocumented.

The bill's implications for children were stunning. The Alabama law required schools to determine and report students' citizenship and immigration status upon enrollment. Supporters said it wouldn't prevent children from being admitted, only that it would allow the state to track the number of "aliens" on each campus and calculate their cost to the public school system. The tally would include classroom instruction, supplies, free or discounted lunches, extracurricular activities, and "other educational impacts" that grew from their presence.[29]

Laws like these, intentionally or not, discourage young immigrants from attending school for fear of outing themselves or their parents. They place an enormous emotional burden on children while turning educators into de facto immigration agents.[30]

And the new initiatives went well beyond primary and secondary school. The Alabama law also prohibited undocumented students from enrolling in the state's public colleges. The University System of Georgia adopted a similar policy around that same time, saying it "was being swamped by thousands of undocumented students," and that "undocumented students were taking seats in college from academically qualified Georgians."[31]

South Carolina had banned undocumented students from its public colleges since 2008. Its SB 20 included many of the same provisions as the Arizona and Alabama bills.[32] Georgia and Indiana passed similar measures.[33]

Scholars and economists said the Alabama bill would come at an alarmingly high price. The state would lose up to $10.8 billion in GDP reductions, hemorrhage up to 140,000 jobs, and sacrifice more than $350 million in state and local tax revenue.[34]

Thousands of immigrants fled Alabama in the days after the law was enacted.[35] Their absence had an enormous, immediate impact. A tomato farmer who relied on immigrant labor to harvest his crop told *The Guardian* newspaper that only eleven of his sixty-five employees turned up to work the day after the bill went into effect. Weeks later, all of them had fled, he said, leaving $100,000 worth of crops to rot in the fields.[36]

And while the region was still recovering from a historic tornado outbreak that severely damaged or destroyed some fourteen thousand homes, prompting a massive cleanup and rebuilding effort, construction suffered for a lack of workers.[37] Churches struggled too with dwindling congregations and new fears about how to help their most vulnerable parishioners.

Episcopal, Methodist, and Roman Catholic faith leaders sued the governor and attorney general in federal court to stop HB 65's implementation, saying, "If enforced, Alabama's Anti-Immigration Law will make it a crime to follow God's command to be Good Samaritans."[38] Even more concerning, crimes went unreported. Doug Pollard, Albertville's police chief, told MSNBC that after the bill was enacted, the Hispanic community stopped talking to police. "If they had a crime committed against them they used to come to us," Pollard said. "Then this new law came out and they got scared."[39]

Schools around the state saw their classrooms empty of Latino students. While some stayed away for weeks, others were formally withdrawn by their parents. A Huntsville school principal, in assessing the damage, said he spoke to a family friend of one of his missing students only to learn that the child and their family had vanished. "They were just gone," he said.[40]

School Superintendent Casey Wardynski tried to assuage students' fears, urging them to return to the classroom. His message, posted on the district's website and on YouTube, delivered a compassionate, if mixed, message. "Our students need not be afraid," Wardynski said. However, he added, students enrolling for the first time would be required to show a birth certificate so the state could gather statistical information.[41]

Across the United States, all of the anti-immigration bills faced immediate legal challenge and many were modified, with some of their harshest provisions scrapped. Portions of the Arizona law were struck down by the US Supreme Court, but its central tenet, often called "show your papers," remained.[42] And the raids continued.

Jennifer Stults, a teacher at the Paradise Valley schools for more than a decade, remembers one particularly disturbing roundup that caused chaos both inside and outside her classroom for an entire week.[43] It happened early in her tenure in the impoverished but tightly knit Palomino neighborhood. Local residents—many of whom were undocumented—were terrified: Parents refused to walk or drive their children to school, fearful they'd be harassed on the street or stopped and arrested for as much as a cracked windshield.

"The neighborhood was a ghost town during this time," Stults said. Only a third of her students showed up to class, and those who did ranged from distracted to inconsolable. They were fully aware of the sweep and knew the sheriff by name. Stults tried her best to comfort them, telling students they were safe inside the classroom even as Arpaio's posse circled the campus. She lost a full week of instruction to the chaos. But the community lost much more.

Prior to the raid, local families, whether they were in the country legally or not, had a positive, open, and cooperative relationship with the school. The sweep broke that trust. Parents stopped coming around, Stults said. When their children had problems or needed referrals to treat conditions like attention-deficit/hyperactivity disorder, they refused to follow through, worried that a new doctor might inquire about their insurance—and then about their citizenship. This fear, born of the infamous sweep, never faded.

"Parents aren't accessing all the things they should," Stults said. "This was how they felt during the raids and how they feel now."

For a while, it looked like Arpaio's days in office might be cut short by the Justice Department, which filed a civil suit against him in May 2012 for discriminatory and unconstitutional law enforcement practices against Latinos.[44] A year later, a federal court found him and his department guilty of racially profiling Latinos during traffic stops and ordered him to stop the practice.[45] In May 2016, he was found in civil contempt with a judge ruling he and his fellow defendants acted in bad faith with respect to ongoing litigation.[46] Convicted of the criminal contempt by another judge in July 2017, he faced up to six months in prison.

Two generations of Maricopa County students came and went from the Paradise Valley schools during Arpaio's tenure. And it was in this same time period that the district began to focus on equity. Former school superintendent Jim Lee, who led Paradise Valley for a decade ending in 2019, met regularly with parents to explain the district's plan. He said it wasn't hard to convince the wealthier among them to support a move toward equity. "It took some conversations and discussions, but I approached it by saying, 'Don't we want all of our students to have the same opportunities?'" he said. "How could you argue with that?"[47]

The school district's work is not over: Some of its efforts have proven successful, and in other cases, the outcome is unclear. But its push for inclusiveness has never waned.

"We have a lot of committed people who want to do what's right for the kids," said administrator Rita Tantillo. "There is really no magic to it."[48]

Like the Paradise Valley Schools, the School District of Lancaster did much to help newcomers. It established a refugee welcoming center inside one of its middle schools in 2015 to assist the parents of refugee children with job training and a host of other educational and health-related needs.

The center would go on to help hundreds of families in the ensuing years. But the district had its limits. Khadidja, Mahamed, and the other refugees who flocked to the school system in recent years were more than it was willing to handle.

CHAPTER 5

HANDLE WITH CARE

THE CASH-STRAPPED SCHOOL DISTRICT OF LANCASTER OUTSOURCED the first of its two alternative campuses in 2009 in a move it said would save roughly $3,000 per student.[1] Like many under-resourced school systems around the country, the district was in serious financial trouble. It faced a $3 million budget shortfall by the end of the 2009–2010 school year, and because of increased pension costs, raises for unionized teachers and staff, health care, and utility expenditures, it was forced to suggest a massive tax hike for local residents for the following year. Additional state funding ultimately saved the district from proceeding with the plea, but its financial woes were not over: it laid off fifty-two teachers and twenty-five support staff in the summer of 2011 in what the teachers' union president said were the deepest cuts he could recall in nearly a quarter century.[2]

Years of fiscal insecurity prompted it in 2014 to join five other school districts in suing the state legislature and state officials for failing to properly support their school district.[3] The suit claimed Pennsylvania's school funding mechanism violated the state's own constitution in that it denied students sufficient resources, equitable access, and opportunity to receive an adequate education.

According to the complaint, the state's leadership knew for nearly a decade that its schools were drastically underfunded and should have received another $4.4 billion in aid. And though it had earlier created a more equitable funding formula, that formula only applied to a small fraction of basic education funding.

Pennsylvania reneged on a promise to address the issue in 2012 when it pulled $860 million in education funding from the state budget.[4] It also limited the amount of money school districts could seek from taxpayers. As a result, elementary, middle, and high school campuses across the Keystone State were forced to cut back on qualified teachers and staff. Class sizes swelled, facilities faltered, textbooks became outdated, and technology was sidelined.

The lawsuit said that because state funding was among the lowest in the nation, school districts were forced to rely on taxpayers to make up the difference, furthering inequity: While poor districts spent less than $10,000 per student per year, rich ones forked over nearly triple, ensuring success for the state's highest-income communities. The suit urged the court to declare the state's funding mechanism unconstitutional and to force lawmakers to come up with a better solution.

The plaintiffs, Lancaster among them, were represented in court by the Public Interest Law Center. Parents and other organizations that had joined in the push were represented by both the Public Interest Law Center and the Education Law Center, a nonprofit legal organization that would loom large in Khadidja's and Mahamed's lives.

. . . .

The United States has a long history of turning to for-profit companies to help educate the nation's youth.[5] The trend has only increased since the 1990s, guided by the controversial notion that schools should be run more like businesses.

The National Education Policy Center found the number of for-profit education management organizations jumped from five to ninety-seven between the 1995–96 and 2011–12 school years. Enrollment shot up from 1,000 to nearly 463,000 in that same timeframe.[6]

To the School District of Lancaster, Camelot Education seemed like a dream. The private, for-profit company ran dozens of schools nationwide, specializing in alternative, special-needs, and at-risk youth.[7] It had already saved the district hundreds of thousands of dollars at its toughest school, Buehrle Academy. The students at Buehrle were among the district's most troubled, with some having committed criminal offenses. The campus had been under Camelot's control since 2009.

Phoenix Academy, which was added to the company's portfolio in 2011, would serve both middle and high schoolers, with a maximum capacity of 350 students. The school district, which at first gave Camelot a yearlong contract for Buehrle, eventually awarded the company a three-year deal for both campuses. The move saved millions of dollars: Camelot employs its own staff, including teachers, freeing the district of costly pension and health-care costs.[8]

Teacher Jandy Rivera remembers the switch.[9] She had visited Phoenix when it was under the school district's control, calling it "laid back, low pressure, and calm." Students learned mostly through computers, with teachers monitoring their progress, she said.

"Then Camelot came in," said Rivera, who taught at the school for eighteen months starting in 2011. "The environment was atrocious."

As part of Camelot's contract for Phoenix, the company agreed to meet strict academic requirements regarding its most at-risk charges. Seventy percent of Phoenix students who were two or more years behind grade level would advance by at least two grades in a single year, the company promised. And 75 percent of students who were one year behind had to catch up to grade level in twelve months. Camelot also was expected to maintain roughly an 85 percent graduation rate.[10] Enrollment was often at 100 percent.

Khadidja and Mahamed, who were denied enrollment at McCaskey, were ultimately admitted to Phoenix. It was a poor fit from the start. The school looked like a prison and made them feel like inmates, distrusted and carefully watched, they said. While all Phoenix students were greeted outside by friendly staff who shook their hands as a means to establish an aura of mutual respect and dignity, the mood quickly shifted when they walked through the front door.

Every child—including the refugees—was made to pass through a metal detector and was patted down by staff of the same gender. The practice was more than alarming to Khadidja and Mahamed, who had no experience with this type of treatment.

"When I was patted down for the first time, I thought there was a chance I'd never see my family again," Mahamed later said. For him, school is an extension of the government. And in his home country of Somalia, such physical contact with a government agent could lead to a life-threatening encounter. He said, "I thought to myself, 'What kind of school is this?'"

Female refugees, who often hailed from cultures where physical contact with strangers is limited, were deeply upset by the practice. But there they stood each morning, allowing staffers to run their fingers down both sides of their arms, starting at the shoulder and underarm, then down the sides of their bodies. A search of their legs reached as high as the crotch before heading down toward their feet. The procedure included a swipe of their bra straps and waistbands and a quick pass between their breasts, where students sometimes hid prohibited items like cell phones and money.

Khadidja's eyes widened when she witnessed the procedure for the first time. "I'd never seen that before," she said. "It wasn't right." She shuddered when it was her turn. Rivera, who often conducted the searches of female students, was equally troubled by the practice. She was saddened to see the shock on the faces of newcomers and even more upset by how easily most of them adapted to it, as if a full-body search should be a regular part of any child's education.

After their initial entry, students were ushered to a large meeting room for what administrators called Townhouse, a sort of daily pep rally. While it was meant to help students and staff focus on their goals for the day, it often devolved into a screaming fest for teachers, who would use the time to berate students for misbehavior, Rivera said. The refugees, unsure of what was happening, would huddle together like emperor penguins, waiting for it to end. Unfortunately for them, Townhouse was held not once but twice daily.

Phoenix rules and policies—including its Handle With Care protocol that allowed staff to place students in a physical hold on the ground or up against the wall with their hands pulled behind their backs—are unlike those of most American high schools. Its students were made to adhere to a strict dress code that required them to wear school-issued dark green polo shirts and khaki pants belted at the waist. The shirts, they were told, must be tucked in and the pants properly fitted—not oversized, baggy, or too tight. Facial hair was required to be neat and groomed, fingernails clean and trimmed. Phoenix students also were not to bring more than ten dollars to school. Anything more would be confiscated. And all were subject to search by authorized personnel at any time.

Book bags, purses, and backpacks were banned. So strict was the policy that girls who had their periods were instructed to ask the school nurse for sanitary napkins and tampons as they had no place to store them. Paralyzed by the notion of approaching an adult—possibly a male—with such a request, menstruating refugees simply skipped school during this time. Rivera kept a drawer full of sanitary products in her classroom for students who were too intimidated to head to the nurse's office.

"Every once in a while, these poor girls would call me aside and I'd go back to my desk and get one," said Rivera, who called the school's policies humiliating, ridiculous, and wrong. "They are punished for going to school. It's a punishment. If they were there for behavioral issues, that's one thing. But many were not."

Camelot's strict policies were well documented. An outside agency hired by the for-profit to assess student safety said, in 2017, "an in-your-face obvious feature of Camelot schooling is the exceptionally tight security, intense control of students." The agency, in its glowing report, described a small aspect of the school day that illustrated its approach to managing children.

"When classes are in session, a student that wants to use the bathroom will be accompanied to the hallway door where the student's teacher will shout 'Male in the hallway,'" the agency reported. "That alerts a behavior specialist in the hallway to accompany and/or monitor that student and, *not* to allow a second student into the hallway until the first returns. There are no blind spots in Camelot hallways or staircases: every adult is in eye contact with at least one other adult throughout the day. To the metal detectors and pat-down searches, Camelot blankets students with rules and expectations that are recorded, publicized, monitored, and consistently and universally applied with rewards and sanctions."[11]

Phoenix Academy teachers and staff use several levels of "behavior intervention" to help students adhere to the rules. The intervention begins with a friendly nonverbal cue, perhaps a teacher pointing out from a distance and with a smile that a student's shirt is not properly tucked or making eye contact with those talking during a classroom lesson. If the issue is not addressed, the cues become stronger, made more serious by facial expressions and verbal warnings.

Only rarely, they say, do staff implement the Handle with Care protocol, and even then, "staff maintain only defensive tactics, never offensive actions, to protect themselves or other members of the school community." Phoenix administrators said Handle with Care is not, as some might believe, an extension of the behavior intervention practice, but an entirely unique protocol used only when a student becomes violent or is a danger to themselves or others. Staffers do their best to avoid it, they said, and instead focus on building a rapport with those in their care.

"At Phoenix Academy, any allegations of mental or physical harm caused to or by students and staff are taken very seriously," Phoenix's administrators said in a statement. "Phoenix Academy staff are extremely dedicated and passionate about their roles as educators and mentors. In many instances, the students who choose to attend Phoenix Academy come from troubled educational, family and personal backgrounds. It takes committed staff and programming to connect with these students and to understand their challenges in order to help them achieve in the classroom."[12]

But for Khadidja and Mahamed, the rules seemed overbearing, hindering their ability to learn. Students also were not permitted to bring books to or from the campus—administrators worried they would not be returned—which essentially meant they had no homework. While some native English speakers enjoyed the policy, the refugees resented it. Desperate to master a new language, they were unable to study English after school, when they returned to households that spoke only their native tongue.

There were other, even bigger problems at the campus. Phoenix was designed for credit recovery, meaning it was meant for those students who needed to make up courses quickly, and it provided students with a no-frills education. It offered only those courses required for graduation and delivered the curriculum at what the refugees considered a breakneck pace, moving at twice the speed of the mainstream high school. "I can't understand what is happening there," Khadidja said.

Despite these challenges, administrators told students their compliance would bring rewards. Those who followed its myriad rules could earn their way to a better standing, one that would be reflected by the color of their polo shirts. Gray-shirted students, deemed trustworthy and responsible by staff, had a degree of independence, privilege, and authority over their peers. They served as sort of mini-monitors, reminding others to adhere to the rules.

Gray shirts were encouraged to confront other students—school officials wanted them to learn to solve their problems verbally rather than through physical confrontation—but the practice was often more menacing than helpful. Critics say the hierarchy led to bullying. Khadidja and Mahamed, for example, had no idea what the gray shirts were saying when they barked orders at them in the hallway.

While the rules and regulations portion of the Phoenix student handbook was extensive, the students' rights section was short. It said enrollees were entitled to fair and impartial treatment, that they had a right to an educational experience free of harassment and could report problems without fear of retaliation. But that's not how Khadidja and Mahamed came to feel.

Burly hall monitors roamed Phoenix like bouncers, popping uninvited in and out of classrooms all day long, intimidating those they were paid to serve. Rivera, who at first welcomed the idea of additional support staff standing at the ready, grew to resent their presence. The monitors caused two key problems: They ratcheted up minor conflicts and they undermined her in front of her students, making them think she couldn't control her own classroom, she said.

"There was a mutual respect between myself and my students, even some of my really tough cookies," she said.

Sure, some occasionally mouthed off, but Rivera felt more than capable of restoring order. But the monitors, she said, didn't allow her the chance.

"All of a sudden, a staff member would come in and say, 'I've got my eye on you,'" she said. "I thought to myself, 'I got this. If I need your help, I'll call for it.'"

Rivera remembers several incidents between staff and students that went too far. In one case, a staffer barged into her classroom and called out a student for sitting sideways at his desk. For Rivera, it was a nonissue: The student was polite, talkative, and fully engaged in her lesson. Plus, she said, he was large in stature and probably didn't feel comfortable with his legs crammed beneath him.

But the staffer wouldn't relent. He pulled the young man from his seat, slammed him against the door, shoved him into the wall, and dragged him out of sight where the altercation continued. "All because of nothing," she said.

Rivera recalls some staff bragging about having previously worked at the infamous nearby Glen Mills Schools. Its campuses were shuttered by the state just a few years later after the *Philadelphia Inquirer* found that staff had beaten students and attempted to coerce them into silence.[14]

Rivera said some Phoenix staffers lamented the fact that they didn't have even greater authority to physically manage students. "They wanted to start a fight with these students so they could take them down," she said.

"They would yell and scream. Certain staffers would call them stupid or worthless, saying things like, 'You're never going to amount to anything. No wonder you're here. You're dumb. You might as well not even be here.'" It was only a matter of time before a child in Camelot's care was seriously hurt, she thought.

In April 2014, a seventeen-year-old student at another of its schools in nearby Reading said he was beaten up by a so-called "behavioral specialist."[15] According to a criminal complaint, the staffer walked into a classroom and told a group of rambunctious students to "shut the fuck up," adding that the next student to talk "would get body slammed through the door."

A child who stood up to sharpen his pencil was pulled into the hallway. A security camera caught at least some of what happened next between the 160-pound boy and the 280-pound man: The teen was swung into a wall headfirst and the incident left him with a string of bruises.[16]

Rivera said that shortly before she left the district, she and her students saw a child return to school who she said had been physically managed by a Phoenix staffer. The middle schooler was visibly injured, Rivera said, suffering a swollen-shut black eye, a fat lip, and marks around his neck. The child missed half a week of school. Phoenix's administrators cast doubt on Rivera's account, saying no such incident occurred. Despite the pushback, Rivera claims the incident was key to her own departure from the school. She remembers clearly, she said, when this child returned to campus.

"He came in with his mom and my kids were rightly freaked out," Rivera said. "They see his black eye and bruises around his neck. We go into the classroom after lunch and this little guy in ninth grade looks at me and says, 'Ms. Rivera, what are we supposed to do if somebody does something illegal?'"

The teacher knew she was in a difficult position and was careful not to disparage the school. "I said, 'Listen to me. If anyone, any adult, does something to you that is against the law, you go to your mother, your father, your grandparents, any person in charge of you and you tell that person they need to go to the police and file a report.'"

Word spread of the conversation, and Rivera was suddenly on the outs with staff and her supervisors. Her reviews, previously solid, were filled with what she says were petty or unfounded complaints.

She quit before Camelot had the chance to fire her, but, in a surprising twist, she was back on campus within weeks: Rivera was hired through the state to work with refugee and migrant students and her new employers, knowing nothing of what happened at Phoenix, assigned her to the alternative campus because of her familiarity with students and staff. She held the position for a year.

Despite its disciplinary issues, the School District of Lancaster touted Phoenix as an excellent choice for students who had already failed multiple courses and who were looking to graduate quickly. Some assigned to the school were grateful for a chance to attend. For them, Phoenix provided exactly the type of environment they needed to succeed. They welcomed the scrutiny as a means to focus on their coursework and their parents were equally happy, believing Phoenix's emphasis on discipline would finally enable their children to graduate.

But others worried about its punitive nature and begged for their children to be transferred to the mainstream high school, McCaskey. They argued that no matter their child's previous infractions, they did not warrant enrollment at Phoenix. One woman, who dropped off a female relative at Phoenix in the summer of 2016, bashfully told a school administrator that she worried about the school's disciplinary nature. "I heard this was a school for bad boys and girls," she said quietly. "She's not a bad girl."

The administrator tried to assure her that Phoenix would make every effort to see the young lady succeed, but the woman was unconvinced. Her face fell when she realized the school wouldn't reconsider. She asked that the girl be allowed to carry a purse and cell phone but the administrator said no. The slender teen standing at her side looked equally bewildered. She took a deep breath and walked toward the school's front door.

Another woman, dropping off her son, had a more hopeful outlook. "I told him, your main focus is to graduate," she told an administrator. "Hopefully, it's a better year for him."[17]

No matter their attitude upon enrollment, there was a stigma attached to Phoenix. Many students who attended the school waited until the last possible second to put on their green shirts. They didn't want to be seen walking through their neighborhood with what they believed was a scarlet letter.

The refugees found little to celebrate at Phoenix. Their English skills were minimal—neither Khadidja nor Mahamed could string together a sentence with more than just a few words—so they didn't understand their teachers. They often did not know which subject was being taught.

"I was scared," Khadidja said. "It wasn't good. I didn't like it. If you don't know English, it's very hard."

Teacher Jandy Rivera left the district before Khadidja and Mahamed arrived. But, she said, their experience lines up with what she witnessed. "The refugee kids at McCaskey were thriving," she said. "The refugees at Phoenix were in survival mode."

Phoenix provided no in-class translators: it would have been impractical considering that its students spoke nearly forty languages. But it also did not use online translation tools or the call-in telephone service that would have allowed students to connect with live interpreters, the refugees said. Both options were available and would have been helpful. Mahamed was enrolled in five classes but couldn't name any of them.

"I tried to learn as much as I could, but it was hard," he said. "It's not a school. It's a jail."

And, the refugees said, Phoenix didn't have nearly enough ESL staff. The only such teacher Khadidja and Mahamed knew was beloved, but also overwhelmed. She was unable to assist them with their other classes, they said.

And Phoenix's other teachers—nearly all of whom had non-English-speaking students in their classrooms—had little training in how to reach them. There were up to forty kids in a class, and none of the refugees assigned to the campus said they had much one-on-one time with their instructors.

And while they were told they could call upon certain designated staff for help, neither Khadidja nor Mahamed felt comfortable enough to confide in anyone at the school. Their limited English would have made it difficult for them to communicate anyway, they said. They couldn't even name their advocates.

When Mahamed was bullied by his peers—one young woman pulled his hair and students would frequently laugh at him, call him names, and pound the door to the bathroom stall while he was using it, yelling words he couldn't understand—he felt he had no one to turn to. "What kind of a school is this?" he'd ask himself. He contemplated dropping out.

By then, he'd lost faith in the system. The district had already broken his trust by initially denying his enrollment and then subjecting him to a program designed for at-risk youth. School officials eventually investigated his claims—they asked a handful of teachers and staff members if they'd witnessed his harassment and they said they hadn't—and found the incidents described were not "severe, persistent, or pervasive" enough to warrant action. They denied Mahamed's request to transfer out of Phoenix.

"We further note that Mahamed's statement that he feels unsafe at the Phoenix Academy is neither credible nor reasonable," said Arthur Abrom, director of student services in a letter.[18]

Khadidja was equally despondent. She didn't have any friends at Phoenix and most of her teachers were unhelpful. "They'd give me books," but they wouldn't help her learn to read them, she said. "I'd try to tell the teacher that I don't understand the words. English is very hard for me."

Khadidja considered quitting school. She and the other refugees were learning nearly nothing from their classroom instruction. Yet, to their surprise, they were somehow being pushed ahead, leaping from one grade to another in a matter of months and receiving good grades—all without speaking but a few words of English.

While some might have thought they would be eager to graduate, the students felt cheated. Their younger brothers and sisters were thriving at other campuses, including McCaskey. But the district opened only one door for these refugees. And with every turn of the calendar's pages, they inched closer and closer to graduation—and into a world they could barely understand.

CHAPTER 6

NOT ON MY WATCH

E LISE CHESSON, THIRTY-SIX, WHO HAILED FROM A FAMILY OF CIVIL rights crusaders, couldn't help but become an activist. It was in her DNA. Her mother, Lorraine Fontaine, of Montreal, Canada, spent sixteen years fighting for women's rights as they related to childbirth. Fontaine also worked for years for a youth development organization when she lived in Toronto, teaching children about social inequality. She and her husband, Dan, had both led social justice committees in and outside their parish, urging people to consider the myriad factors that create unequal opportunity for minorities and the poor.

But the root of the family's activism lies with Chesson's seventy-seven-year-old grandmother, Adèle Fontaine, who believed, well ahead of her time, that all women should be free to explore their passions outside the home. A mother of seven, she spent years working with delinquent youth and also teaching at the university level.

In the later part of Adèle's career, she worked with a nonprofit that served French-speaking African immigrants looking for employment. Ever independent, she moved to Korea at age sixty-two to teach English. Her husband, Normand, a radio announcer and artist, visited her overseas until she returned nearly two years later.

Chesson's mother started taking her to various protests beginning when she was just a baby, filling her tiny ears with chants of "Hey, hey! Ho, ho! Nuclear arms have got to go!" or "Free Nelson Mandela!" Years later, fueled by her growing interest in Canada's indigenous population, Lorraine took the family to visit the First Nation Community of Sheshegwaning on Manitoulin Island in Lake Huron. Though they were initially suspicious of her motives—Canada, just like America, frequently trampled the rights of indigenous people—the group eventually warmed to the family. Twenty members of the community, including the chief, later visited them in Toronto. It was an important cultural exchange, one that Lorraine hoped would make a lasting impression on her family.

She wanted her children to be exposed to other cultures and also to recognize their own ability to change the world. So it's no wonder that Chesson would be compelled to call out injustice as she grew into adulthood. "She sees every opportunity as a chance to open minds," Fontaine said of her daughter. "She will not back down when it comes to standing up for people's rights."[1]

Chesson eventually married a man who hailed from Liberia and had two children of her own. The family moved to Pennsylvania in 2007 so that her then husband could pursue a job opportunity. Chesson had other goals: She put her academic and career ambitions on hold to raise a family.

But her interest in social justice never waned. In 2008, she became involved in Obama's presidential campaign, spending several hours each week going door-to-door in Reading to convince mostly Spanish-speaking voters to take a chance on a relatively unknown candidate. She was proud of her participation. Obama's victory wasn't just about politics, but about social change, she told friends and family.

Chesson went on to earn an associate's degree in cultural anthropology from Reading Area Community College in 2013 and a bachelor's degree in political science from West Chester University two years later. She landed a job at Lutheran Immigration and Refugee Service in November 2015, hired as the organization's employment program manager. Another team within her agency was charged with school enrollment, but the task soon fell to Chesson and her colleagues.

It took only a few weeks on the job for her to realize there was something wrong with the School District of Lancaster's enrollment policies.

"The initial red flag was Mahamed," said Chesson, who first met the teen when she was assigned through her job to help the adults in the family with employment. "He was denied entry to school and there was some confusion as to whose responsibility that was."[2]

Chesson was determined to find the root of the enrollment problem and tried to enlist the help of Sheila Mastropietro of Church World Service, who had worked with the Lancaster schools for decades. But Chesson found Mastropietro surprisingly unwilling to pursue the matter.

Mastropietro had worked with Lancaster refugees for decades and was a fixture in the community. She couldn't afford to burn bridges. But where, Chesson wondered, did that leave Mahamed? She didn't want to become part of a bureaucracy that left students like him with no advocate. "I didn't want to be that person who saw something that I could change . . . and turned away," she said.

Chesson's initial contact with the district came in the form of a conference call in December 2015 when she tried to learn more about its enrollment procedures. She wanted to know who decided each child's fate and whether such decisions could be appealed, but the call did not go well.

The district was resolute. Administrators suggested that Mahamed enroll in a GED program, but Chesson knew that was no substitute for a high school education. "It's two different worlds," she told school officials. "And if we all have the goal of self-sufficiency and building up a community that is work-ready, then I think you guys know what's the best route."

Chesson worried that the district was admitting students based on what she considered unrelated factors, including a child's perceived demeanor during meetings with administrators. School officials' response did little to change her mind: They said Mahamed was uninterested in school, that he backed away from a conference table during a key meeting with enrollment gatekeeper Jacques Blackman and didn't want to engage in a discussion about his future.

Chesson doubted the story, not only because Mahamed denied it but also because, she believed, it made no sense. Even if Mahamed had seemed aloof or remote, what frustrated teenager doesn't seem standoffish from time to time, she wondered? Especially one who had such a challenging childhood and who felt so poorly treated by the district?

She and other advocates brought this up at a contentious meeting with school officials on February 11, 2016, when they asked administrators whether personal observations factored into their decision-making process regarding enrollment. School officials conceded but also cited the refugees' ages, lack of language skills, limited school credits prior to arrival in America, and potential for dropping out as factors in their placement. They insisted, the program manager said, that older refugees wanted to find work rather than attend school.

Chesson knew they were wrong, at least about Mahamed, but she wasn't gaining ground, so she and her colleagues moved on. They told school administrators that Phoenix made too little effort to help students learn English or provide them with translation services and that the documents sent home to their parents were often written in a language they did not understand. But nothing seemed to compel the district to address these issues.

Eager to learn more about Phoenix Academy, Chesson attended the alternative school's orientation in the winter of 2016 alongside Khadidja and another resettlement caseworker, Bilal Al Tememi. The district did not provide a Fur or Arabic translator. Al Tememi, who spoke Arabic, served as Khadidja's interpreter.

Chesson described the atmosphere at the school as unsettling. "It seemed very stale," she said. "Every level had behavior specialists. I would have described it more like a detention center."

The orientation focused almost entirely on student discipline, with the presenter telling the crowd that Phoenix was "a school of last resort," Chesson said.

"'This is your last chance,'" Chesson recalled her saying. "'We don't know where you are, where you're coming from, or what you've been through, but we need to keep order in this school.'"

Chesson said the woman went on to outline the ways in which a child might be reined in by staff, including the Handle with Care protocol, which was demonstrated on a female student picked from the crowd. Chesson couldn't believe the refugees would be subject to such treatment having no prior record of disciplinary problems.

Swallowing her shock, she began to inquire about Phoenix's academic offerings, asking for key educational statistics, including the school's dropout rate and percentage of students who go on to college. But the presenter didn't have the answers.

Chesson moved on to the school's English language program and its homework policy. She was told there was no homework.

"What about the pat-downs and dress code?" she asked.

Chesson also inquired about the school's curriculum, which seemed to mostly focus on satisfying basic, general educational requirements before moving on to the campus's fast-paced learning environment.

That's when the conversation took a surprising turn. Chesson said the presenter told her that school staff—including an overwhelmed ESL teacher—didn't believe Phoenix was the right place for refugees. The woman said they had already brought this to the attention of the district but that nothing changed. She said she hoped Chesson and her colleagues would have better luck routing the students to a different location.

Astonished, the program manager immediately fired off a series of emails to other refugee advocates, including Mastropietro. Convinced that the alternative school was not the appropriate setting for traumatized young refugees, she pushed for yet another meeting with school officials.

Chesson, Mastropietro, other refugee advocates, and school officials met yet again in mid-March 2016. Chesson urged the district to take action in Mahamed's case, to investigate the bullying that drove him off campus. School administrators vowed to inquire but said it would take time.

Chesson could hardly believe what she was hearing: by that point, the school year was almost over. The caseworker warned that students were already falling through the cracks and implored administrators to look into specific cases. But school superintendent Damaris Rau refused.

"Why couldn't these students go to the International School instead of Phoenix Academy?" Chesson asked.

Increasingly irritated by her tone, Superintendent Rau, new to her post, told Chesson to be patient as the district reevaluated its admission policies the following school year. But the caseworker would not let go.

Chesson knew that Mastropietro, head of Lancaster's other major resettlement agency, had already inquired about the very same issue years earlier and nothing was done. There was no way she was going to allow the district to squander yet another year of a child's education. Time had already run out. Mahamed had fallen into a deep depression and Khadidja considered giving up her fight entirely.

"There were multiple opportunities for them to make changes, but they didn't want to," Chesson said. "It's often the case that people who don't have money also don't have a voice and are easy to brush aside."

Chesson knew that students who failed to graduate high school qualified only for dead-end jobs. She knew, too, that low-skilled workers, including those who populated the region's many poultry plants, often toiled in wretched conditions. "Sometimes they're exposed to harmful chemicals or freezing temperatures," she said. "It's horrible."

And they were easy to replace, leaving them virtually no leverage with their employers. Such uncertainty, she said, does not allow for a happy, fulfilled life. "You are so consumed by that and you are so emotionally and physically drained that when you come home, you have nothing to give," she said.

Chesson needed outside help if anything was to change at the school district. By the spring of 2016, she was staying up for hours each night, sometimes until 3:00 a.m., compiling data she hoped would win the attention of the media or of attorneys who could intervene on the students' behalf.

After she prepared her pitch, she reached out to the State Board of Education but had little faith that it would take action, especially considering its leadership. Pedro A. Rivera, nominated as the state's secretary of education on January 20, 2015, was formerly the superintendent of the Lancaster school district. He was at the helm when the district outsourced its alternative schools to Camelot and when it set up its enrollment procedures.

Even if the department did take action, Chesson feared it would only make recommendations and that it would be years before the situation was truly corrected. And she worried that she would be forced to share with the school district all of the information she had amassed, allowing administrators a chance to undermine her claims.

Chesson called statewide advocacy groups and a national news outlet but wasn't making any progress. As the weeks passed, she grew increasingly worried that the problems in Lancaster would remain unnoticed. "I felt we were going to be in this spinning spiral of endless nothing," she said.

But Chesson was made for this moment. She had the drive and ability to see this fight through. She just couldn't do it alone.

CHAPTER 7

BIG LEAGUES

THE ACLU OF PENNSYLVANIA RECEIVES THOUSANDS OF CALLS EACH year, but nearly all are cast aside. Most involve disputes between neighbors, complaints about city services, or are made by residents who say they hear voices or who suspect the government has implanted microchips in their brains. Only 1 percent are ever truly considered and just seventy-five to a hundred make it to trial each year. Some are quick, easy wins, like those fought on behalf of students forced to stand for the Pledge of Allegiance. Others are massive and time-consuming, like the battle for marriage equality or against overly restrictive voter identification laws.

Elise Chesson, program manager at Lutheran Immigration and Refugee Service, had to make it through at least three screenings before she was able to talk to an intake lawyer. It was a frustrating process, but her persistence paid off when her claims were laid out before statewide legal director Vic Walczak.

Walczak was so incensed by what he heard that he spent the afternoon pacing around the office conference table, his face tightening as he learned the facts of the case. He jumped on the chance to represent the refugees.

Luckily for Khadidja, Mahamed, and the others, Chesson called at exactly the right time. Had she reached out just a few months earlier, the refugees might have gotten lost amid the office's preparation for a different lawsuit, one filed on behalf of hundreds of severely mentally ill people who had been languishing in the state's county jails for months at a time.

And the Lancaster case met another important criterion: it angered just the right person. Walczak was outraged by what he felt was clear discrimination against the refugees who had already suffered so much in their home countries. "I was bonkers on that—and even more bonkers after we met the kids," he said.[1] They reminded the attorney, in many ways, of his own family, which had faced similar persecution in an earlier era.

Witold "Vic" Walczak was born in Sweden and came to the US when he was three years old, brought by his Polish mother and father. He's Jewish on his mother's side, meaning half of his family was marked for execution by the Nazis during World War II and most died in the conflict.

His grandmother perished in Treblinka, a forced labor camp in Poland, along with at least seven hundred thousand other Jews. His grandfather, a member of the Polish Underground State, a resistance group loyal to the Government of the Republic of Poland, was among only a small number of people who escaped the death camp. He left for Sweden in the mid-1950s and would go on to spend the rest of his life testifying about the war crimes he'd witnessed. Walczak's parents joined him, and the family eventually moved to Canada and then to Tennessee, Oklahoma, and New Jersey, where Walczak attended high school.

As a young child, Walczak didn't fit in with the other kids in his neighborhood in Nashville. He was embarrassed by his Polish-speaking parents and their ethnic cuisine. "It was really hard," he said. "We had different customs, a different language. My parents spoke funny, and still speak funny, with heavy accents." Like many immigrants, they struggled to merge the old with the new. Walczak recalls one particular incident involving his birthday. His parents had made him a traditional Polish dessert—a flourless, walnut-based treat with mocha frosting—that his Tennessee friends wouldn't dare touch. "We're sitting at the table and I'm scarfing this down and I look at all of the little kids in Nashville—most wouldn't even try it—and I remember thinking, 'Man, we're really different,'" he said. "It's a silly little story but it's so true. I have always been cognizant of being different, not so much today but certainly growing up as an immigrant. As a kid, you just want to be like everybody else."

In many ways, Walczak had it easier than the refugees he would come to represent. Not only was he white, but he also came to America as a toddler. While he spoke only Polish upon arrival, he was quick to pick up a new language, accent-free. But life had other challenges for him. Walczak's parents divorced when he was a child and he became estranged from his father. He tried to reach out to the man when he was seventeen but was rebuffed: his father's new wife, pregnant at the time, chased him out of their home with a kitchen knife.

Lost and dejected, Walczak was desperate for direction. He found it at Colgate University in a course called Leaders in Non-Violence. Mahatma Gandhi, Martin Luther King Jr., and the men behind the Polish resistance movement became his mentors, at least in theory. "I was this really kind of screwed-up kid," said Walczak, who would go on to major in philosophy. "I needed a guide in my life. I had this insatiable thirst to figure out what was right and wrong."

While in college, Walczak worked as an investigator for the public defender's office in Washington, DC, and eventually for the agency's juvenile probation program, which was filled with young Black boys trying to distance themselves from the crime, poverty, and despair that swept their neighborhoods in the mid-1980s.

As Walczak came to know these children and their families—helping them with their homework, job searches, and cantankerous probation officers—he became aware of the systemic racism that left many poor and minority teens with few options outside of crime. "Seeing the difficulties these kids had in trying to make something of their lives was just unbelievably revealing," he said. "It really inspired me even more to want to go to law school."

But his enrollment would have to wait. After graduation, Walczak visited Poland for a month in support of the anti-communist Solidarity movement. The mood in the country was tense. Fearful that they were being secretly recorded inside their own homes and offices, Poles would turn up their radios before engaging in conversation. When they headed outside, they'd cover their mouths when they spoke. It was Walczak's first experience with what he called a wholesale decline of civil liberties. "You never knew who was on your side and who wasn't," he said.

During his trip, Walczak photographed police officers beating demonstrators in the port city of Gdansk. Seconds after his shutter snapped, secret police knocked him to the ground and demanded his camera, but the twenty-two-year-old refused to hand it over.

His friends chased off his attackers and likely saved him from a weeks-long prison stay, but he wasn't entirely out of trouble. He was strip-searched at the border on a train from Poland to Slovakia, his bags cut with a razor blade. Thankfully, he had ensured his photos would make it out of the country, even if he didn't: he had earlier asked a friend who worked at a consular office to mail them to him in the States and was reunited with them when he returned home.

Between growing up as an immigrant, his DC experience, and his frightening encounters with authorities in Poland, Walczak knew he wanted to be a civil rights attorney and went on to graduate from Boston College Law School. He applied to the ACLU of Massachusetts as a summer intern but didn't land a spot. After working for a short time in environmental law, he spent the next several years at Legal Services in Maryland, fighting for prisoners' rights. It was there that he won an important case in 1987 that challenged the state's practice of allowing the governor to override parole board decisions. The state ultimately was forced to set free several convicted rapists and murderers, including a man who had killed three people.

Walczak stood by his work, but that didn't keep him from scanning the local newspapers for the next five years to see if any of the men he'd freed went on to commit serious crimes upon release. They didn't, at least to his knowledge.

After gaining years of trial experience, Walczak joined the Pennsylvania ACLU as its assistant chapter director in 1991 at an annual salary of about $21,000. It wasn't that he was short on job offers, only that he picked the one that paid the least.

But what Walczak lacked in salary he gained in a sense of purpose. He recalls with pride two cases filed in 1996 that led to long-lasting change. The first focused on police corruption in Pittsburgh, including allegations of false arrests, unreasonable searches and seizures, and excessive force. The second involved the defunding of the public defender's office in Allegheny County, a move that left many defendants without legal representation. "They didn't have enough lawyers for each courtroom, much less for each defendant," Walczak said. "We ended up settling the case. They doubled the budget, added a ton more lawyers, investigators, and social workers."

While many of Walczak's clients drew public sympathy, others, like the Ku Klux Klan, elicited only scorn. But the attorney had no problem defending hate groups, even those that singled out Jews. While his family's history instilled in him a strong sense of empathy for the oppressed, it would never come before his love of free speech and assembly. It was because of this that

he considered it an honor to stand up for the rights of prisoners who identified themselves as Nazis and also for members of the KKK, knowing that every case he cited in their defense stemmed from the civil rights movement.

"That's the thing about rights," Walczak said. "They don't exist unless
they are a reality for everyone."

The ACLU of Pennsylvania wins 75 to 80 percent of its cases, but
that's not as impressive as it might sound. The organization is choosy
and won't often take on battles it knows it will lose. Sometimes, though,
Walczak will take a chance on a case, especially if he considers the alleged
civil rights violation particularly egregious. Add to that a bit of wisdom
he gleaned from an old friend and mentor who told him early in his career that if he's winning all of his cases, he's not taking the right ones.
"Sometimes you've got to push the envelope," he said. Occasionally, he
admitted, you lose.

Walczak still winces over a particularly painful defeat involving an
Egyptian-born scientist who lost his security clearance in what the attorney
called "post-9/11 hysteria." The man, who worked for a nuclear contractor,
was active in his local mosque and gave a number of talks about America's
poor treatment of Muslims. The scientist said he was unfairly targeted and
that the government failed to give him due process. Walczak lost his case in
district court—and on appeal.

Like most lawyers, he has a hard time accepting failure and doesn't always know when to give up. His persistence often tests the patience of the
attorneys who work alongside him. They try to reel him in before he spends
time and money pursuing those doomed to failure, but they don't always
succeed. He once lost a case nine times, sticking with it long after his colleagues told him to abandon ship. "People inside and outside the organization were like 'Vic, give it up. Give. It. Up,'" Walczak said. "And I'm like,
'No, I'm right.'" He eventually won on appeal.

But righteous indignation is expensive. Losing cases can be a major financial drain. The nonprofit ACLU had just four full-time lawyers and a $2
million budget in the spring of 2016 when Elise Chesson's call was finally
patched through.

The Lancaster case was no slam dunk. The ACLU did not merely have
to prove that the mainstream high school, McCaskey, was better than
Phoenix—that would have been easy, Walczak said—but also that Phoenix
wasn't equipped to meet the refugees' needs.

This was an extraordinarily difficult task considering that all public schools are regulated by the state. The Pennsylvania Department of Education, the highest educational authority in the state, gave Phoenix its stamp of approval year after year after year. Who was Walczak to say the department was wrong?

The ACLU had little experience with education law. So Walczak called upon the Education Law Center for help—the same group that backed the School District of Lancaster in its push for more school funding. But even with their assistance, Walczak needed another pair of hands. He called on an old friend, one with whom he shared the biggest victory of his career, to shoulder the burden.

Walczak first met Eric Rothschild in 2005 when the pair teamed up to fight against the teaching of creationism in a small Pennsylvania school district. Their victory made headlines around the world and led to a lasting friendship between the two men. And while they had much in common— both are outspoken progressives married to pediatricians—Rothschild didn't always let his ideals drive his work. A lawyer for the massive Philadelphia-based firm Pepper Hamilton (now Troutman Pepper Hamilton Sanders), he'd spent much of his career representing the nation's largest pharmaceutical companies.[2]

The work kept him busy and made him rich. The only reason he was free to help with the Lancaster case was because he had recently settled more than a dozen lawsuits against Eli Lilly and Company, maker of Prozac. The company had been battling for nearly three years with a group of mothers who said the drug caused birth defects in their children. Rothschild argued that their evidence was weak: he said the defects could have been caused by a number of other factors, including genetics, and that the women were probably better off for having taken Prozac because it might have spared them the torment of postpartum depression.

Rothschild believed in his argument but was glad the case never made it to trial. It would have been almost impossible for a jury to decide against the women in a courtroom filled with photos of kids with birth defects, he said.

Rothschild joined the firm in 1994. While he didn't lament a life spent defending large corporations, when he looked back at his career, he was proudest of those cases he fought pro bono and was itching for just such a fight when Walczak called.

· · · · · · · · ·

The attorneys for the refugees, desperate to resolve the matter before the start of the new school year in August, were under a massive time crunch. They had just a few months to prepare for court. In an effort to meet their deadline, they set a backbreaking schedule that called for the sped-up collection of more than a dozen depositions and nearly a hundred exhibits in a matter of weeks.

Fired up and ready to pounce, Rothschild was eager to start interviewing witnesses in the summer of 2016, but then he got a call that forced him to drop everything. His mother, who had been suffering with Alzheimer's for years, was dying.

With time running out—and with a lead attorney gone—the ACLU and the Education Law Center hit yet another roadblock: The refugees didn't trust them. And why would they? How could this group of polished white professionals, not a Black or brown face among them, possibly understand what the refugees stood to lose? New to the country and afraid to speak up, they were fearful of being kicked out of the school district entirely. Sure, Phoenix was a nightmare, but at least it was something.

And they had other reasons for their silence: They carried with them fresh memories from home where pleas for freedom, fairness, and equal treatment were met with force. Some had lived in countries where simply holding a public gathering could land a person in jail. They didn't know their rights in America and their experience with the School District of Lancaster left them feeling powerless.

One by one, they sat and listened to Walczak's pitch, nodding their heads at all of the appropriate moments, yet few were convinced the lawsuit was their best option. "It was a lot of discussion," Walczak said. "The distrust level was quite high." In the end, just six refugees and their families signed on as named plaintiffs, though many more were facing similar problems in enrolling at the school district or trying to make their way through Phoenix Academy that year alone.

The case was filed as a class action on behalf of past, current, and future limited English proficient immigrant students excluded from McCaskey. At the time it was filed, there were more than 517 refugees resettled in the district, including twenty at Phoenix. Their attorneys say there was evidence that more than 100 had been turned away or had been sent to the alternative school in the years prior to the trial.[3] While the figure may seem small, the impact is large.

The United States has a shockingly low rate of social mobility considering its overall wealth. Most of these hundred students will marry and have children, with poverty passed down like a dominant gene. A recent study shows it would take five generations for a child born to a low-income family in America to earn the country's average income, meaning that the Lancaster school district's decision to turn them away impacted not only the students it had refused possibly one hundred years' worth of descendants.[4]

Even after the six refugees committed to the lawsuit, linguistic and cultural barriers made it difficult for their attorneys to have simple conversations with them, let alone extract their complex stories. Khadidja spoke a language called Fur. Mahamed spoke Somali and Arabic, but his dialect was tough for local translators to follow. The other students spoke languages that were similarly obscure in the United States. And even if they somehow could speak English, cultural differences made it difficult for them to talk honestly about their feelings or their families' hardships.

Asked what it was like to flee their home countries, some of the most famously distressed places in the world, they clammed up. "I remember the first time we met with them and said, 'Tell me what life was like in your home country,' and they said, 'It was fine,'" Walczak recalled. "Really? 'Fine?' It really wasn't until we were preparing them for trial several months in that they were all of a sudden divulging things to us that were just mind-blowing."

Elise Chesson was the lawyers' most critical on-the-ground contact. Dubbed "the chain rattler" by Rothschild for alerting the ACLU to the students' plight, she spent dozens of unpaid hours coordinating meetings between the attorneys and their new clients, staking her own reputation on theirs.

After weeks of scrambling, the ACLU and Education Law Center filed suit in July 2016, arguing that the School District of Lancaster provided the refugees with an inferior education in violation of their civil rights. They said, too, that the school district failed to provide adequate language instruction as is legally required and that its decision to place the students at the alternative campus denied them due process. The refugees were largely unable to learn and had no means to fight back. "With its highly restrictive and overly confrontational environment, Phoenix is run more like a disciplinary school than a traditional high school," they told the court, alleging that Phoenix was "academically inferior by all measures" and unable to meet the educational and language needs of newly arrived immigrant students.[5]

But even before those issues were to be debated at trial, the lawyers wanted the court to grant an emergency injunction that would keep the students from being sent back to Phoenix at the start of the next school year, which by then was a mere six weeks away. Judges do not grant such requests easily—especially not the one assigned to this case. Edward G. Smith, a twenty-seven-year veteran of the United States Navy, was a self-described conservative who abhorred government overreach.

Nominated by President Barack Obama in 2013, Smith, a Republican, was well regarded by the attorneys who argued cases before him. But his political leanings worried the ACLU and the Education Law Center. Smith was a highly disciplined, letter-of-the-law judge who believed federal justices should never decide cases based upon their own personal agendas or what they wished the law would say.

Instead, he said, their job was to simply "apply the law to the facts as you find them." The judge has not one but two Antonin Scalia quotes etched in glass bolstering the claim. "The judge who always likes the results he reaches is a bad judge," read one such trinket, a gift from his clerks.

Smith was no activist, no crusader for the poor or disenfranchised. He believed federal judges who wanted to change the law should step down from the bench and run for office.

In their brief interactions with him prior to the trial, attorneys for the refugees say it was clear the judge had no desire to tell a local school district how to run its programs. Smith warned the legal team three times in one phone call that their burden of proof for keeping the refugees out of Phoenix would be exceedingly high.

"That just immediately told me what his mindset was," Walczak said. "He seemed to be erecting a very high barrier."

Sharon O'Donnell, hired to represent the school district, said it would be almost impossible for the ACLU and Education Law Center to prove it placed the refugees in Phoenix unlawfully. She argued that the judge should deny the team's request for a preliminary injunction because the refugees and their attorneys failed to prove the students would suffer irreparable harm if they were not immediately admitted to the district's main high school, McCaskey.

O'Donnell said the school district did not discriminate against the students based on their country of origin, as the refugees' lawyers alleged, but that they were assigned to Phoenix based on their age and the number of credits they could earn before aging out at twenty-one. She said the students had no legal right to appeal the district's decision.

· · · · · · · · · ·

While the ACLU and the Education Law Center had a small army of attorneys making their case, O'Donnell worked alone. An experienced lawyer and a sharp, eloquent speaker, she was victorious in a number of hard-to-win cases, several of which were highly publicized.

Married at age twenty when she and her husband were still in college, O'Donnell was a small-town girl from northeast Pennsylvania who would go on to spend the next several years raising their two sons and working as a paralegal.

She always knew she could achieve more professionally, but it wasn't until she turned thirty that she decided to pursue a law degree. "I was tired of being a paralegal," O'Donnell said. "I was just tired of doing all of the grunt work. I wanted the trials; I wanted all of it."[6] Her husband did not support the decision, but she forged ahead anyway, tired of her subjugated position in their marriage and in the law firms where she worked.

O'Donnell graduated from law school in Harrisburg in 1996 and was immediately scooped up by a Philadelphia-based firm, Marshall Dennehey Warner Coleman & Goggin.

Independent and self-assured, she considered herself an outlier. No one would have guessed while she was chasing her children around the yard in her late twenties that she would one day become a sought-after attorney, she said. And while her career has been a success, her marriage never recovered from her decision to pursue law. She and her husband split amicably in 2009 after thirty years.

Although she's practiced in other areas, O'Donnell has spent most of her time on school-related cases, including that of a Philadelphia-area teacher who blogged about her students, calling them "utterly loathsome," "rat-like," and "disengaged, lazy whiners," on a website she thought no one would find. The woman was eventually fired and sued the district, saying her online comments were protected by the First Amendment. O'Donnell argued that she had no right to speak disparagingly of her students, considering her position with the district. The case was eventually thrown out.

In another instance, O'Donnell convinced a jury that an African American teacher who left his school district after his superiors exchanged racist text messages about him had no right to sue over his departure. The man had resigned under threat of termination, the attorney said.

The incendiary missives—O'Donnell acknowledged they were "dripping racism" and included the N-word—were blown up to the size of billboards inside the courtroom. The attorney knew the exhibits would be impactful, but she had faith in her argument and was victorious.

"I always felt we could win that case," she said, hoping to direct the court's attention on the man's job performance rather than the racist texts. "We just had to stay focused."

She hoped the Lancaster case would turn out similarly: O'Donnell's goal was to keep the judge focused on the educational issues at hand, not on the personal lives of the students involved. Yes, the refugees lived challenging lives, and yes, they survived difficult circumstances on their way to America. But the case wasn't about their tortured journeys or the violence that overtook their homelands. It was about whether the Lancaster school district provided them with a decent education, one that met state and federal standards—and, more broadly, whether such determinations should be made by a federal judge rather than the local school board.

"We had, in this particular case, lots of overlap between the politics and the education," O'Donnell said, but there was a more pointed issue at hand. "We are talking about seventeen- to twenty-one-year-olds who typically are not part of the K–12 curriculum."

The attorney contended they "don't really mix well" with younger students. "Their whole lives are different," she argued. "And so, educationally, the question is . . . what do we do with these two groups?"

O'Donnell also wanted the court to acknowledge that the School District of Lancaster was not rich. More than 80 percent of its students received free or reduced lunch, a key indicator of poverty. It had thousands of underprivileged students to worry about, including children who had seen violence and dysfunction in their own homes. "We have little kids who've seen their parents shot in a drug deal gone south," she said, "or who have seen their siblings raped. All of that exists—in lots of places."

Most importantly, she contended, Lancaster did not route the refugees to the alternative school because of racial discrimination, as the ACLU and the Education Law Center had alleged. Instead, their admissions policies were driven by data: statistics showed that non-English–speaking students who arrived late to the country and with limited educations had extremely low graduation rates. The district was making its enrollment decisions based on numbers, O'Donnell said.

"Regardless of where you come from or what you've been through, if you are in this age group and you have no credits, the odds of you finishing, according to national statistics and the statistics in this community, are that you will drop out in a year," she said. "And they're trying to prevent that."

· · · · · · · · · ·

While lawyers on both sides were building their cases in Pennsylvania, a third immigrant education battle was brewing further down the Eastern Seaboard in Florida, this time involving mostly Guatemalan and Haitian children, some of whom were US citizens.

In that instance, the Southern Poverty Law Center (SPLC), an Alabama-based nonprofit advocacy organization, sued a Collier County school district on behalf of several students who spoke limited English and who were pushed into adult education classes with no chance to earn credits toward a high school diploma.

The plaintiffs were just a small sample of the several hundred children between the ages of fifteen and eighteen who had been turned away by the mainstream high school or sent to a local technical school, their attorneys said. The students had no access to the mainstream school's academic enrichment or extracurricular activities and were completely segregated from their English-speaking peers. Their claims were thus not unlike those of the Lancaster refugees.

"The Collier County school district is shirking its responsibility to educate these students," said Tania Galloni, SPLC managing attorney. "Let's be clear: An adult English language class is no substitute for a high school education. Collier County has a responsibility under state and federal law to provide these children with a high school education."[7]

The attorneys said the so-called surge of newcomers from Mexico and Central America prompted the Collier County School Board in 2013 to lower the maximum age at which a student could enroll in school if they were not on track to graduate in two years.

The new cutoff was sixteen, although students as young as fifteen were alleged to have been turned away. School officials, in response to the claims, said the students in question were academically unqualified for school and that enrolling them in the mainstream campus "would have set them up for failure, with its attendant psychological and social consequences."[8] They said the students were free to pursue adult education classes and that the district was acting within its rights when it refused those who would not graduate before they turned nineteen.

But immigrant advocates knew this wasn't true. All school-aged children have the right to enroll, even if their school districts believe they'll drop out before graduation. Walczak believed both the Collier County and Lancaster schools were shortchanging the very children who had come to them for help. "It's like kicking people when they're down," he said. "It's just cruel. If anybody in the world deserves a break, it's these kids."

CHAPTER 8

NOT IN OUR NAMES

N EWS OF THE LAWSUIT SPREAD QUICKLY, ESPECIALLY AMONG LAN-
caster's tight-knit refugee community. The more established transplants—many from Africa who had been living in the States for more than
a decade—had long ago become organized. The elders among them had
been meeting for years to share resources and work toward greater representation in local and state government. For them, the case against the school
district was a major development, though not necessarily a good one. The
group, which included many Muslims, feared that lifelong residents would
think Khadidja, Mahamed, and the others were asking too much, that the
lawsuit was a cash grab when it wasn't. They worried the entire refugee
community would be labeled ungrateful. And that's exactly what they told
Vic Walczak when he came to visit them in the spring of 2016.

Walczak had heard that the elders were wary of the suit and wanted the
students, the ACLU, and the Education Law Center to drop the matter,
even though their own children had been treated similarly by the school
district. "Nobody hires a troublemaker," they told him.

The elders had lived in America long enough to know their relationship
with the United States was tenuous: They loved their adopted country, but
it didn't always love them back. Islamophobia was on the rise, just as it was
post 9/11. No one wanted to raise their hand and end up risking their head.

Trump and his followers had been making it clear for several months
that America's Muslims were on borrowed time. "If you have people coming out of mosques with hatred and death in their eyes and on their minds,

we're going to have to do something," Trump said in the wake of the San Bernardino shootings in December 2015.[1] By then, he was spreading a false claim that a quarter of all Muslims living in the United States supported violence against Americans.[2]

A week later, he told Fox News they were "sick people." "There's sickness going on," he told the conservative news outlet. "There's a group of people that's very sick, and we have to figure out the answer."[3]

While Trump's xenophobic rants outraged his detractors, they exhilarated his supporters. "I think Islam hates us," he said in an interview in March 2016. "There's something there that—there's a tremendous hatred there. There's a tremendous hatred. We have to get to the bottom of it. There's an unbelievable hatred of us."[4]

Two weeks later, after three suicide attacks in Brussels, Trump said Muslims refused to blend in. "This all happened because frankly, there's no assimilation," he said. "They are not assimilating for whatever reason. They don't want laws that we have, they want Sharia law, and you say to yourself, at what point, how much of this do you take?"[5]

His remarks made headlines around the world. Lancaster's elder refugees heard every word and shook their heads in disbelief.

"At least he's not the president," they said.

. . . .

Mustafa Nuur, a twenty-four-year-old Somali refugee and activist who regularly attended the Lancaster refugees' organizational meetings, understood their reluctance to support the lawsuit. But he knew some of the plaintiffs personally and assured the others that they were not asking for special treatment. "The atmosphere in the whole refugee community was scared," Mustafa said.[6] "Everybody was like, 'Don't do it.' And then you think about it and . . . it has to start with somebody. Somebody has to fight for the future of all of the refugee children."

But when the case was made public, the vitriol in the comments section of the local newspaper left refugees aghast. The pushback confirmed their worst fears.

"Some gratitude," one man wrote. "Looks like it took them no time at all to learn the culture of entitlement."

The remarks grew so hate-filled that the paper removed them and later placed the story on a Facebook page where those who wished to offer their opinions were identified by name. The move did little to curb the animosity. "The government doesn't have the funding to help our own war vets because they spend it all on people who shouldn't be here in the first place!!!!" one woman wrote. "I'm so sick of all those 'foreigners' coming into the U.S. and bleeding us dry!!!!!"

Another woman, whose Facebook page identifies her as a graduate of McCaskey High School, the school Khadidja, Mahamed, and the others hoped to attend, said the young refugees had no right to ask for equal treatment. "They are refugees!" she said. "That they come here and demand to be treated as citizens is deplorable. They have been given homes when so many Americans have lost theirs. They are given cash when the government decided seniors didn't need a raise in their Social Security benefits because their [sic] was no money . . . Then, they have the nerve to file a lawsuit because they feel slighted, what kind of thank you is that for a roof over their heads and food to eat?"[7]

Mustafa was stunned by the comments and, for a moment, questioned his own position on the lawsuit. "All of these adults were saying horrible things about children and you think, 'My God, maybe you don't have a right and maybe you should just keep quiet,'" he said. "But there has to be some change. Of course you are a refugee, of course you came from a foreign land. But you are also a human being and you deserve the same opportunities in education as anyone else."

. . . .

In an effort to foster understanding between refugees and locals, Mustafa spends his spare time telling his family's story at area churches and inside cramped living rooms across Lancaster County.

His talks, often delivered to Christians, Quakers, and Mennonites, are typically preceded by a prayer or story from the Bible. Mustafa, who is Muslim, listens politely before taking his cue.

He starts his presentation much the same way each time by passing around a photo of himself as a preteen in Mogadishu. Mustafa's father, Omar, was a successful businessman who was able to afford a large home for his family, one that protected them from the violence in the surrounding community. "I was somehow blinded to the way other people lived," Mustafa said. "I was a foreigner in my own land and didn't know things outside my comfort zone."

But as the terror group Al-Shabaab began to grow in number and influence in Mogadishu, Omar, a longtime activist, felt compelled to speak out against it. He urged the young men in his community not to join the organization, and soon he was marked for death. Omar's family pleaded with him to stop, especially after he started receiving threatening messages, but the missives only left him emboldened. "If I'm dying, I'll at least die being true to what I believe," he would say.

Omar was stabbed to death inside the family home in broad daylight just a few months later, assassinated by six members of the terror group he derided. Mustafa was twelve years old at the time. The photo he'd passed around at the start of his talk, worn at the edges and blurred by his fingerprints, was taken just a month before the murder and remains the only picture he has of himself in his youth.

Mustafa's mother, Sadia, had given birth to the couple's youngest child, a girl named Siham, just two days before her husband was murdered. All of the children were present for his execution, but none was given the chance to mourn him. Fearful that the assailants would return, they fled Mogadishu just hours after Omar's death.

Taking what little cash they had, they started out on what would be a weeks-long trek to neighboring Kenya, traveling more than 430 miles by any means they could—by car, by donkey cart, and often on foot. On the rare occasions that they slept, it was in open-air clearings under the stars alongside scores of other families fleeing similar perils.

Midway through the trek, they ran out of both cash and food and the outcome looked bleak: Most large families do not survive such journeys intact. Mustafa and his mother worried about the little ones, especially his days-old sister, but the family was blessed with the generosity of others. Those who were sympathetic to their plight, or who had known his father, gave them food, clothes, and blankets.

Mustafa was lucky. Others were not. He recalls one young mother traveling with three children who was forced to abandon her oldest boy in a well-worn clearing a few miles back, hoping another family could bring him to safety. With two other young children to usher, she simply could not take the boy, who looked to be about eight years old. "She left him with a note and her last bag of food," Mustafa said.

Mustafa and his family returned to the spot where she had left him but could not find the child. Haunted by what might have happened, Mustafa tried hard not to think about it. At the time, he didn't allow himself to feel much of anything at all. Numb with shock and grief about the loss of his father, there was no time to process anything that happened after, only time to walk.

To his great surprise, everyone in his family survived the fourteen-day journey to the Dadaab refugee camp in Kenya. But at the time they found little to celebrate. Soon after they arrived, they were told by other refugees that the killings were not over: Whatever death had found them in Mogadishu would surely find them again in Dadaab.

The sprawling tent city, established in 1991, would grow to hold more than 463,000 people by 2012, making it for a time the largest refugee camp in the world, its population rivaling that of Miami, Florida.[8] "Dadaab is huge and it is full of a lot of people," Mustafa said. "You don't know who to trust. You don't know who is real. You don't know who is helping you. Everybody scares you. So we left."

The family moved southwest to Nairobi after just a few weeks, settling uncomfortably in a city of more than three million people. It was a difficult adjustment: in Somalia, they could spread out in a seven-bedroom home, but in Nairobi, all nine of them shared a one-bedroom apartment.

But it wasn't the cramped living conditions that troubled Mustafa. It was his new role as the eldest male. "All of a sudden, it hits you that you really have to provide for your family," he said. "You are only twelve. But you don't have a choice." With this realization, Mustafa's childhood ended. He and his brother started selling water bottles on the street for $2 a day. Their mother, Sadia, eventually joined them, selling tea.

Two years into his new life, Mustafa made a fateful sale to a group of humanitarian volunteers from America who invited him to a local community center so he could learn English. To his surprise, a tide of emotions erupted in him during what was the first period of calm in his life since his father's killing. He spent the ensuing months tacking back and forth between expressing and controlling his anger. As he shared his story, he slowly began to heal.

So much had happened, not only in his own life but also in the one he left behind: his house in Somalia, the one he and his brothers and sisters once filled with laughter, was being used as an orphanage for those whose parents were killed in conflict. Some fourteen children had come and gone from the residence in the years since he and his family fled.

Though he was grateful for this growing sense of emotional stability, Mustafa had many practical concerns. He and his brother were regularly shaken down by thieves—including the police—as they walked home at the end of their workday.

They and other refugees were even more vulnerable after high-profile terror attacks. The Nairobi Westgate shopping mall massacre of September 2013 only emboldened local authorities in their quest to squeeze even more cash from the newcomers. Police burst into the family's apartment shortly after the killings, Mustafa said, placing all of the boys, including those under ten, under arrest for their suspected involvement. The officers told his mother they could all be released for a fee.

Mustafa watched helpless from the couch as she handed over what little money she had. "You just live every day waiting for some miracles to happen," he said.

He and his family lived in Nairobi for six years before they learned they were accepted for resettlement to the States.

For Mustafa, the joy came in waves. "You get excited for your baby sisters and your baby brothers—they will have all of these opportunities and they won't have their childhood robbed from them," he said. "And you feel excited for your mother because she has been so scared for the past eight years. She didn't have a sense of security. And then maybe you feel like you can celebrate for yourself to have the opportunity to have a life again."

But the news was bittersweet. It meant an end of his family's time in Africa. "You get excited, like 'Oh my goodness!'" Mustafa said. "But then it hits you. You are really leaving your whole continent. That's the last chapter. That's when you really close your book as far as home."

The family moved to Lancaster in 2014. Mustafa found a job in information technology and devoted the remainder of his time to activism, raising money and awareness for refugee families. He was one of the first friendly faces Khadidja and Mahamed met upon their relocation. Though he had been in the country for just a year, he became a one-man welcoming committee for new arrivals and a treasured liaison between refugees and their neighbors. Jovial and soft-spoken with kind eyes and an inviting smile, Mustafa often uses humor to build bridges between the two.

Speaking at a June 2016 story slam, where audience members volunteer to tell compelling true stories on a select topic, Mustafa used his time to tell a rapt crowd what it meant to live on foreign soil.

Standing before a microphone, white lights beating down on his temples, he explained how his family arrived in the States the day before Halloween, having no knowledge of the tradition. When a group of children approached his family's apartment in costume, holding bags of candy, Mustafa thought they were some sort of strange welcoming committee.

"So I opened the door and they're like, 'Hi! Trick or treat!' and I'm like, 'Thank you very much!'" he said, mimicking how he tried to grab the candy from the kids. When the children explained they were there to get food, not to give it, Mustafa was even more confused. He raced to the refrigerator and returned with the only thing he had to spare—a handful of carrots. Placing the vegetables in their baskets, he thanked them and closed the door.

His second story was about his struggles with technology. In Africa he never needed electronic navigation to get from one place to another. "That's what feet are for," he said. But in America, everyone plugs an address into their smartphones before heading out the door. Phone in hand, Mustafa embarked one afternoon on a journey his phone told him would take just twenty minutes. But the directions seemed odd: When Mustafa came up to a highway, the phone instructed him to keep going and he obeyed.

Roads like that in Africa have multiple exits, he reasoned, so even if he was wrong, he could change course a few hundred feet away. Not so in the States, he learned. The highway he chose ran all the way to California, with exits several miles apart. Motorists gave Mustafa strange looks as they passed him and he waved in return. Finally, after walking for miles, he called for a cab, but the driver didn't understand what he meant when he said he needed to be picked up *on* the highway.

The cabbie insisted on an address. "Just come on the highway, I'm the only person really walking there," Mustafa told him. But the driver refused, forcing Mustafa to get off the road and walk up to a local house where he made the mistake of demanding an address from its surprised inhabitants.

"These people are having this backyard party and here comes this guy coming up the mountain," he told the audience. "So I come out and they are like, 'Umm, hello,' and I say, 'What address is this?' And they say, 'We're not going to tell you. You can't just show up in our backyard and ask us.'"

They wondered if he was being chased. "Chased?" he thought. He didn't even know where he was. The story slam audience roared. Mustafa had made exactly the type of connection he'd been hoping for.

CHAPTER 9

THIS LAND IS YOUR LAND

T HE NUMBER OF IMMIGRANTS LIVING INSIDE THE UNITED STATES both legally and illegally reached a new high in 2015, the year Khadidja and Mahamed arrived, hitting forty-three million for the first time.[1]

Young immigrants' impact on the public school system could not be ignored: Nearly 10 percent, or 4.8 million students, were classified as English language learners that year alone, including one in five children in California. Two years later, immigrants and their US-born children would account for more than one in every four US residents.[2]

And unlike decades past, when they flocked to major American cities before fanning out to smaller locales, these newcomers were landing directly in small-town America, in places often unprepared for the challenge they posed.

. . . .

Within the immigrant student population, three major groups are at a particular disadvantage: refugees, unaccompanied minors, and the undocumented. Each face their own unique challenges, though they share a number of similarities.

Child refugees, uprooted from their homes by catastrophe, often arrive in their host countries badly traumatized. Half of the 12,600 Syrians admitted to the United States in 2016 were children, and many—including several in the School District of Lancaster—had witnessed at least one parent's execution.

Some of these children wrestle with anxiety and sadness and have a hard time managing their behaviors and emotions inside the classroom.[3] Amelia Hererra, a California teacher with a PhD in education, has been working with all three groups of students in the Modesto City schools for more than a decade.

She marvels at their resilience but also recognizes their challenges. Some have difficulty managing their anger while others find it hard to relax and must be kept busy with puzzles and games. Silence can bring back unwanted memories. "When they do sit still and stop and breathe, they start thinking about their past," she said.[4]

Hererra is at an advantage: she works exclusively with this population and knows what to expect. But many teachers across the country are not alerted to the refugees in their midst and are often unaware of the hardships or what might make them uncomfortable in the classroom.

Mahamed's teachers knew little about him when one of them asked the class to read an essay about a teenaged boy who faced enormous obstacles in his youth. The tale was meant to inspire, but for Mahamed, it was too much. "I didn't like it," he said. "I didn't want to read it, so I stopped."

In addition to their emotional burdens, many refugees, including Khadidja and Mahamed, come to the States with little formal education. Both were at a disadvantage when it came to learning English. Literacy is a transferable skill, meaning that children who can read and write in one language can more easily learn a second.

Barbara Marler, director of English language services at Skokie School District 68 just outside Chicago, serves students from across the globe. Skokie, a once predominantly Jewish community made famous by a planned neo-Nazi rally in 1977, has long since diversified, adding Muslim holy days to its school calendar even before New York City did.[5]

The district has recently welcomed dozens of Syrian families along with others from the Philippines and the Northern Triangle of Central America. Some have missed years of school prior to coming to the States and arrive illiterate, even in their native language, while others have had a more consistent education.

The difference between the two is immense. Children who can read, write, and speak in any language have already "broken the code of literacy," Marler said, so it's relatively easy to teach them English.

"You are, generally, just giving them new labels and new frameworks . . . for what they already know," she said.[6] In that case, teachers focus on things like the sounds letters make, semantics, and grammar while also showcasing the similarities and differences between the student's native tongue and English.

For those who are illiterate and have missed years of school, Marler believes it's best to first teach them to read and write in their mother tongue, the language they already speak and understand. "This is fairly commonplace in Spanish," she said. "It is relatively simple, if you have the materials and a teacher fluent in the language."

But this is nearly impossible when it comes to students who speak uncommon dialects or when the native tongue does not have a written component like Hmong and other more indigenous languages. In that case, teachers must focus on English, homing in on oral language development before tackling things like grammar.

Some schools are more artful in their approach than others. Many place these children in English-only settings and fail to translate report cards, alerts, and permissions slips to languages they and their families can understand. This lack of communication leads to problems in nearly every facet of a child's education, which is why non-English–speaking students sometimes show up to school on snow days and miss out on summer enrichment, tutoring programs, and extracurriculars.

And young refugees' concerns extend far beyond school. These children, who often arrive in the United States with little to no money, worry about their family's financial frailty. Some feel pressure—be it internal or external—to cut short their education so they can join the workforce.

At just eighteen years old, Khadidja knew every one of the family's bills, from rent to water to electric. She frequently considered dropping out of school and pitching in financially. "It's hard not to help," Khadidja said, especially because her mother was already so overwhelmed.

Mariam's morning routine was particularly stressful: Tasked with delivering her two youngest children to daycare each morning without a car, she then had to scramble to catch the only bus that would deliver her to work on time. She panicked about missing it, so much so that she developed crippling migraines, the kind that could keep her out of work for days.

"Everything is so expensive," Khadidja said one summer afternoon, sitting at her family's donated living room table with her baby sister on her lap, a stack of bills in front of them. "It's hard to keep up," Khadidja said, trying to keep Howa from grabbing the pile.

Mahamed, beset with the same problem, chose a different solution. He toiled for dozens of hours each week at a local supermarket, contributing mightily to his family's income while his attendance and grades suffered. It was not just himself, his mother, and his siblings that he worried about; there were new mouths to feed. His sister's husband, who suffered a serious shoulder injury, was unable to work for several months. The couple had young children. "I have to help," Mahamed said, his face taking on the worn expression of a much older man. "There is no money."

....

Unaccompanied minors in custody at US Department of Health and Human Services shelters are prohibited from attending their local school districts during their confinement. They do receive some educational services while detained, but the quality of the instruction is questionable.[7]

An English teacher who worked in a Harlingen, Texas, shelter for two years ending in 2013 said she was forced to deliver the same eight-week curriculum over and over to her middle school students despite the fact that some of them had been on site for more than a year.

"Whenever I would finish, I had to start all over again," she said. "Some of the kids were bored and ended up misbehaving." She told her boss, but he did nothing. "He told me to stick with the lesson plan," she said. "So that's what I did."[8]

Like the refugees who flock to the States from far-flung lands, many unaccompanied children have skipped a year or more of school in their home countries before enrolling in the nation's public schools and, as a result, are often far behind their American-born peers.

Some buckle under the strain and drop out; no one wants to be the oldest kid in ninth grade. Others merely count down the days until they are legally allowed to exit, no matter their potential. Veronica Calderon Speed, the daughter of migrant farm workers, knows this feeling well.

She signed herself out of school at age fourteen to work alongside her parents in Indiana. "It was hard seeing them exhausted all the time, coming home every night covered in mud," she said, so she decided to join them.[9]

But the sacrifice was too much. Veronica was a bright student. She grew angry at herself and her circumstance and broke down in the field one morning while picking radishes alongside her mother and father. "I was just so mad," she said. "My dad, in his infinite wisdom, said, 'What are you going to do? Nobody told you to quit.'" He was right, but by that time, Veronica had missed three full months of school.

It took her more than a year to make up her missed coursework but she persevered, going on to graduate from college and earn a master's degree, the first in her family to achieve either goal. A teacher for nearly two decades, she currently works with English language learners, including many unaccompanied minors, at Hardin Valley Academy in Knoxville, Tennessee.

Many of her students work at area restaurants or in the construction industry and tell her that those who speak English earn more money and are spared from the most grueling physical labor. She uses this fact, coupled with her own life experience, to keep them in school as long as possible. "I tell them to take advantage of the classroom while they're here," she said. "And that they might not have the time or energy after a full day's work."

It's Veronica's job to provide her students with an education, but she can't help but wonder about all that happened to them prior to their arrival in Knoxville. Sometimes they tell her about their journeys. One student, a sixteen-year-old from Guatemala, shared his story in book form, complete with text and hand-drawn pictures.

"Monday at 4 in the morning, I said goodbye to my mom, dad and sister to travel to the United States," he wrote above a crude rendering of a family in tears. A "guide," he said, took him and three others on a five-hour car ride to the Mexico/Guatemala border. The trip included a three-hour boat ride, a brief stay on the coast, and another long journey to Chiapas.

"The next day, we left at 2 o'clock in the afternoon hidden in a cabin of a bus for 19 hours until we reached Matamoros," he wrote above a drawing of a crowded highway. The image included a picture of a green bus with several bodies lying up top, as if spotted through an X-ray. He and his group stayed in a warehouse for two days without eating until they crossed the Rio Grande into Texas, he wrote next to a drawing of several people swimming across the waterway.

The teen endured another two-day stay in a warehouse before the final and perhaps most treacherous leg of his journey when he walked in the desert for two days, once again without food or water. The sun appears hundreds of times its normal size in the corresponding drawing, scorching the earth beneath the boy's feet.

The teen's story is linear, at least to a point. He omits his time in "the freezer," the frigid detention center where he was held before arriving in Tennessee. It was just too difficult to discuss, he told Veronica, so he skipped ahead to when he was reunited with his brothers, who had already survived a similar journey.

．．．．．．．．．．

Two doctors assigned to monitor young immigrants' care inside several US Immigration and Customs Enforcement (ICE) family detention centers starting in 2014 were compelled to alert Congress to the harsh conditions they found. Children were not being properly vaccinated, life-threatening conditions went unnoticed, and tiny fingers were being crushed by cell doors meant for adults, they said. But the problem was larger than one single malady. "The fundamental flaw of family detention is not just the risk posed by the conditions of confinement—it's the incarceration of innocent children itself," wrote the doctors, an internist and a psychiatrist. "Detention of innocent children should never occur in a civilized society, especially if there are less restrictive options, because the risk of harm to children simply cannot be justified."[10]

As biting as their criticisms were, their observations didn't come close to capturing the scope of the young detainees' turmoil. The Office of Refugee Resettlement, part of the Health and Human Services Department, received more than 4,500 complaints about sexual abuse against immigrant children held in the detention facilities between October 2014 and July 2018, with the claims ranging from unwanted kissing to rape.[11]

The Justice Department received 1,300 similar complaints. Together, they revealed a nauseating abuse of power with 178 allegations made against staff: One boy said a staffer grabbed his crotch while another child said they were offered shoes in exchange for allowing a worker to fondle their genitals. Others reported they were watched while showering or were provided pornographic material by the adults in charge. One girl said a male staffer told her he was falling in love with her and couldn't stop thinking about her, while another said a worker touched her breasts during a restraint. Some children reported that they were involved in sexual relationships with staff or that they knew of others who were. Some of the cases were investigated while others were not. Some accused staff members quit or were terminated while others were reinstated.[12]

In addition to the sexual abuse, some children were given psychotropic drugs without their parents' consent while others were placed in foster care against their parents' wishes.[13]

But housing was only part of the problem. Unaccompanied minors often had no legal representation in immigration court.[14] Children as young as three years old were made to defend themselves despite the enormous consequences of the legal proceedings.[15] Those represented by attorneys were allowed to remain in the United States roughly 73 percent of the time compared to only 15 percent for those who were not, according to records from fiscal years 2012–2014.[16]

While many child advocates believe it is a travesty for children to appear in court without lawyers, Jack H. Weil, a longtime immigration judge and senior Justice Department official, said even toddlers could represent themselves successfully. "I've taught immigration law literally to 3-year-olds and 4-year-olds," he said in March 2016. "It takes a lot of time. It takes a lot of patience. They get it. It's not the most efficient, but it can be done. . . . You can do a fair hearing."[17]

A month later, 177 child and immigration advocates joined forces to implore US Attorney General Loretta E. Lynch to halt the practice, citing Weil's claims. "A system that deports children who do not have counsel is a system that is willing to sacrifice integrity and justice in the name of expediency," they said in a letter dated April 29. "Children, by definition, lack the competency to represent themselves in court proceedings. Most children appearing in immigration court do not speak English and have no understanding of any legal system." They said many of the youngsters have strong claims of asylum and that "for these children, an attorney can be a matter of life and death."[18] But the practice continued.

Human Rights Watch, a nonprofit, nongovernmental human rights organization made up of 400 staff members around the world, has regularly condemned the way the United States has detained young immigrants, saying in 2014 that the American government flouts international standards and that it should explore alternatives used by other nations.[19] A report five years later was even harsher. "These unconscionable abuses against children are not what America should stand for," two of the group's representatives wrote after interviewing children in several border facilities.[20]

Even after they make it out of shelters and holding cells and are placed with sponsors, these children often face enormous obstacles. Some are pressured to join stateside gangs while others fall into the hands of unscrupulous smugglers who seek to profit from their vulnerability.

In one infamous case, six Guatemalan youths were lured to the States in 2014 by traffickers who promised their families they would have a chance to attend school. They were instead enslaved at a Marion County, Ohio, egg farm, where they were forced to work twelve hours a day under threat of death. One boy who complained about the nature of the work was moved to a vermin-ridden trailer with no bed, no heat, no hot water, and no working toilet. The traffickers then called his father and threatened to shoot him in the head if his son did not resume his duties.[21] The ringleader of the group was eventually sentenced to more than fifteen years in prison.[22]

Perhaps even more disturbing than the boys' treatment was the fact that they had been handed over to the traffickers by agents of the federal government, albeit unknowingly.[23] The case prompted a six-month-long congressional inquiry examining how such youths are placed with their caretakers. It found that the US Department of Health and Human Services had failed to conduct background checks on sponsors or any other adults living with the youths and also did not verify their relationships to the children.

The agency did not conduct follow-up visits, nor did alarm bells sound when sponsors took in multiple unrelated children, an obvious sign of human trafficking.[24] The department also permitted sponsors to cut off contact between the agency and the children it placed, greatly hampering the opportunity for a child to reveal abuse.

"It is intolerable that human trafficking—modern-day slavery—could occur in our own backyard," said Senator Rob Portman, Republican of Ohio. "But what makes the Marion cases even more alarming is that a U.S. government agency was responsible for delivering some of the victims into the hands of their abusers."[25]

Portman wondered how many other children have met a similar fate: The department had only conducted home visits for 4 percent of its placements in the prior three years. The senator said he was disturbed by the fact that the agency had no way to determine how many children were placed with convicted felons, what crimes those sponsors had committed, or how the youths were faring in their care. He called the department's conduct "unacceptable," adding that it already has a model in the American foster care system, which requires home visits.[26]

The investigation turned up several cases of abuse and exploitation. In one instance, a sixteen-year-old girl was brought to the country by a man claiming to be her cousin. He wasn't and instead pressured her to have sex with him. The teen was eventually removed from his care by Child Protective Services.

In another case, a sponsor falsely accused an unaccompanied minor of watching child pornography, telling the boy he owed her $10,000 to keep her from telling police. Though the allegation was false, the sponsor forced him to work for four months without pay and took away his identification papers. The child subsequently ran away.[27]

Senator Claire McCaskill, Democrat of Missouri, upon learning of the crimes committed against these children, questioned the nation's commitment to them. "The bottom line is when a child is admitted into our country, the United States of America should be an example for the world of how we care for those children."[28]

Even those who manage to escape this fate can experience other problems related to their transition, experts say. Yearslong separation from family can make it difficult for them to form proper attachments to their parents and caregivers. Some children, who had acted as guardians to their younger siblings for years, have found it hard to take orders from their long-absent mothers and fathers.[29]

Studies show they may suffer from low self-esteem, substance abuse, and self-injury. Lorna Collier, writing for the American Psychological Association in 2015, said these emotional problems will manifest in different ways, depending on the age of the child in question. "Young children may be clingy, fearful of new situations, frightened and difficult to console, while older kids may display problems with aggression and impulsivity," she wrote.[30]

Mental health experts say school would be an ideal place for children to get the counseling they deserve, but many districts don't have the staffing or funding to help these students—nor are they familiar with their needs.

. . . .

Jerome J. Schultz, a former middle school teacher turned clinical neuropsychologist, is the man schools turn to when they're trying to understand why a six-year-old overturned every piece of furniture in his classroom and spat on his teacher, or why a teen has threatened violence against himself or others.

An experienced and respected clinician, he has devoted nearly his entire professional life to understanding the relationship between the physical brain and behaviors. A lecturer on psychology at Harvard Medical School, he's been a member of the faculty for nearly two decades and also works in private practice. He's served thousands of students in the United States and abroad and describes two different kinds of trauma they can face.

The first is acute, resulting from a short-term event like a serious car accident. In that case, the trauma is confined to a single day and can be buttressed by long periods of stability.

The other is insidious and can be more damaging and complex, like the stresses associated with homelessness, abuse, poverty, or neglect.

Child refugees and unaccompanied minors often experience at least one of these hardships spread across many years. All are at least temporarily homeless and many have witnessed or suffered violence. Nearly none arrives in their host countries with any degree of wealth. For them, Schultz said, their emotional pain can be ongoing. This is true even for those children who arrive with their parents. "Even if you feed the family, put money in their bank account, and give them a place to live, the effects of that trauma live on," he said.[31]

Older children are sometimes better able to recover from catastrophe because they have a longer memory and can recall past periods of stability prior to a major life disruption. They've also had more time to develop positive, loving relationships with relatives or caregivers who can help them through hard times, he said. But most, no matter their age, remain vulnerable to long-term trauma. And, after decades of study, the medical community has come to a consensus regarding its impact.

Trauma activates the midbrain—sometimes called the primitive or ancient brain—which is tasked with keeping us alive in times of crisis, he said. The midbrain regulates heart rate, breathing, and body temperature and biochemically determines where to allocate the body's precious internal resources, sending blood to our legs in times of trouble so we can run, rather than to our stomachs for digestion.

"When those primitive centers are activated through stress or trauma, they send out cortisol and other hormones that help us either flee, fight, or freeze," Schultz said. "At the same time, the parts of the brain responsible for thinking and learning shut down in the service of survival."

Continually traumatized children live in a chronic state of high alert. "These kids are on the lookout for danger," he said. "They have been hurt and they—and their brains—don't want to be hurt again."

But, Schultz said, the midbrain has a sort of counterpart in the new brain, the prefrontal cortex. Located just behind the forehead, it's responsible for executive function. It's where we analyze the nature of a task, organize and plan a strategy for dealing with a challenge, filter relevant from irrelevant information, decide what should become a long-term memory, and make judgments about safety.

In normal circumstances, these two very different parts of the brain communicate with one another to achieve a balance, he said. But when people face chronic stress or trauma, the prefrontal cortex deactivates. "You can see it clearly in brain scans," Schultz said. "Under extreme or prolonged stress, the part of the brain responsible for cognitive skills goes dark."

Children who live under unrelenting stress for months or years, including those who have been pushed from their homes like refugees and unaccompanied minors, can have a decreased ability to analyze, store, consolidate, and retain new information. "Their memory is impacted," Schultz said. "If you can't process new information and can't analyze what goes through your brain—and the more complex the information, the more difficult this will be—you can't store or compare new information to old. You can't learn."

School can be overwhelming for these children. And their failure in the classroom only compounds their problems. "They can't focus, can't get any rewards for learning, can't be successful, constantly experience failure, embarrassment, and frustration, and all of that only further activates the fear centers of the brain," Schultz said. The only means to combat this is through long-lasting, powerful interventions that can once again make the brain available for learning.

Trauma-informed education, in which all of the adults inside a school building are trained to serve children who have experienced trauma and stress, offers hope to students who have survived significant life challenges. "This approach to education acknowledges that schools must be aware that children who experience trauma might have difficulty learning and behaving," he said.

When a child has experienced trauma, schools must learn as much as they can about their past. Ideally, they should create a short-to-intermediate-term specialized intervention, assessing the child's skill level, psychological history, and coping skills along with the amount of support they get from home and their community so they can make a prediction about how long it will take them to heal. After that, Schultz said, they must share their findings with the school staff so that every teacher who comes into contact with the child can help.

And this can't be done just once, he said. These assessments must be updated over time and the effectiveness of the intervention has to be reexamined "so you don't keep doing the wrong thing."

Schultz acknowledges that schools rarely have the resources to support such a complete inquiry, especially when they receive dozens or even hundreds of traumatized students at the same time. Still, he said, they must rise to the challenge. Even those with tighter budgets can send a handful of staff to learn helpful techniques they can share with their colleagues.

"If you have a train wreck with forty injured people and your ER is overwhelmed and you run out of beds, you don't turn patients away," he said. "You create a field hospital, enlarge the triage unit, and stabilize them. You start treating the most severely injured patients first. Then you start with the highly individualized plans. Only in that way will these patients/kids get better. It takes money, time, commitment, and a new way of thinking about what education really means."

CHAPTER 10

UNDACAMENTED

L IKE UNACCOMPANIED MINORS, AMERICA'S 725,000 UNDOCUMENTED children live in constant fear of deportation.[1] They worry not only about themselves but also about their parents' status, wondering whether a simple traffic stop might one day take them away, plunging the remaining family into even greater emotional and economic instability.

Nineteen-year-old Herlinda (her middle name) makes the sign of the cross every time she gets behind the wheel, driving as carefully as she can to avoid the police. Herlinda was born in northern Mexico and came to South Texas with her family at age seven. They arrived in the States with six-month visas but overstayed by well over a decade.

A dedicated student, Herlinda pushed herself to earn near-perfect grades in high school so she could qualify for a scholarship specifically for undocumented youth. She graduated valedictorian of her class with a 3.97 grade point average and immediately enrolled in state college to study civil engineering. "I always loved the idea of building my own house," she said.[2]

But she has no idea what her future will hold. In her valedictory speech, Herlinda told the crowd she and other undocumented students are bound by invisible chains. She worries about finding a job, considering her citizenship status. "That's honestly the biggest challenge for me," she said, her voice breaking. "I'm constantly figuring out 'plan B.' Currently, my main worry is DACA."

Undocumented youth have long stood on unstable ground. Their hopes for acceptance by the United States were dashed in 2001 when the

DREAM Act failed to pass in Congress. The legislation, reintroduced several times through the years, would have secured lawful permanent residency for some undocumented youth. So-called Dreamers took a chance in 2012 by outing themselves to the federal government in order to partake in the Deferred Action for Childhood Arrivals (DACA) program, which promised to spare them from deportation. It grew to include more than eight hundred thousand people who arrived in the States as children.[3] The Dreamers' wish was simple: to study and work in the only country they ever called home.

Herlinda never enrolled in DACA. Her parents worried that if it didn't come to fruition, she would have outed herself to the federal government for nothing and set herself up for deportation. But she monitors the program closely. She would like to apply in the future, hoping to somehow benefit if Dreamers gain citizenship.

"If that doesn't work out, I don't know," she said. "It is an ongoing fear." For now, she and many thousands of others remain "unDACAmented."

If Herlinda is not granted citizenship before she earns her bachelor's degree, she'll go on to graduate school to earn her master's, she said. And if the matter is not sorted out by then, she has another, final plan: marriage.

"But it's the last thing I want," said the career-minded Herlinda.

· · · · · · · · · ·

Because of their low graduation rates, students who don't speak English are a tempting target for being denied admission to the nation's public schools. The statistics are not inconsequential: graduation rates can help determine a district's overall reputation in the community. If the percentage falls low enough, more affluent parents will pull their children out of the public school system, reducing the district's funding and leaving it with a poorer, needier population, one that could bring ratings down further still through low test scores.

In Pennsylvania, while the state monitors graduation rates, funding is not tied to those numbers.

In some parts of the country, including New York City, dropout rates can help determine whether a campus will be permanently closed, making some administrators wary of students they believe will be low-performing. A former Bronx middle school principal who asked not to be named said this category includes children who enroll long after the school year begins—including immigrants—because statistics show they need more support and are more likely to earn poor grades.

"Most families with the choice or ability would avoid transferring kids during the school year," she said, adding that their admission sparks two key concerns. "One was that we didn't have the staffing or money to give them what they needed, and two was that they would bring our scores down and make us labeled as 'failing.'"[4]

Despite these concerns, the district welcomed these children, the former principal said. She added that she and her staff often found that these students enriched the school community and learned at a rapid pace.

But it's not just immigrant students' academic shortcomings that pose a challenge. There is little agreement on how best to teach young immigrants English, leaving schools across the country to seek out their own methods. At issue, at least in part, is whether to separate them from their English-speaking peers—and if so, for how long.

Approaches vary from district to district, with some isolating newcomers for a few hours a day and others for months or even years at a time. Critics, including those in the federal government, believe some have gone too far.

A popular Newcomer Center in Buncombe County, North Carolina, designed to ease non-English-speaking students into middle and high school, was in heavy demand before it was shuttered in 2015 for its failure to offer college-level courses and sports.[5]

But the standard doesn't appear to be universally applied. A Riverhead, Long Island, school that opened in 2015 targeting a similar population has remained open, even though it doesn't offer sports or extracurriculars. Both the Buncombe County and Riverhead programs were voluntary; students had to opt in.

Julie Lutz, chief operating officer of Eastern Suffolk BOCES, which runs the Riverhead school, downplayed the disparity between her program and the regular public school system. "High school sports to them don't mean a lot," she said of the immigrants in her program. "They come here to make a life for themselves [and need help with] English, soft skills, resume writing, and finding employment."[6]

Some two hundred students have passed through her program's doors since it opened. Not a single one has earned a diploma, she said. She insisted this isn't a problem, saying educators have to be careful not to put "our white people values" on these students. "They don't have the same appreciation for a New York State high school diploma as we do," she said. "They are here to make money to send back to the folks that were left behind."

. . . .

Unaccompanied minors have landed in numbers in nearly every state in the last several years.[7] More than 8,500 such children arrived in Long Island, New York, between 2014 and 2017, with many turning up in the region's poorest school districts.[8]

Nassau County's Hempstead High School had just a 48 percent graduation rate in 2014 when more than a thousand unaccompanied youth arrived in the district in a single year.[9] The beleaguered high school refused the kids at the door: administrators told the children they had no room for them and to go home and wait for a slot to open. The state eventually forced the district to admit the young immigrants and the district later opened a "transition school" for them. But the crisis didn't end there.

School employees were confused about who should be admitted to the new program. The newcomers were not properly assessed upon enrollment. The district didn't have a standard protocol to evaluate foreign transcripts, and little effort was made to determine the newcomers' linguistic ability. A vast majority of the new arrivals were placed in the ninth grade regardless of their prior academic attainment. Some were made to review the alphabet by cutting letters from construction paper, state auditors found, adding that the students "appeared insulted at the level of the instruction material" they received.[10]

The unaccompanied students' arrival also stirred long-simmering racial tensions in the community. Hempstead was changing demographically, with Hispanics making enormous population gains since the year 2000. For some, the change came too fast. Black residents who spoke out at the school district's infamously raucous board meetings said they resented the "burden" of being forced to educate these children, whom they said were unfairly "dumped" on their doorstep. They called the unaccompanied youth "outsiders" and said the school was right in refusing them. Why couldn't the children be routed to other, more affluent school districts like nearby Garden City, they asked?

But the unaccompanied youth did have their advocates. School board member Maribel Toure, a Mexican immigrant who was so badly harassed about her ethnic background that she was forced to publicly reveal her passport to local media outlets as proof of American citizenship, said it was the school district's legal responsibility to admit the students. "We cannot play with this," Toure said. "Enough is enough. We are liable for this. We cannot keep denying an education to these children."[11]

Still, other school administrators said the responsibility was simply too great. The Hempstead school district had been in financial and academic trouble for years and in 2015 was singled out by the state for possible takeover. Longtime residents were frustrated that the district had failed their community for so long. The few students who managed to graduate each year were unprepared for college and were no better off than their parents and grandparents. How could they possibly be expected to share what little they had with students who lived in the country illegally, parents wondered.

. . . .

A 2015 study showed that only 5 to 10 percent of undocumented youth go on to college and far fewer graduate.[12]

Research shows undocumented students' obstacles are many as they relate to higher education. According to a study out of the University of California at Los Angeles, undocumented undergraduates are "more likely to grow up in poverty, crowded housing, lacking health care," and to live in homes where families "have trouble paying rent and affording food."[13] Held back by their inability to get a driver's license or work legally, they often attend college closer to home because of the perceived affordability, even if they qualify for better schools elsewhere.[14]

Ineligible for federal financial aid, they are more likely than their documented peers to delay enrollment after completing high school, enroll in college only part time, and take time off from their studies because of lack of funds. Not surprisingly, undocumented students take longer to graduate.[15]

Even the US-born children of undocumented parents don't escape disadvantage: They have lower preschool enrollment rates, are less likely to speak English at home, and are more likely than their peers to grow up in poverty and experience little social mobility as they grow older. Nearly four million public and private school students in America fell into this category in 2014, according to the Pew Research Center.[16]

Sunil Samuel, associate vice president of enrollment at a major Long Island university, said undocumented students are ideal candidates in that they are hungry for an education. But they are often unprepared for the cost. "Unfortunately, what ends up happening is that a lot of undocumented kids and first-generation students go through the college process on their own," he said. "They fall in love with a school and maybe three-fourths of the funding is there. They say, 'Okay, I need only this much to make it work.' What we find is they get enough funding for year one, but can't pay for year two, three, or four. They don't see the long term." [17]

Samuel, who has worked in college enrollment for two decades, said these students might not factor in books, living costs, or transportation. Once they have outstanding bills, they have to withdraw or drop out until they can pay up. At that point, Samuel said, they can't attend any college and their transcripts are held.

"They end up working as hard as they can for a year trying to get out of debt and are then a year behind," he said. "It gets into an ugly cycle."

Even if they do come up with the money to attend—some qualify for state financial assistance and private scholarships—they are not always welcome. Some state school systems, including Georgia's, bar their enrollment. But a vast majority of colleges and universities throughout the country are glad to add these students to their roster: Roughly a quarter million are enrolled nationwide.

Many, though, including thirty-year-old Marissa of Denver, Colorado, feel isolated on campus, unsure of whom they could trust regarding their immigration status. They report being treated unfairly by staff, counselors, financial aid officers, and other students, and they are uneasy about advocating for themselves because they are in the country illegally.[18]

Born in Western Mexico, north of Guadalajara, Marissa crossed into the States with her family when she was a little girl. She didn't know she was undocumented until she was a teenager and wanted to get a job.

Her mother said she couldn't. A job would require a Social Security card, she told her, and Marissa didn't have one. Her mother offered to obtain fake credentials but Marissa couldn't fathom why this was necessary. Nor did she know why she was forbidden by her parents from applying for a driver's license—or why her mother started curtailing her time with friends, warning her about the dangers of getting arrested.

Pressed to explain, her mother finally told the truth. "If they go to jail here, they get out here," she said of Marissa's American-born friends. "But if you go to jail, they are going to take you to Mexico and we don't know when you are going to come back."

Marissa grew up fearful of her own deportation and stayed close to home. She graduated from high school in 2007 and took a job at a local Walgreens, saving money for college. But her path was far from linear. She would spend more than a decade chipping away at an associate's degree, navigating a system that often seemed bent on her failure. She enrolled in community college in Denver in 2009, but back then, she said, there weren't many resources for undocumented students. "I was able to take one class a semester," she said. "It was all I could afford. I was paying out-of-state tuition. It was just crazy. I felt like the world was against me, like I was getting nowhere."

Though she had a scholarship, Marissa was overwhelmed by out-of-pocket costs. She would have continued with her studies, she said, but she lost her job. Walgreens didn't ask for proof of citizenship when she first applied, but when a woman from the corporate office visited her store and told employees they would have to show their papers, Marissa outed herself to avoid the humiliation of being fired.

She worked a string of odd jobs before re-enrolling in community college in 2018, hoping, like Herlinda, to become a civil engineer. After years of watching her city balloon in size, she is eager to improve its infrastructure, starting with its aging roads. She wishes that critics could understand her plight and her desire to become the first in her family to graduate from college. Marissa wants to honor her older brother, who sacrificed his own education to keep the clan afloat, and to inspire her nieces, for whom she sets an example.

"I know there are a lot of people out there who won't accept me," said Marissa, who remains undocumented and works in a local hospital. "I try to stay under the radar. That is all I can do. If they only knew this is my home and I want to better this country, I would hope they would understand."

· · · · · · · · · ·

The Lancaster lawsuit, filed in July 2016, had been hurtling toward federal court at a speed that left attorneys on both sides scrambling to keep up. As they focused on their cases, the rest of the nation was fixated on what had been a particularly vitriolic presidential race.

By the time the refugees' case went to court, Hillary Clinton was predicted to win the election, though even longtime Democrats regarded her with suspicion and disdain. Meanwhile, Trump's anti-Muslim and anti-immigrant rhetoric had somehow made him an outspoken champion of white working-class voters who felt left behind by the Democrats.

On the day before the pretrial hearing in the Lancaster lawsuit was to begin, the nation's most influential media corporations had all but announced Clinton the victor. Nate Cohn, writing for the *New York Times*, said she had an 88 percent chance of winning. "It's about the same probability of hitting a field goal from the 20-yard line," he wrote in The Upshot. "That's a pretty good way to think about it. If Mrs. Clinton ultimately wins, we will probably look back and say she had more or less already won it by this point."[19]

Nate Silver, writing for FiveThirtyEight, said Trump should be worried. His position in the polls had moved from "middling to dire," Silver wrote. But the candidate continued to draw crowds. Speaking out against terrorism at a rally in Youngstown, Ohio, on August 15, Trump promised to crack down on "radical Islam" if elected. But his talk somehow morphed into an attack on immigrants in general. "The common thread linking the major Islamic terrorist attacks that have recently occurred on our soil—9/11, the Fort Hood shooting, the Boston Bombing, the San Bernardino attack, the Orlando attack—is that they have involved immigrants or the children of immigrants," Trump said.[20]

On that same evening, Trump blasted Clinton on social media for what he said was her stance on refugees. "CLINTON REFUGEE PLAN COULD BRING IN 620,000 REFUGEES IN FIRST TERM AT LIFETIME COST OF OVER $400 BILLION," he wrote in all capital letters.[21] It was no matter that he was wrong: Clinton had not entirely revealed her plans in this area, and refugees and asylum seekers were not the burden he declared. Researchers with the Department of Health and Human Services found that between 2005 and 2014, refugees contributed $63 billion more to government revenues than they used in public services.[22]

Nevertheless, Trump's misinformation took root. Khadidja, Mahamed, and the other refugees who had filed the Lancaster lawsuit had only a limited understanding of what the candidate was saying, but the roar of his supporters was starting to scare them.

CHAPTER 11

OPENING ARGUMENTS

THE US DISTRICT COURT IN EASTON, PENNSYLVANIA, SITS unmarked on the fourth floor of a simple, modern red brick building with a Bank of America at its base. Inconspicuous by design, it's impossible to spot from the street. But for Khadidja and the five other young refugees in the Lancaster lawsuit, no place was more important in the summer of 2016. It was there that they hoped a federal judge would intervene in a civil rights battle that had been quietly simmering in their community for years.

For the refugees, the case was much more than a dispute about enroll-ment: it was about fairness, equity, and the promise of their newly adopted country. The outcome would determine the trajectory of their entire lives. A quality high school education would equate to literacy, a path to college, a shot at a decent job. A defeat could mean decades of low-wage work, sub-standard health care, and an unstable foundation for their own children.

Lancaster school officials had a far narrower view of the case. For them, the issue boiled down to local control. They believed the lawsuit threatened their ability to make even the most basic decisions about education, in-cluding who should be admitted and where those children or young adults should be sent.

The district served a total of 11,300 students, including hundreds of refugees. What if the community was suddenly inundated with hundreds of immigrants in a single year, as had happened before? Could administrators not decide, with their limited resources and space, to send the students to whichever campus could house them?

School officials, who had hoped to avoid a costly, embarrassing trial, were resentful of the ACLU and Education Law Center for filing the lawsuit. The district believed the organizations pushed the refugees to make the claim. And they might have been right, at least in part.

Khadidja, Mahamed, and the others knew nothing of the American legal system, so they wouldn't have turned to the courts as a means to resolve their dispute without the attorneys' intervention. But even before the organization became involved, the refugees believed the district's decision to refuse them or send them to Phoenix Academy was inherently unfair. They just didn't know how to fight back. They also knew their time in the public school system was finite. Every month of their education counted as they steadily crept toward age twenty-one, the state cutoff.

The refugees' attorneys, who wanted the matter resolved before the start of the new school year, had little time to prepare witnesses or choose court-savvy experts, so they went with what they had: non-English-speaking teens who struggled to relate their true feelings for fear of offending their host country and an expert witness largely untested on the stand. Even though they believed the law was on their side, the case remained a multimillion-dollar gamble with the tab increasing by the day.

....

Khadidja was the only member of her household who was awake in the early morning hours of August 16, 2016, opening day of the court proceedings in her case. She went about her chores in eerie silence, and though she might have wanted to, she refused to wake her mother, whose sleep was rare and precious. Khadidja, slowly morphing into a typical American teen, sent her a goodbye text and headed out the door.

She and the other refugees arrived at court early and quietly took their seats in an empty gallery. Molly Tack-Hooper, an attorney with the ACLU, used the time to talk to her clients about the day's proceedings. She told Khadidja where the judge would sit and what he would be wearing. "You'll know him," she said, smiling and speaking softly into the girl's ear. "He's an old white guy." As if on cue, Judge Smith emerged from a side chamber and took his seat. Khadidja and Tack-Hooper shared a knowing glance.

Though the refugees had only a limited understanding of the proceedings, the formality of the hearing was not lost on them. Each sat in a stony silence as another of their attorneys approached the bench. Nearly a dozen lawyers fought on their behalf.

It was up to a nervous Eric Rothschild to deliver opening arguments in a case he and his team thought they had a good chance of losing.[1] Rothschild had spent most of his professional life defending pharmaceutical companies and was well paid for keeping his clients out of the courtroom. He had argued only one other case at trial and was easily tongue-tied on opening day.

Plus, he was in mourning: his mother had died just weeks earlier after a long battle with Alzheimer's. Rothschild had swiped a quarter from her hospice care room after she passed and kept it in his right pocket during the trial. He rubbed it between his thumb and index finger whenever he thought of her, which was often.

In an effort to boost his confidence and lift his mood, he spent the morning listening to the score from the hit Broadway musical *Hamilton*, a perpetually sold-out show about one of the nation's founding fathers. Nearly all of its numbers proved inspirational, a fact he repeated to his colleagues with annoying frequency. "My Shot," the third song from act 1, gave Rothschild a much-needed burst of adrenaline. But it was another song, one about the Siege of Yorktown, the last major battle of the Revolutionary War, that was on Rothschild's mind as he prepared for court that morning.

Quieting the soundtrack that played in his head, the attorney stepped up to the lectern, cleared his throat, and made his case. "Your Honor, each of these young people came to this country with his or her family as a refugee pursuant to the United States Refugee Convention to escape war, strife, persecution in their native country," he said. "In addition to the freedom and safety that this country provides, each one of them is seeking education. They want to be educated so that they can create a better life for themselves and their families in America."

Though they hailed from different places and each had their own unique experience with the school district, all were turned away from the mainstream campus, McCaskey, in favor of the alternative school, Phoenix. And the loss was tremendous, Rothschild said. "What they're missing is what this case is all about," he told the court.

The attorney said he would be presenting evidence that would persuade Judge Smith to come to two important decisions. The first was to expand the group to which the judge's ruling would apply so it wouldn't be confined to just the six refugees who had filed the lawsuit, but so it would apply to any child in the school district who faced similar language and educational hurdles.

The second was for the judge to grant a preliminary injunction that would keep the refugees out of the Phoenix Academy as the case made its way through the courts and instead place them at the mainstream campus, McCaskey.

But Smith didn't immediately hear the second request. He had trouble accepting the first. Just minutes into the trial, Rothschild hit a major stumbling block, one that could undermine the entire case.

"I apologize for interrupting you during your opening statement, but I am concerned about this class designation issue," said the ever-polite judge. "Here, you've identified six children. You've even indicated each one had an independent, different experience than the others." So how, he asked, could they and other students be grouped together?

What they had in common, Rothschild said, was discrimination: none of them was given a fair chance. The school district's decision to turn them away or place them in the alternative school, the attorney argued, amounted to a violation of Title VI, which prohibits racial and other forms of discrimination against students and the Equal Education Opportunities Act, a federal law established in 1974. The law had already served to help secure better educational opportunities for students learning English in *Idaho Migrant Council v. Board of Education* (1981) and in *Flores v. Arizona* (1992).

Another case, *Casteñeda v. Pickard*, decided in 1981, would figure prominently in the Lancaster lawsuit. But Rothschild wasn't there yet. He was still trying to convince the judge that the refugees and other non-English-speaking students in Lancaster constituted a class.

Rothschild argued the district's bias was so pervasive that he wanted the class to include any immigrant within the district's boundaries who was between the ages of seventeen and twenty-one and who spoke limited English, including the eighteen refugees who were assigned to the alternative school at the time of the pretrial hearing.

Now was the time for action, he argued: children were suffering. The education his clients received at Phoenix constituted irreparable harm. Nothing could fix what had been done.

One of the refugees was slated to graduate that very night and another had already reached the cutoff age of twenty-one. In both cases, they no longer qualified for a public school education.

But Khadidja, Mahamed, and two others named in the lawsuit still had a chance. And there were scores of additional refugees who had been treated similarly in recent years, either turned away before their time or pushed through the alternative school with lackluster results. Rothschild was arguing not only for them but also for the new arrivals who no doubt would be coming in the future. The court had both the time and opportunity to turn it all around, he said.

The attorney painted a vivid picture of two entirely dissimilar schools that he said the district wanted to pass off as equal. He asked the judge to study photos of each, starting with McCaskey, which is made up of two beautifully manicured campuses spread across acre upon acre of kelly-green grass, its pristine athletic fields the envy of lesser schools.

"So, McCaskey is like what we kind of typically would see on TV as your regular high school," Rothschild said. Its appeal went well beyond its appearance. McCaskey offered a full course selection, including college-level classes, a world-renowned honors program, numerous electives, and a wide array of extracurricular activities.

Not so at Phoenix Academy. There was almost nothing about the building that resembled a typical high school, he told the court. From the street, Phoenix looked almost like a prison.[2] Sterile and uninviting, its aging pale façade lined with black trim, it lacked the warmth and promise of the district's main campus.

But his problem with the school was less about aesthetics and more about curriculum. Phoenix was not suitable for the refugees, and witnesses would prove it, the attorney told Judge Smith.

According to the alternative school's own website, Phoenix was an "accelerated" campus, meaning, in this case, it provided a sped-up curriculum for those who were at risk of dropping out. This included students who needed temporary placement because of behavioral infractions. None of this applied to the refugees, the attorney argued, so they should never have been assigned to campus.

"Every day these students come in . . . and have to take off their shoes," he said. "Their shoes are searched. They are patted down by hand by an employee of the same gender. They can't bring in personal belongings like bags or backpacks. And one of the consequences of that, or at least a related aspect, is that they don't bring books home from school."

As a result, Rothschild said, homework was almost never assigned, so there was no way for a student to continue with their studies once they left school.

And Phoenix's rules, which made up a bulk of its student handbook, extended far beyond the norm, the attorney said. While the Handle With Care physical restraint procedure and daily pat-downs might be the most alarming elements of the school's disciplinary tools, its attempt to control its students went much further. Those assigned to Phoenix had to adhere to a strict dress code of school-issued polo shirts and khaki pants with myriad other do's and don'ts regarding their appearance and attire.

But it was another policy, one in which students were encouraged to confront one other in an effort to resolve grievances, that created an intimidating environment for newcomers, especially those who didn't speak English. "This is not the way students are treated at McCaskey or most high schools," Rothschild said.

He went on to tell the judge the school district had a long history of denying, discouraging, or delaying the enrollment of older non-English–speaking immigrants. "Everything I described violates the law, so that's very problematic."

Students were placed in the district based on two factors: the amount of credits they had obtained before enrolling and their age. If the district determined an immigrant student could not fulfill the degree requirements at the mainstream high school, they were sent to Phoenix. There was no consideration of their language proficiency, aptitude, or whether they would be able to grasp the material, Rothschild argued, and all of this was in violation of their rights.

But the judge pushed back. He wondered if students' placement in Phoenix was the permanent dead-end that Rothschild described or if they had the opportunity to transfer to McCaskey as school officials had indicated before the pretrial hearing began.

Rothschild conceded that transferring was a theoretical possibility, but it almost never happened. "It's so vanishingly rare . . . that it doesn't change our case," he said. And even if the refugees were eventually moved to the mainstream high school, how would they have benefited from attending

Phoenix? The notion that these newcomer students, who spoke almost no English, would somehow gain something by starting their education with sped-up instruction—the only type offered at the alternative campus—made no sense, he said.

Rothschild's argument was solid and he appeared to be gaining ground. In what seemed like an early breakthrough, Judge Smith started to question the value of graduating a student who might not have the education or skills they needed to succeed in life. "I'm also curious as to the relationship between getting that piece of paper known as a diploma, and actually, truly, educating someone, such that they could be a productive member of our society," the judge said.

Here was the opening Rothschild had been looking for all morning. It was his chance to plant the seed that Phoenix wasn't living up to its promise.

Rothschild said that in order to judge the merits of the alternative program, the court must consider the *Castañeda v. Pickard* court case. Filed against the Raymondville Independent School District in Texas by Roy Castañeda, a father of two Mexican American children, the case was tried in the United States District Court for the Southern District of Texas in 1978. Castañeda, through his attorneys, argued that the district grouped children in such a way that those with Mexican heritage received a substandard education.

A major outcome was a three-pronged test to determine whether schools were taking "appropriate action" to address the needs of English language learners as required by the Equal Education Opportunities Act. According to the Castañeda standard, educational programs for non-English–speaking students must be based on a sound educational theory, implemented effectively with sufficient resources and personnel, and evaluated to determine whether they are effective in helping students overcome language barriers.[3]

Phoenix failed by every measure, Rothschild told the court. And the diploma its graduates received at the end of their time there was dubious because many could not read or write English and had not advanced in their other coursework because of it, leaving them unprepared for the future, whether they wanted to attend college or join the workforce.

Rothschild said the district's decision to send the refugees to the alternative school was badly misguided and would ultimately backfire. "They need to have a slow start, building on the basics, so that they can really understand English and then access the curriculum," he said. "And here's the important thing: The district knows this, and they've known it long before we filed the lawsuit."

Judge Smith was amenable to Rothschild's argument, but he had one final question: if Phoenix was as deficient as the attorney claimed, why hadn't the Pennsylvania Department of Education or the Attorney General's office taken a position on the case as had their counterparts in other states, including New York?

The explanation was simple, if surprising. Pennsylvania's Secretary of Education, Pedro A. Rivera, was previously the superintendent of the Lancaster school district. The refugees and their advocates and attorneys felt he could not be trusted to be impartial or to dismantle a system created under his leadership.

As for Pennsylvania Attorney General Kathleen Kane, hers was an even more extraordinary tale: Kane was awaiting sentencing on multiple felony charges for her attempts to smear a political rival. No one in the courtroom knew it at the time, but she resigned from her post that very day.

. . . .

Next to the lectern was Sharon O'Donnell, who waited through the introduction of six lawyers on the refugees' side before uttering her first words in court.

Although she was outnumbered, O'Donnell was more than a formidable opponent. Sharp, incisive, and direct, the school district's lawyer opened with a jab. "I am not going to take anywhere near the amount of time that my colleague has taken to present their case," she said. "This really boils down to a couple of issues, and one is whether or not this court is going to act as a Super Board of Education and tell this Board of Education where some of its students should be educated—in the pretty high school or in the Phoenix Academy, where they are receiving their accelerated education."

O'Donnell said Phoenix can act as a bridge for students wishing to transfer to McCaskey, but many refugees choose to stay at the alternative school, preferring its quickened pace. The program is a proven winner for many non-English–speaking students, including one of the refugees named in the lawsuit. Anyemu Dunia was to graduate from Phoenix later that very day, the attorney told the court.

But, she added, school isn't for everyone. Some of the students the ACLU and Education Law Center sought to defend—immigrants between the ages of seventeen and twenty-one—don't want to enroll at all. And that's their right, she said.

"They don't have to come to be educated," O'Donnell told Judge Smith. "But once they show up at our door and they request enrollment, then the idea is to assess them for where they could best be educated and receive their diploma."

O'Donnell said students are placed in the district based on their age and "ability to graduate." The attorney admitted that students have the right to stay on until twenty-one, "but the idea is to get them educated on time and on task with their similarly situated peers."

Judge Smith took immediate issue with her assessment. What if a non-English–speaking immigrant comes to the district at age twenty to pursue a year of education, he asked. While it's obvious they won't be able to graduate before aging out, isn't there value in providing the newcomer with even a single year of schooling at the mainstream campus as opposed to not enrolling them at all or pushing them through an accelerated program?

The short answer, O'Donnell said, was no. School officials didn't see the point in placing a child in an educational setting from which they would not earn their diploma.

O'Donnell said the district has a sound plan for older students in referring them to the Literacy Council of Lancaster, a private, nonprofit adult educational center not affiliated with the school district. There, she said, they could learn English, apply for a general education diploma (GED), and eventually swap it for one offered by the school district.

"Again, the mission, the goal here is to get them educated and graduated," she said. "That's what the funding is about. That's why public schools are in business: to graduate kids."

Walczak and Rothschild, who made little effort to conceal their joy over even the smallest victories, noticeably bristled at her remarks. School as a business? No, they said as they shook their heads.

But the concern for the district was real. A low graduation rate could damage its reputation in the eyes of the state, requiring it to comply with an improvement plan, forcing it to spend money in areas it might not wish to. In addition, underfunded districts often seek additional money through increased taxes, a big ask from local residents, who might be less likely to support such a request if the district's graduation rate drops.

Asked by the judge if any state or federal law allowed the district to turn away a child under the age of twenty-one, O'Donnell skirted. Regardless of where they come from, non-English–speaking students who have reached the age of twenty are going to have a hard time enrolling, she said. "It's a dead-end for them, and we're trying to prevent that dead-end," she told the judge. "We're trying to get them on their way to something better."

But would the same strategy be applied to an American student who had failed the tenth grade year after year, the judge asked. O'Donnell said the student would have the right to stay on until age twenty-one but the district might encourage him to seek another path. Besides, she said, Phoenix is "not the prison some people would make it out to be." With 350 students and thirty-six staff members, it's much smaller than McCaskey and is an ideal learning environment for those who might be distracted by a typical high school, she said.

As for the refugees' complaints about the pat-downs, O'Donnell dismissed them. Such security is commonplace in various settings around the country, she said. Everyone who came to federal court that morning had to remove their shoes and reveal the contents of their bag, she told the judge, adding that neither request is unconstitutional or unlawful. "I believe the government has the right to keep the folks in their building safe, and I think that's what the law encourages as well."

O'Donnell added that McCaskey has even more rigid guidelines than Phoenix. "If they don't like security measures here, they're definitely not going to like security measures at McCaskey, where they have two full-time school resource officers that use more than just de-escalation techniques with their hands," she said unapologetically. "They have Tasers, and yes, that's lawful. And yes, sometimes they have to use them."

The attorney reminded the court that all of the district's schools are monitored by the Commonwealth of Pennsylvania. So, while the refugees' attorneys might bring in outside experts to tell the judge how these children should be educated, "the fact is, Pennsylvania, through its Department of Education, has told us that the magnet school, Phoenix Academy, is just fine," she said.

She also said that the refugees' national origin was not a factor in the district's decision to place them at Phoenix. And unlike the Utica, New York, school system, which was cited for steering immigrant youth into programs that would not result in a diploma, the School District of Lancaster was working hard to graduate all of its students, including those who brought the lawsuit. "So, we do the best we can and put them in the program where we think they'll be most successful towards getting that diploma," she said.

The district understood the refugees wanted to be enrolled in McCaskey's International School, but administrators felt it wasn't an appropriate setting for them, the attorney told the court. O'Donnell said McCaskey's offerings are similar to what is available at Phoenix, where students are "spoon fed" their English language instruction.

"Now if you hear testimony this week from any of the kids that say, 'I'm not getting any help,' they're not asking for help," she said. "It's there and it's there in copious amounts. We make sure that there is. We're well staffed. They're well qualified, they're well trained in ESL and they know what the kids need."

But the case wasn't about the quality of the alternative school's English language instruction, she said. It was about "whether or not these children are being funneled to a different school because of their national origin," O'Donnell told the court. Indeed, they were not, she said. In fact, Phoenix presented a great opportunity for new arrivals: its administrators prided themselves on getting to know every single child admitted to the program.

The school's director, who greeted students at the door each morning, knew every attendees' name and face, "so, it really isn't as if they're getting lost or they're being pushed aside," the attorney said.

. . . .

Sheila Mastropietro, director of the Lancaster office of Church World Service, was the first witness to give testimony in the case, introduced to the court by ACLU attorney Vic Walczak. Mastropietro used the time to outline refugees' needs upon arrival as well as her organization's efforts to meet them. She said the newcomers arrive with almost nothing and that it's up to her agency to find and furnish their first apartment and supply them with clothes.

Resettlement workers then help families register their children for school, find jobs for the adults in the household, acquire Social Security cards for all, and orient the refugees to their new community, she said. The adults also must register for English language classes.

The goal, as established by the federal government, is for refugees to become self-sufficient within three to six months. But the timeframe is ambitious, particularly for the youngest newcomers, all of whom have experienced at least some trauma as a result of leaving their home country and culture, Mastropietro said.

"Depending on where they're from, they've also been through a civil war or a breakdown in their country's government where there's chaos or they've lived in refugee camps where there's not as much order as in a stable country," she told the court. "The atmosphere for their parents is not good either."

Mastropietro said most of the children she resettled in recent years did not speak English upon arrival to the States and many had been kept from the classroom for years in their home countries. "I can't remember anyone who didn't have a break in their education, whether it's Iraqi or Syrian or the Somali or the Congolese," she said. Most of these children did not have school transcripts, report cards, or other records, she told the court.

But no matter their educational attainment prior to arrival in America, the refugees had one thing in common. "Everybody seems to want to go to school," Mastropietro said, from the youngest newcomer to the oldest entrant. "They expect to go to school, I would say."

Even the so-called Lost Boys of Sudan, who wandered East Africa for years starting in the 1980s, pushed for enrollment upon arriving in America, she said. Some forty such children resettled in Lancaster.

"Their story was really tragic," Mastropietro told the court. "The northern Sudanese army would come into southern Sudan and go through the villages and take young boys because they could turn them into soldiers."

Desperate to escape this fate, more than twenty thousand boys, some as young as six, fled the region. Only half survived the thousand-mile trek out of Sudan, through the length of Ethiopia, and on to Kenya. Many of the boys died of disease, starvation, or dehydration; some were shot to death or eaten by lions. But even after all of this, after their parents, friends, and siblings had been slain, the surviving children held out hope for a better life.

Those who came to the States had high ambitions, Mastropietro said. "They all wanted to go to college," she said. "I know some, personally, who did."

Judge Smith, impressed by the Lost Boys' perseverance, wondered if their expectations were on par with other refugees. He asked Mastropietro if the older teens she resettled wanted to attend school or if they preferred to find work instead.

Mastropietro, who had been resettling refugees since the mid-80s, re-called only one group, young men who had come to the United States from the former Soviet Union, who preferred to join the workforce. These new-comers had already completed their education in their home country, she said. It was their parents who thought a diploma from the States might be helpful.

"So, what's your sense of most of the seventeen-to-twenty-one-year-olds?" Judge Smith asked. "Are they interested in pursuing an education?"

Yes, she said: "They want to learn." And their desire extended well be-yond merely understanding English, she told him. They wanted to build a future.

Khadidja had long wished to become a nurse and Mahamed hoped to perhaps join the police force or the military as a means to make money and continue his education.

Despite this, the School District of Lancaster was reluctant, Mastropi-etro told the court. She first noticed it was discouraging or denying refugees' enrollment back in 2010. She investigated the students' educational rights and learned that all children, no matter where they come from, are per-mitted to attend the state's public schools until the semester in which they celebrate their twenty-first birthday. But somehow, she said, Lancaster was not honoring the rule. "So, the school district discouraged them, actually in some cases told us they couldn't be enrolled because they were too old," she told the judge.

Refugees' admission was stalled for all sorts of reasons, she said, includ-ing a lack of school transcripts and disputes about immunizations. Mastro-pietro said that administrators would make appointments and then cancel them—or schedule admissions-related meetings months out, causing the refugees to miss weeks of schooling. They wanted the newcomers to pursue a GED instead, she told the court.

Not only did the practice deprive the students of a chance to learn, but the delays also violated protocol. Mastropietro's organization, Church World Service, was required by the Department of State to enroll young refugees in school within thirty days of their arrival. "We keep really good case notes about that," she told the court, firing a sort of warning shot to the school district that it could not deny the postponements.

Mastropietro went on to say that the school district's problems with older refugees extended well beyond enrollment. Many of those assigned to Phoenix reported problems, she told Judge Smith.

"There were a few Bhutanese and some Burmese students who said they weren't learning English," she said. "They were basically bored. We had some drop out. They didn't want to go back because they weren't learning anything. They couldn't understand their teachers and they didn't have enough ESL."

Mastropietro said the admissions process itself seemed arbitrary. She recalled the story of a nineteen-year-old student who was admitted on what seemed like a whim. "The enrollment counselor was kind of flippant," one of her staffers told her, adding that he said something to the effect of, "'I'm feeling good today. I'm going to enroll you.' And then he enrolled him at the Phoenix Academy."

By that point, Mastropietro and her staff were wary of the alternative school. If one of their clients was assigned to the campus, her office wanted to know why, she told Judge Smith. But the answer never seemed to justify their placement. "Usually, they would tell us that it was because they were overage and under-credited," she told the court.

Although school enrollment was critical to the refugees' success, her office didn't have time to pursue the matter, she said. The problem seemed to die down for a while until it resurfaced in 2012 and again 2015, right around the time her agency was approached by Elise Chesson of Lutheran Immigration and Refugee Service, who reported similar issues.

Mastropietro suggested a meeting with school superintendent Damaris Rau and scheduled one for March 2016, during which the women shared their concerns about what they believed was a lack of English language instruction at Phoenix and about the alternative school's punitive nature.

Rau told the pair she wanted to study the issue and scheduled another meeting for April. In that second roundtable, school district officials were asked to describe, in detail, their enrollment policies but they declined, Mastropietro said. The resettlement staff also wanted to know whether the students had a choice in attending the alternative school but a district administrator said she wasn't sure.

Mastropietro met with school officials again in July when she pressed them about the dress code, pat-downs, language services, and policies on books and backpacks, but most of her questions went unaddressed. She did manage to get an answer to one query about homework: School officials told her that students were welcome to come to school early or stay late to complete their coursework.

"So, there's homework, but it's not done at home?" ACLU attorney Vic Walczak asked.

"Well, they don't call it homework," Mastropietro said. "They call it 'assignments.'"

As for the Handle With Care restraint procedure, Mastropietro said she was concerned about refugees having to witness the technique, given the violence they had seen in their home countries. Superintendent Rau, in attempting to make a concession, told her that Phoenix staff wouldn't demonstrate the hold during orientation, though it would still be employed at the school year-round, she said. The minor change did little to assuage Mastropietro's fears.

Pressed about the quality of instruction, administrators bragged about Phoenix's graduation rate, which did not, in Mastropietro's opinion, address her concerns. Students were simply not being admitted on time, she said, adding that she once tried to enroll a student in March only to be told he should wait until the following school year, a move that would be considered outrageous for an American-born child.

In explaining their decision to route older refugees to Phoenix, school officials told Mastropietro the campus allowed students to obtain credits far faster than they would at the mainstream school. But their standards seemed alarmingly low, Mastropietro told the court. School superintendent Rau seemed to say that students at the alternative school could earn credit for simply attending class, what school officials called "seat time."

Mastropietro didn't understand.

"And so, I even asked her, 'Just being there?' And she said, 'Yeah,'" Mastropietro told the court.

Walczak asked her if she believed the young refugees could learn in an accelerated model like the one offered at Phoenix. The school district's attorney objected to the question because Mastropietro was not an educator, but the judge allowed it.

"So, I have worked with a lot of students and I talk to, I mean, a lot of refugees," she said. "When they don't understand English well, I don't know how they could be in an accelerated class and learn."

CHAPTER 12

IN THEIR OWN WORDS

K HADIDJA ISSA, THE FIRST STUDENT TO TESTIFY IN THE CASE THAT bore her name, sat quietly through four hours of court proceedings before walking to the witness stand with her chin held high. Though she was racked with nerves, the teen didn't let it show. Eager to be heard, she scooted as close as she could to the microphone, speaking with the aid of a translator who called into the courtroom by phone.

Kristina Moon, an attorney with the Education Law Center, one of the groups representing the refugees, started by asking about Khadidja's past. The teen told the court she and her family left Sudan because of political instability, which she called "problems with President Omar al-Bashir." Characteristically circumspect about the most painful elements of her life, she did not elaborate, and the judge, perhaps sensing her discomfort, didn't push for details.

Khadidja told the court she came to Pennsylvania with a sixth-grade education, that she had missed years of schooling and could not read or write in English upon arrival. Still, she said, she wanted nothing more than to attend school.

"When you first came to the United States, what was your goal?" Moon asked.

"We came to get a better education," Khadidja said.

The teen first tried to enroll at McCaskey in November 2015, but was rebuffed. "They told me that I was too old for schooling, that I should get a job," Khadidja told Judge Smith. School officials offered her no means to appeal their decision, she said, and it took another three months for them to agree to admit her to Phoenix.

Khadidja started her high school career in the eleventh grade, she told the court. Her attorney suggested the placement was dubious.

"Did anyone at the school ask you what grade you had completed before coming to the United States?" Moon inquired.

"No," Khadidja said. "Nobody asked me."

Khadidja told the court she attended the alternative school's orientation—both Elise Chesson and caseworker Bilal Al Tememi went with her—but that she didn't understand the presenters, who spoke only English. Al Tememi, who speaks Arabic, was able to offer some translation, but not in her native language of Fur, so she had a limited understanding of what was being said.

But no matter what he told her, nothing could have prepared Khadidja for her first day at Phoenix, she said. She was shocked to see every student searched upon entrance to the building.

"I have never seen a place where they pat you down in order to enter school—and they actually do it every day," Khadidja said.

She added that the school's no-homework policy left her jealous of her younger sister, Nouracham, who attended McCaskey's International School. Nouracham brought home assignments every night, her English constantly improving. Khadidja, however, was excluded from her own academic experience. Unable to talk with her teachers or fellow students—most of her classmates were native English speakers—she felt completely alone, she told the court.

Asked by her attorney to recall a typical school day, Khadidja said her mornings started off with math before moving on to English. After that, her classes were a blur. "They speak and write in English and I don't understand," she said. The school made no effort to use phone-in interpreters like the one employed by the court that day and also did not use computer-based translation tools to make the material accessible. Nearly all of the meetings Khadidja had with school officials did not include a translator provided by the district, so she understood only fragments, she told Judge Smith.

But her coursework indicated something different, at least on the surface.

The refugees' attorneys knew the school district would use the students' own assignments against them in court. Moon wanted to get ahead of the matter and invited the judge to read some of Khadidja's written work in which the teen appeared to write long sentences in English.

Moon asked Khadidja how this was possible if she had no command of the language, as she claimed.

"I copied from the board," Khadidja said.

"Do you understand what you wrote there?" Moon asked.

"No, I don't understand," the teen said.

The idea that a student's own work might not reflect their knowledge was disturbing enough, but it was Khadidja's answer to another question about testing that stunned the courtroom.

"When you take tests in class, do you receive help from the teachers?" Moon asked.

"Yes, they help me," Khadidja said.

"And how do they help you when you're taking a test?" the attorney asked.

"If there is a test and I don't know the answers, I tell them that I don't know the answers," the teen said.

"And then what do they do when you say you don't know the answers?" Moon asked.

"They answer for me," Khadidja said, seemingly unaware of the bombshell she had dropped.

As Khadidja grew more at ease on the stand, her frustration with the school district started to shine through. Her answer to a simple question about the Phoenix Academy was a jumble, but her exasperation clear.

"I don't like this school," she said. "I don't like Phoenix, this school, because it's a bad school and since I started, I was told that I will study there until the people who are helping me, and who can find me a different school, and it's better to find a different school than go to a school where you don't understand anything and just go and sit there."

Moon asked Khadidja about the fast pace of instruction at Phoenix. Fast or slow, the teen said, she didn't understand any of it.

"And Khadidja, why is it important to you that you learn at school?" Moon asked.

The teen's answer reflected her earliest memories of watching and later joining her mother, Mariam, in picking crops at a farm field near their refugee camp in Chad. The hours were long, the weather punishing, and the pay abysmal. Even after moving to the States, Mariam could not escape manual labor because she had little formal education and spent her afternoons making and unmaking hotel beds, lifting the corners of dozens of heavy mattresses until her back ached. She told her daughter to stay in school as long as she could to avoid a similar path.

"In America, if you don't get an education, you'll have a very hard life," Khadidja told the court.

Moon thanked the teen before handing her over to O'Donnell.

The school district's attorney asked Khadidja how she came to know so much about McCaskey, having never attended the school.

"I know because I hear things," Khadidja said.

"Do you know that if you transfer to McCaskey, you would not have enough time in order to graduate?" the attorney asked.

Khadidja's response surprised even this most seasoned lawyer.

"I don't just want to graduate," she said. "I want to receive an actual education. Now, even if I graduate, I know nothing."

Khadidja's words landed like a thunderbolt. Even the poised O'Donnell appeared flummoxed. In an effort to move on, she asked the court to once again examine the teen's schoolwork, using assignments Khadidja had completed at Phoenix.

With the judge's permission, O'Donnell walked to the witness stand and pointed at several images on a piece of paper—they included a hat, a heart, and a camera—and asked Khadidja to identify them. The teen did so successfully, to the surprise of the court. O'Donnell was back in control and Vic Walczak was starting to sweat.

. . . .

Mahamed Hassan had never stepped inside a classroom before arriving in America. He was unable to attend school in Mogadishu because it was too dangerous for him to leave the house and was shut out again in Egypt because of the cost.

After Lancaster refused to admit him, he broke down to his mother, asking why his education was always out of reach. His testimony, brief but powerful, was facilitated by a live translator, a grandmotherly woman in an oatmeal-colored sweater standing dutifully at his side. With her help,

Mahamed told the judge about leaving Somalia after his father had been murdered and about his experience in Egypt.

He described his failed attempts to gain entrance to McCaskey, mentioning by name the man who stood in his way. Mahamed said it was Jacques Blackman who told him he would not be permitted to attend any of the schools within the district—including Phoenix Academy—because he did not speak English.

Blackman, Mahamed said, was dismissive, barely invested in the conversation that would determine the teen's entire future.

"How much could you understand of that first meeting with Mr. Blackman?" Mahamed's attorney, Molly Tack-Hooper, asked.

"I understood my name, that's all," the teen replied.

When the attorney moved on to his time at Phoenix, Mahamed told the court it was disastrous. None of his teachers spoke Arabic or Somali and they made no effort to provide translation services. Mahamed told the court he was enrolled in art, English, gym, mathematics, and some sort of computer course, but much of what was said in class was lost on him.

"I tried to learn as much as I could, but it was hard," he told Judge Smith. The only teacher he understood was his English language instructor. The woman was patient and kind, but her time was limited.

"Did your English teacher ever come into your other classes if you needed extra language help to understand them?" Tack-Hooper asked.

"No, only her class," Mahamed said.

"How often did the school bring in an interpreter to help you understand something?" she inquired.

"Never," he said.

Mahamed was unable to keep up with his coursework, he told the court. Nearly all the students in his other classes were native English speakers.

If Phoenix "spoon-fed" newcomer students their English language instruction as O'Donnell said earlier, it somehow skipped Mahamed. He studied English for only an hour each day, he told the court, and it wasn't nearly enough.

The disconnect extended to his mother as well, he testified. The district failed to send home documents that he and his family could understand. And if the alternative school provided extra help, Mahamed was unaware of it. He was never told he could participate in extracurricular activities and none of his teachers offered to photocopy texts for him to bring home, he told Judge Smith.

But perhaps the worst part of his time at Phoenix was the daily pat-downs, which ate at his self-esteem.

"Do you have to go through security screening in the morning at Phoenix?" Tack-Hooper asked.

"Yes," Mahamed said.

"What is that like?" she asked.

"It makes me feel like I'm a bad person," he said.

"How do the pat-downs make you feel about the school you go to?" she asked.

"It makes me hate the school and hate the system," he said.

"How do they make you feel about yourself?" Tack-Hooper asked.

"It makes me feel bad," the teen replied.

"Why does it make you feel bad?" she pressed.

"Police only search those who carry illegal things," Mahamed said.

"So, it makes you feel like they suspect you of having illegal things?" she asked.

"Yes," he said.

And then there was the bullying, Mahamed told the court. A female student yanked his hair in class, and a group of boys would kick at the bathroom door whenever he was in the stall, screaming and yelling in English.

"I didn't know what to do," he told Judge Smith. "I'm not in my country."

The teen said he was afraid to tell anyone for fear of retaliation. He tried to avoid using the bathroom altogether, but soon realized the plan was impractical.

"I'm alone here," he told the court.

The bathroom harassment continued and Mahamed felt increasingly vulnerable. The third time it happened, he vowed not to return to campus.

"I stopped going to school, period," he told Judge Smith.

"Mahamed, what do you want to do with your life?" Tack-Hooper asked.

"I want to pursue my education and to help my family," he said. "I want to be a policeman."

But the alternative school didn't bring him any closer to his goal, he told the court.

"I believe if I stay in Phoenix, probably it will take me ten years to graduate," he said, his voice tightening and his shoulders rising.

"Let's set aside when you graduate," his attorney said. "Do you feel that you learned at Phoenix?"

"No," Mahamed said. "It's impossible."

"Did anyone ever suggest to you that if you got some credit at Phoenix, you could transfer to McCaskey?" Tack-Hooper asked.

"No," he said.

But the school district's attorney had a different view. Sharon O'Donnell, during her cross-examination, implied that Mahamed didn't give Phoenix a fair chance. He attended the alternative school for only six weeks and didn't do enough to solve his own problems, she said.

O'Donnell told the court Mahamed once told school officials he wanted to work instead of attend school, a claim the teen denied in court. She said, too, that Mahamed's English teacher offered to help him with his other courses and that additional staff members told him to reach out if ever he had a problem. Mahamed recalled none of this, he told Judge Smith.

O'Donnell asked the teen if he remembered being told about a program at Phoenix that would allow him to earn extra credits and learn English. Mahamed didn't recall any such program, nor did he know about summer school.

But one thing was clear, Mahamed told the court: Phoenix was no longer an option for him. If given the choice between graduating from the alternative school or attending McCaskey where he might age out before earning a diploma, Mahamed opted for McCaskey.

"I would choose the better school," he said.

As for the help O'Donnell claimed was available to him, either it never materialized or was presented in such a way that he could not understand, making it irrelevant.

While his time at Phoenix was over, Mahamed never formally withdrew from the school district. He still held out hope he would one day win admission to the mainstream campus.

His wish was not lost on Judge Smith.

What happened next alarmed attorneys on both sides. The judge had questions of his own. No one knew his motive, how the students might respond, or how their answers might factor into his decision. All the attorneys could do was wait and worry as Smith probed Mahamed's past, unearthing information that even the teen's attorneys didn't know. Vic Walczak feared he was losing control of his witness and of the case in general.

"You don't ever like judges doing the questioning," he later said. "It's not inappropriate, but it's out of your hands. This was as extensive a questioning by a judge that I've ever seen."

O'Donnell was equally concerned. Judge Smith, she believed, should have been focused on the school district's educational programs, not on the journey of any one plaintiff.

But that was not her decision to make. The judge wanted to know exactly why Mahamed came to the States—and how he felt about his reception in Lancaster.

"Can you describe what life was like in Somalia as best you can remember?" the judge asked, turning in his chair to face the teen as if they were sitting alone at a quiet bar.

"There was fighting," Mahamed said softly. "My mother hid us in the house so nothing could harm us."

The judge moved on to Mahamed's time in Egypt. "Did you have enough food?" he asked, looking genuinely concerned.

"It was not much," the teen said.

Mahamed told the judge that he, his mother, and his siblings lived together in a single room of a house owned by another family.

"When did you hear that you were going to be resettled in the United States? How and when?" the judge asked.

Mahamed said the family with whom they lived had applied for asylum on their behalf. All Mahamed and his family had to do was survive. "We waited many years to get acceptance to come to the United States," the teen said.

"Okay," Smith said. "And when you got that news, was it good news?"

"I was the happiest person," Mahamed said, a faint smile crossing his lips for the first time since he took the stand.

"What did you know about the United States?" Judge Smith asked.

"That America's number one," the teen said.

"And once you arrived here, was it what you expected?" the judge asked.

Mahamed was silent. His interpreter turned her face and started to cry.

"Take a moment," the judge told her. "That's fine."

"No," Mahamed said, when the interpreter resumed her duties. By this time, the warmth was gone from his voice. "I did not find what I expected."

"And why was that?" the judge asked.

Mahamed said the school district's decision to deny his enrollment colored his experience in the States. "I did not find the support that I deserve," he said.

"And when you were at the Phoenix school, did you basically sit there all day long without understanding anything except that one hour with the English teacher?" the judge asked, the question a gut punch to the defense.

"Yes," Mahamed said.

. . . .

Next to testify were two sisters from Burma who told the court they left their home country after their father was forced into labor there. Neither girl spoke a word of English when they arrived in the States in November 2015. One of the sisters had completed school until only the eighth grade. Like Khadidja and Mahamed, she was routed to Phoenix Academy and did not understand her teachers or fellow students. She was hungry for additional language instruction and wanted to become a doctor, she told the court.

Her nineteen-year-old sister had just a ninth-grade education when she arrived in America. Like the others, her enrollment was delayed by months. Her caseworker, who had advocated for her admission, told her that her age was a factor in the school's decision. She, too, was sent to Phoenix and was so upset by her slow progress at the alternative school that she considered giving up on her education entirely, her hopes of becoming a teacher dashed.

Judge Smith thanked the girls for their testimony before turning to the lawyers on both sides of the case and urging them to settle their differences rather than continue with the pretrial hearing.

"I hope there's a dialogue between you two," said Smith, not knowing how badly their relationship had soured.

CHAPTER 13

CAPS AND GOWNS

D ESPITE JUDGE SMITH'S WISHES, LAWYERS ON BOTH SIDES OF THE case were unable to reach an agreement, so the second day of testimony began as scheduled with Elise Chesson telling the court there was no doubt Mahamed Hassan wanted to attend school.

Chesson, who had worked as a program manager for Lutheran Immigration and Refugee Service of Lancaster, represented Mahamed's mother, Faisa, and had come to know the family well. Her organization kept detailed notes on each new client. An intake document written upon the family's arrival to the States said that although Mahamed worried about the language barrier, he was "eager to start school as soon as possible."

He first attempted to enroll in October 2015, about a month after he arrived in America, Chesson told the court, but his admission was held up because he had not completed his vaccinations. A month later, having received his shots, he once again tried to take his seat at McCaskey, but district officials erected yet another barrier in forcing him to meet with administrator Jacques Blackman.

There was only one catch, Chesson said: Blackman wasn't available until December 10, nearly two months after Mahamed first tried to enroll.

Chesson said the district's delays and initial refusal to admit Mahamed were a problem not only for him but for his entire family. His mother received state aid, money she risked losing if she and her family failed to meet certain requirements.

"If her school-aged children are not enrolled, that would affect her bene-fits," Chesson told the court. The fight for Mahamed's admission would drag on for months, she said, recalling a January 2016 conference call in which school officials pushed for Mahamed to forget about McCaskey.

District officials questioned the teen's age—they thought he was older than he said—and his enthusiasm for school, Chesson said. They said his attendance "would represent a big commitment and would take a lot of time," adding that his "body language and demeanor" in the December meeting with Blackman indicated he wasn't invested in school, she testi-fied. School administrators told her Mahamed wouldn't graduate on time and was a dropout risk.

Chesson, recounting the conversation to the judge, said cultural and communication barriers often make it difficult for refugees to express their true feelings. She said she reminded them of how difficult it is for non-English-speaking immigrants to find work, especially without a high school diploma.

It was around this time that her organization received an email from Jacques Blackman that appeared to be sent by mistake. It referred to a case-worker who had been advocating for Khadidja's admission to the district. It read, in part, "This guy is nuts. Makes me say no all the time. Decisions are made on a case-by-case basis."

Chesson and her agency were appalled by the note. It wasn't what they expected from a community partner, especially one charged with school ad-missions. Even more upsetting was the notion that the district's enrollment policy wasn't universally applied. If all Pennsylvania schools operated under admissions guidelines established by the state, why would they vary from one child to the next, she wondered?

Chesson told the court of another case involving a brother and sister from Burma. The district agreed to admit the pair to Phoenix but later rescinded the offer upon learning they had "certificates of leave" from their Burmese school district. Lancaster school officials said such documents dis-qualified them from enrollment.

But the certificates were not high school diplomas, only acknowledge-ments that they had completed the eighth, ninth, or tenth grade, Chesson told the court. If the Lancaster school district refused to admit them, what would be their educational path, she asked the administrators. Were they somehow expected to enroll in college even though they had not yet graduated from high school? Yes, they told her.

Chesson said the school district invited the pair to meet with a high school guidance counselor who would help them with complicated financial aid forms. But when Chesson and the siblings visited the counselor, a staffer merely handed them an application to the local community college, a document they could have retrieved on their own.

"There wasn't much assistance or follow-through," Chesson told Judge Smith. Neither of the siblings received an offer of financial aid and, as a result, neither pursued their education.

But even as she fought for her clients' rights, Chesson faced an enormous obstacle of her own. Her organization, Lutheran Immigration and Refugee Service, laid off nearly all of its staff, including Chesson, in mid-May, just a few months before the pretrial hearing began. The office shuttered in late June.

Its closure made Chesson's testimony less relevant, the school district's attorney contended. Sharon O'Donnell told the court that because of her dismissal, Chesson no longer had an official role in the students' lives. "What actual relationship do you have now to the Hassan family?" O'Donnell asked, referring to Mahamed.

"Just advocacy," Chesson said.

"Friend?" O'Donnell asked, minimizing her tie to the case.

"Advocacy on behalf of their education," Chesson pushed back, undeterred.

But whatever work Chesson was doing was without the backing of an agency, O'Donnell reminded the court.

The former caseworker concurred, but said the organization's closure didn't end her relationship with her clients. "I don't believe you need an agency to advocate on behalf of someone," she told the court, never taking her eyes off the attorney.

O'Donnell homed in on the December meeting between Mahamed and Blackman, the one the district said reflected the teen's lack of interest in school. Mahamed refused to sit at the table and discuss his academic future, the attorney told the court, asking Chesson if she ever questioned him about his performance that day. "Did you confront or speak with Mahamed about his body language at that meeting?" O'Donnell asked.

"Yes," Chesson said.

"And did you agree with the district representatives that as a person who was interested in attending school, he should have been sitting at the table with his family . . . in order to get him enrolled?" O'Donnell asked.

"I did ask what occurred at that meeting and he said that at some point in time, Mr. Blackman was very rude and flippant and slammed the door on him," Chesson said. "So that could have contributed to the interaction. I don't know."

The attorney wouldn't let the moment slide. "Do you know whether Mr. Blackman left the table after Mahamed refused to sit down?" she asked.

"No, I don't know," Chesson said.

"Did you ask anyone whether Mr. Blackman was offended by Mahamed's lack of interest in enrolling in the school district and his body language?" the attorney pressed.

Chesson told the court Blackman's hurt feelings were irrelevant to Mahamed's future. Even if the administrator was somehow offended by the teen, he still had a job to do.

But O'Donnell was unimpressed: Mahamed was old enough to advocate for himself, to show school officials he was sincere in his pursuit of an education, she said. He wasn't playing the role.

"So, if Mahamed never set down at the table and turned his head away and refused to engage in any discussion with an interpreter, would that suggest to you that he was being a willing participant as a community partner to get himself enrolled in school?" O'Donnell asked.

"I don't know whether the door slamming occurred before or after that," Chesson answered.

The attorney soon moved on to Chesson's knowledge about Phoenix itself. "We learned from your direct testimony though that you're a very good researcher and you were able to find laws and all sorts of other things to help your client and to advocate," O'Donnell said. "Did it ever occur to you that perhaps you might look at the curriculum and see what's being offered to your clients in order to help advocate for them to stay in school?"

Chesson said such information can be difficult to access online and that the school district itself was not particularly helpful in explaining its own programs.

O'Donnell looped back to Mahamed's meeting with Blackman. The student was obtuse, the attorney said. But his behavior was, in a way, not unlike that of other teens. Wasn't it true that any child, regardless of where they were born, could have a difficult time speaking to adults and could present themselves much the same way that Mahamed did that day, O'Donnell asked. Chesson agreed. Although she didn't say it explicitly, O'Donnell was trying to chip away at the idea that the district was discriminating against Mahamed. Any would-be student who behaved as he did would be perceived the same way, she insinuated.

O'Donnell shifted her focus to cast doubt on Chesson's familiarity with McCaskey. "Do you have any idea that school resource officers [at McCaskey] do handcuff, arrest, and put to the floor any student they feel needs to have that treatment, including girls?" O'Donnell asked.

Chesson said she knew families whose children had attended both schools and had learned through their experiences about each campus. And even if students at McCaskey were handcuffed in extreme situations, that didn't negate the problem at Phoenix, she told the court.

· · · · · · · · · ·

Alembe Dunia, one of the six refugees named in the lawsuit, told the judge he was nineteen years old when he first attempted to enroll in school in the fall of 2014. His father hailed from Congo but was eventually forced to leave the troubled country, he said with the help of an interpreter. His parents fled to Tanzania, where Alembe was born, but the family remained unsafe: his father's tormentors could easily cross the border between the two Central African nations.

"My family life was very bad because my father was running for his life," Alembe told Judge Smith. "People were coming after him, so we were running here and there."

He, his younger brother, and their parents moved to a refugee camp in Mozambique in 2003. It was there that Alembe attended school for the first time, but it was difficult for him to understand his teachers because they spoke Portuguese.

Despite this, he remained in school until the eighth grade. His brother, Anyemu, also a plaintiff in the lawsuit, stayed on until the ninth grade. Neither spoke English when they arrived in Lancaster in November 2014, but both were eager to continue their schooling.

"Education would open doors for me," Alembe said.

In an effort to enroll in school in Lancaster, he completed all of the district's required paperwork and was told he would be contacted at a later date. But the call never came, he told the judge. He spent the next six months waiting for a reply before trying again with the help of an advocate. School officials eventually told him he had aged out of the system. Every other school-aged child in his family was enrolled. The rejection stung, he told the court.

"It didn't feel good in my mind, you know?" he said. "Being home when all my family members go to school."

Though he was desperate to learn English, Alembe couldn't afford to pay anyone to teach him, and he had little faith that the local literacy center could provide him with all he needed. The classes were free and he worried they were of poor quality.

O'Donnell reminded the court that if he entered high school at age twenty, Alembe could not possibly have graduated before aging out at twenty-one.

While this was true, the young man said, he still would have wanted to enroll: he would rather receive some schooling than none at all.

His brother, Anyemu, seventeen when he came to the States, told the judge he didn't understand why he was assigned to the alternative school. Speaking through an interpreter, he said it was nearly impossible for him to communicate with his teachers or fellow students. He said he was not provided translation services, did not spend enough time learning English, and his classes moved too fast. "I couldn't keep up with them," he said. And he was distracted by his peers' poor behavior. Students were kicked out of the classroom on a daily basis, he told the court.

Anyemu also missed out on sports. An avid soccer player, he would have loved to join the high school team but was never told he could participate. He also was not offered a chance to take college prep courses and never spoke to a counselor about applying to college, he told the court. And none of the documents sent home to his family were written in Swahili.

Just like Mahamed, Anyemu also faced bullying. He tried to ignore it, "but when they hurt me very bad, hurt my feelings very bad, then I go see the teachers and tell them," he told the judge. His appeals went largely unanswered. When classmates called him the N-word, staff told him to talk to his tormentors and work it out, he said. Absent adult intervention, nothing changed.

But the most damning part of Anyemu's testimony was the speed in which he was pushed through Phoenix. He graduated less than a year and a half after enrolling, having no idea he was a senior.

"Anyemu, do you know what grade you were in this past spring semester at Phoenix?" his attorney, Molly Tack-Hooper, asked.

"I don't know because the classes were mixed with people from the tenth grade, ninth grade, so I don't know what grade I was in," he said.

"Had you ever seen your school records showing when you advanced from grade to grade?" Tack-Hooper asked.

"I never saw them," he said.

If he had seen his records, they'd show he had catapulted from one grade to the next with remarkable speed.

Anyemu completed ninth grade in June 2015 and tenth grade just seven months later. He finished eleventh grade by May of 2016 and twelfth grade a week after that, according to his transcripts.

School officials would later testify that the last entry was misleading—they say it reflected when the information was entered into the system—but whether or not this is the case, the teen was ushered out far before he was ready, he and his attorneys argued.

Anyemu attended his graduation ceremony on August 16, 2016, opening day of the Lancaster trial. There he stood, diploma in hand, unable to communicate with the outside world.

So long gone was his dream of working in science that his attorney spoke about his ambitions in the past tense.

"What did you want to do with your life, Anyemu?" Tack-Hooper asked.

"I would love to study biology," he said.

"Now that you've graduated from Phoenix, do you feel prepared to pursue a career as a biologist?" she asked.

"I don't think so," he said.

O'Donnell, in her cross-examination, told the court that while Anyemu had graduated, he could continue to call on his teachers, including the school principal, for help. She wondered why he hadn't reached out to anyone from Phoenix to assist in his acquiring a driver's license.

The attorney moved on to Anyemu's graduation ceremony the previous evening. Did he recall telling Phoenix's principal that he was ready to graduate, she asked.

"No," he said, adding that the lawyer had it all wrong. "I don't remember telling her that. But I heard her telling me I'm ready to graduate."

Judge Smith, quiet through much of the brothers' testimony, waited until the end of O'Donnell's questions to interview Anyemu himself.

"I just have a few questions," he said, before diving into the student's trek from Tanzania to Mozambique. Where did he learn to speak Swahili? How long did it take him to pick up Portuguese? What was his exposure to English? Did he have much training in math?

"Not to put you on the spot, but what is ten times ten?" Judge Smith asked.

"One hundred," Anyemu replied in English.

"You are speaking through the interpreter here, but can you understand a lot of what counsel have been saying and what I am saying?" the judge inquired.

"I understand a little bit," the teen replied.

Judge Smith asked Anyemu to refer to his schoolwork, particularly an essay he had written on what it means to be a hero.

"Did you write that?" the judge asked.

"Yes, I wrote that," Anyemu replied.

"And that is your handwriting?"

"Yes," he said.

The judge complimented Anyemu on his penmanship before asking him to read the document aloud in English. The sheepish teen waded through the text with a thick, almost impenetrable accent. A third of what he said was indecipherable but the narrative was coherent, showing a level of advancement that surprised the court.

"What is a hero?" Anyemu began. "A hero has to make you strong or happy. A hero wants you to (sic) good future. It is important to have a hero . . . I like to be a hero because I like to help people. My mother is (sic) hero because she works hard and she is strong . . . My mother goes (sic) work everyday. Here (sic) only day off is on Sunday . . . My mother gives me good advice. She loves me very much . . . There are many heroes in the world . . ."

Vic Walczak, the refugees' lead attorney, was beginning to worry. Once again, Smith had control of the testimony. Worse yet, Anyemu seemed far more advanced in his command of the English language than anyone in the courtroom had thought, including the judge.

"Obviously you are very bright, very smart," Judge Smith said.

"I was a little bit smart," Anyemu replied.

"Who is smarter, you or your brother?" the judge asked playfully.

Anyemu was reluctant to answer, saying, essentially, that he didn't know.

"Right," Judge Smith said. "You've got to be careful because you don't know what's going to happen at home. But in less than a year you went from speaking no English at all to being able to write that clear, basic English."

The judge asked Anyemu if he was disappointed by the school's decision to refuse his brother, Alembe.

"I was very, very upset," the teen said. "I didn't feel good about that."

The judge, turning back to Anyemu's own accomplishments, noted that he appeared to rank high among his peers. "You finished number six out of 107 students," the judge remarked, referring to the school's own records. "Did you know that?"

No, the eighteen-year-old said, he didn't.

It was unclear whether Judge Smith believed Phoenix provided Anyemu a satisfactory education or whether he gave credence to his high ranking. But one thing was obvious: The judge believed the teen might have benefited from additional schooling. If he could come so far in just sixteen months, Smith said, it was likely he could have gone even further if he spent a full four years in high school. Anyemu agreed, saying he wished to learn as much as he could.

"And you think you could have learned even more if you were at Mc-Caskey?" the judge asked.

"I think McCaskey would be better for me because the school is big and they have more teachers and they don't go fast like at Phoenix," he said.

Asked if there was anything more he would like to tell the court, Anyemu urged for change at Phoenix. The no-homework policy put students like him at a terrible disadvantage, he said. Without after-hours assignments, he was tempted to simply watch TV or fall asleep when he returned home from school. "I want to make sure changes happen so people who would come after me, refugees who come after me, they can be in better shape than me," he said.

Judge Smith, almost as if delivering a soliloquy, wondered aloud how a non-English–speaking student could complete his entire high school career in just sixteen months. How could he have satisfied the school's academic requirements and still need an interpreter to speak on his behalf in court?

O'Donnell told him that the teen was able to exit the program quickly because it offered only the basic, required courses—just enough for him to earn a high school diploma. And Phoenix's classes were significantly longer in duration than those at McCaskey, allowing teachers to cover more material each day, she said.

But Judge Smith was skeptical. He could not understand how a student from a foreign country with little formal schooling could complete in sixteen months what an English-speaking child who attended school in the States throughout their entire lifetime would need four years to finish.

Anyemu, the judge said, came from Mozambique and was unable to say anything outside "hello" in English upon arrival. But somehow, he was able to earn a high school diploma—even though he couldn't speak on his own behalf in federal court.

"It's a little hard to understand," the judge said, moments before urging both sides to settle. "I would again suggest to counsel that you discuss to see if there's any meeting of the minds or if you're at complete loggerheads with respect to resolving some or all of the issues by agreement and consent."

CHAPTER 14

TOUGH CROWD

I T WASN'T UNTIL THE THIRD DAY OF TESTIMONY THAT THE COURT finally heard from an adult who worked inside Phoenix Academy. Jandy Rivera spent a year and a half teaching ninth- and tenth-grade English and literature at the alternative school before she quit in January 2013. Asked to describe its atmosphere, she called Phoenix "loud, chaotic, and violent," telling the court she was so troubled by its disciplinary tactics that she left in the middle of the school year with no other offer of employment.

In explaining how Phoenix was run, Rivera described a school that was, on some level, separate from the rest of the district. She said Camelot Education, the for-profit company that ran Phoenix, set the campus's disciplinary policies, while the School District of Lancaster established the curriculum. Both had unrealistic expectations: Camelot required disciplinary perfection from students while the school district demanded teachers cover their topics at double the speed of the mainstream high school, she said.

Rivera taught four classes at Phoenix. Some had more than forty students—though school officials said the average class size was twenty-five—and many of the teens in her charge had significant behavioral issues.

"I had students who came in far below grade level with reading," she told the court. "They were high school students, but they were reading at an elementary school level . . . And then I had refugee students who were coming in who had no English background whatsoever. So trying to meet each and every one of their needs while teaching the curriculum at an accelerated pace was impossible."

The no-homework policy was particularly challenging for her subject matter. Normally, she said, students are permitted to bring home novels and short stories so class time can be used to study the works in detail. But at Phoenix, much of her instructional time was spent simply reading the texts. It was hard for them—and for Rivera—to keep up.

"How did the administrators, if at all, verify how much of the district curriculum was covered in your class?" asked attorney Kristina Moon.

"They didn't," Rivera replied.

"And in reality, did your students master the material in Phoenix's accelerated model?" the attorney asked.

That all depends, Rivera said. Those who came into the school at or above grade level managed to digest the material, but those who came in behind—either because they had missed school or did not speak English—were hopelessly lost. They would have benefited from what she called a "regularly paced" atmosphere or an even slower model, adding that this was particularly true of the refugees.

"There were some who were coming in who had been born in refugee camps," Rivera said. "So, their education needs I felt were very unique . . . It wasn't just about putting a pencil and a piece of paper in front of them and, 'Here's the English alphabet.' It was about figuring out a way to somehow try to slow down the educational process enough for them to learn some of the material."

And her responsibilities extended well beyond classroom instruction, she told the court. Rivera and the rest of the staff were expected to help new immigrants understand how school worked: how to come in each morning, find the cafeteria, acclimate to a new atmosphere, and adapt to a brand new country—all while making them feel welcomed and safe. Phoenix fell short in matters large and small, she told Judge Smith.

"There was one instance where we had a young man from an African country come in and he spoke no English," Rivera said. "I was in the entranceway in the morning and he was standing by the restrooms . . . I wondered what was he doing." Rivera soon realized the child didn't know which was the boys' room and which was the girls' because neither included a corresponding image. After pointing him in the right direction, Rivera quickly printed clip art for all of the school's restrooms.

The former teacher had a hard time communicating with the many students in her care who did not speak English. She was not certified to teach

English as a second language and had almost no outside assistance. Phoenix had only one ESL teacher during her tenure, she told the court. And Rivera recalled only one instance where the instructor offered any guidance to the remainder of the staff in the form of a twenty-minute lesson. Her instruction offered no help in how to teach in an accelerated model like the one used at Phoenix, Rivera said.

Rivera told the court her problems with the school were many. She said staff would misuse the Handle With Care protocol, even in cases where students had committed no infraction at all. "Staff members would suddenly pick up a child for no reason, slam a child against a wall, slam a child against a door, scream at a child, yell at a child, curse at a child," she said.

The result, she said, was that many students were "wary, fearful, and tense" around those employees who could not control their anger. "There were staff members who would provoke students with words or with their hands, even though the students hadn't done anything," she said.

Rivera went on to tell the court about a Phoenix student who had been restrained by staff and who came back to campus with bruises on his face and neck. The students who saw him were frightened by his appearance and asked Rivera what they should do if they were similarly treated. The teacher told them to alert their parents and file a police report, adding that it was this bit of advice that put her on the outs with management and eventually led to her early exit.

Phoenix administrators say Rivera never claimed to have directly witnessed the student's alleged encounter with staff. She couldn't have, they said in a statement, "because no such incident occurred at Phoenix Academy."[1]

Rivera, like many teachers at the school, told the court she was made to conduct the morning pat-downs, her hands running down the students' sides, arms, legs, and back. She said staff went so far as to feel girls' underarms and bra straps for illicit items, adding that the refugees were particularly sensitive to the procedure and would stiffen immediately upon being touched.

They were equally disturbed by another element of life at Phoenix Academy, a morning meeting for students and staff called Townhouse. Though it was meant as a sort of daily pep rally, it would often devolve into a venting session for teachers, Rivera said. One instructor used the meeting to scream and curse the students, "often saying things like, you know, 'You guys can't do this, you're not going to accomplish anything, you're not going to learn,'" she told Judge Smith.

The school district offered no interpreters for Townhouse, leaving the non-English–speaking students to cower in fear, unable to understand what was taking place. "It was awful," Rivera said. Day after day the refugees sat "hunched over, heads down, eyes on the floor, shoulders forward—and they appeared terrified," she told the court.

After leaving her job at Phoenix, Rivera went on to work for Pennsylvania's Migrant Education Program, which offered added educational support for migratory children at home, in the community, and at school. She was assigned to several campuses within the School District of Lancaster and visited Phoenix at least monthly, checking in on migrant and refugee students' grades and meeting with their English language teacher to assess their progress, she told the court. Through her work with the program, she also had the opportunity to teach summer school for English language learners.

It was a far more relaxed environment than the one at Phoenix, she recalled. She taught a dozen students at a time and was much better able to address their needs. She said the experience taught her that if she slowed down the pace of instruction and allowed time for conversation and questions, newcomers learned far more effectively.

The school district, through Sharon O'Donnell, challenged Rivera's testimony, saying she had no firsthand knowledge of the day-to-day goings-on at Phoenix after she left. She did not teach at the school while Khadidja, Mahamed, and the other plaintiffs were present and could not offer testimony as to their experience. The attorney went on to say she should have asked for assistance in teaching students with varied abilities, including those who were new to the country.

O'Donnell told the court Rivera had been placed on an "improvement plan" by her supervisors, meaning that they took issue with her performance, though she did part with a recommendation letter written by one of her superiors.

As for Rivera's description of Phoenix as "chaotic" and "loud," O'Donnell wondered what would lead her to believe McCaskey was any different. But Rivera held firm on her point that Phoenix's disciplinary practices were unusual, especially in comparison to the mainstream campus.

Phoenix stationed two or three "behavior specialists" on each floor in addition to a "team leader" for each level during her tenure, Rivera told the court. Their purpose was to keep order. An additional worker oversaw the behavioral staff as a whole. "That's a lot of people," Rivera told Judge Smith.

And the greater community was well aware of the school's disciplinary focus, she said. If one were to walk down the street in Lancaster and ask about Phoenix, local residents would say, "That's where the bad kids go."

The judge asked Rivera, based on her experience, if there was any advantage to educating refugees at the Phoenix Academy.

"No," she said without hesitation. "By having them go through the material really quickly and then give them an A or a B for being there every day doesn't mean that they're actually mastering the material and mastering the English language."

Judge Smith homed in on the point. "And would students, refugee students who couldn't speak English, sit in class without any interpreter or any way of understanding what the teacher was teaching them and get a credit just because they were sitting there?" the judge asked.

Yes, Rivera said. Attendance was factored into what the school called "participation points."

"Was there a lot of effort to focus on the unique challenges that these refugee students had, in particular with their language barriers?" the judge asked.

"I didn't see that coming from the top, as far as Phoenix Academy," Rivera said. "I only saw that really driven home by our ESL teacher. She's the one who went above and beyond in trying to meet the unique needs of the refugee students."

Finally, Judge Smith focused on the crux of the case against the school district—whether or not Phoenix truly served the educational needs of the refugees assigned to the campus. Did the alternative school help students overcome their language barriers, he asked.

"Absolutely not," Rivera said.

While her testimony was damaging to the school district, it still wasn't clear from her comments whether McCaskey would have been a better choice for the refugees.

O'Donnell was not about to let the court think the former teacher made a strong case for the mainstream campus.

"Ms. Rivera, would you have any knowledge that a student age seventeen to twenty-one, if enrolled at McCaskey, would overcome those language barriers before he or she finished at age twenty-one?" O'Donnell asked.

"I can't say that I do," Rivera said.

. . . .

While Rivera's testimony focused on the tone and atmosphere of the alternative school, Helaine Marshall focused on the speedy delivery of Phoenix's curriculum and whether it was a good fit for the refugees.

Marshall, director of language education programs at Long Island University, was the Education Law Center's expert witness, and for good reason. She spent much of her career focusing on a particular subset of newcomer students: non-English speakers with little formal education and limited literacy in their native language who were at least two years behind grade level upon arrival to the States. All six refugees in the Lancaster lawsuit fell into this category.

Educators sometimes refer to these children as students with limited or interrupted formal education or SLIFE. This was the same group at the heart of the Utica, New York, and Collier County, Florida, lawsuits, who had been targeted by schools all across the country for years.

Marshall's testimony was essential, if only she could withstand the questioning. An academic, she prioritized accuracy and completeness above clarity and brevity, and the halting manner in which she spoke tested attorneys on both sides.

But her knowledge was unmatched. Marshall was the director of her university's language education program and taught eighteen credits per year, centering around a curriculum known as Teaching English to Speakers of Other Languages or TESOL. She earned a doctorate in the topic from Teachers College at Columbia University, where she had also taught. She was certified to teach kindergarten through twelfth grade in the state of New York and had supervised more than two hundred teachers of English as a second language during her decades-long career.

But the work that led to her expertise with this particular category began in 1987 when she served as a faculty member and assistant professor at the University of Wisconsin–Green Bay.

She spent six years training prospective teachers in how to teach English as a second language and took great care in sharing her knowledge and the rationale behind the methods she promoted.

But, she told the court, she had it all wrong.

"So, my students would approach me after class, you know, and they'd say, 'Look . . . none of what you've been teaching me is working,'" she told Judge Smith.

Though her methods had been successful with other groups of English language learners, they had somehow failed in Wisconsin when applied to Hmong refugees. Hmong, who hail from the highlands of Laos, arrived in the States by the thousands following the end of the Vietnam War, with many settling in Minnesota and Wisconsin. Desperate to learn more about this group, Marshall began observing teachers and students in the classroom.

"I started to realize that we were dealing with a very different population here," she told the court. After much research, she learned the Hmong hailed from an oral culture with limited literacy, making reading in English particularly difficult. "The transition to literacy was a major shift for them," she said.

Many came to the States with little to no formal education and learned through rote memorization. Traditional ESL teaching methods didn't work with this population.

The professor's observations caused a stir in Wisconsin and she started presenting her findings at conferences. Her work was well received and she eventually started publishing on the topic, spending the next several years assessing school districts' English language programs.

Her exposure to these children and their teachers showed her that some ESL students, particularly those who have missed years of schooling and are more than two grades behind their peers, require far more from their schools than to simply learn English. They need to understand the culture, customs, mores, and expectations of their new homeland. "Language and culture go hand in hand," the professor told the court. "When you're teaching an ESL student, you're also teaching the culture of the country."

Marshall's early work focused mainly on Hmong students. It was because of this that she came to believe, albeit erroneously, that their academic challenges were unique to their culture. Only later did she come to understand that other groups of refugees and immigrants—including Haitians, Vietnamese, and Somalis—wrestled with similar issues. But she still didn't entirely understand why, so she began studying how these children were taught in their home countries. Her efforts led her to an important conclusion.

"The way we're teaching and the way they're learning doesn't match," she told the court. "And so what's important to understand is you can't simply double down on your way of teaching and just go slower. It doesn't work. You have to incorporate some strategies that they feel comfortable with at the same time."

After this revelation, Marshall devoted the remainder of her career to spreading the word about this group. She'd written two books and several peer-reviewed articles on the topic. By the time she appeared in court, she'd presented her findings hundreds of times and was a sought-after expert in this area.

The ACLU and Education Law Center believed she was more than capable of assessing the School District of Lancaster, but district officials disagreed.

Marshall hadn't visited any of the district's schools and had not spoken with a single administrator. The professor interviewed only one former teacher, Jandy Rivera, and even more important, the school district's attorney said, Marshall had never actually taught students like the ones in the Lancaster lawsuit.

"Throughout the course of your career, your very long career, you've never delivered ESL instruction to students K–12 in any public school," O'Donnell said. "Is that correct?"

Marshall tried to hold up her work with teachers as a means to bolster her experience with children but the answer was no, she told the court.

And, just as important in the eyes of school officials, she never considered the cost of the changes she called for either.

"So, when you make recommendations to superintendents or boards of education, do you also give them recommendations in terms of how they're going to fund [them]?" O'Donnell asked.

"No," Marshall answered. "That was not my purview."

"So, your purview was just to come in, evaluate, and give some advice about how they can improve a system," O'Donnell said. "Is that correct?"

Marshall bristled, saying she gave more than advice. She told the court she was hired to make sure schools were in compliance with state and federal regulations. But the core of O'Donnell's criticism still stood: Marshall never factored in the cost. Her ideas might have had merit, but without funding, they were merely pie-in-the-sky suggestions, ones the school could not afford.

Regardless of cost, students like the ones in the Lancaster lawsuit required intensive English language instruction upon arrival to the States, Marshall said. But even before the instruction begins, schools must determine whether they can speak, read, and write in their native language. If so, they'll find it much easier to learn English. If not, teachers must take on the tough task of teaching the child literacy in a language they're unfamiliar with. It's a major challenge for educators, Marshall conceded, one that requires time and training.

But while language acquisition is an important focus, these students also must learn other subjects, including math, science, and social studies. "You don't avoid that," Marshall told the court. "They need that."

These children can be taught at grade level, but their teachers must constantly incorporate background information to build their knowledge, the professor said.

Above all, they must have access to the education they are entitled to, Marshall told the court. Their mere admission to school is not enough. These students can't learn the material if they can't understand their teachers—and if that's the case, they don't actually have access, Marshall said.

This was a critical distinction, reflecting so much of what was being argued in court, whether the students' admission by the district equated to their receiving a quality education.

Once enrolled, teachers must be sensitive to the students' learning styles, Marshall said. Multiple choice, matching, and true/false tests are often completely alien and utterly confusing to children from other countries.

"Students like this look at these kinds of tasks and they think we're trying to confuse and trick them," Marshall said. "We say, 'Compare, contrast, analyze, summarize, define,'" but SLIFE students often don't understand these concepts.

Marshall also said that students must feel a sense of belonging at school, that the environment must be safe and welcoming. If not, their fear will take over. "If you're not comfortable in your learning situation, you have anxiety, you're not going to be a risk taker," she told the court. "Your feelings are blocking your ability to access learning . . . and you kind of shut down."

The professor added that while she had not visited Phoenix Academy, she read its online description and other written materials. She interviewed all six refugees in the lawsuit in addition to local resettlement staff. She studied the state's own educational guidelines and the standards established by the WIDA Consortium, a national group devoted to providing critical resources to those who teach the type of students represented in the lawsuit. WIDA, part of the University of Wisconsin–Madison, boasted dozens of member states, including Pennsylvania. Based upon this and other lessons she had gleaned through the years, Marshall said Phoenix's program is unlikely to help seventeen-to-twenty-one-year-old immigrant students overcome their language barriers, adding that its fast pace of instruction is "totally inappropriate for this population."

The best way to explain it, she told Judge Smith, was to imagine an airplane taking off on a runway: Phoenix was asking the refugees to soar into the air without first building up speed.

Marshall thought the school's approach was ridiculous, but that's not what she said in court. Instead, she said Phoenix's program was not built on sound educational theory, that it ran counter to what had been long-accepted practice for newcomer students. What they needed, she said, was time. Repetition and redundancy helps students understand new material. While Marshall empathized with the district's desire to move fast because the refugees' time in school was running low, the accelerated model actually held these students back.

"It backfires," she said. "It's misguided."

Marshall told the court the district regularly placed immigrant students in settings in which they could not learn. Phoenix's computer class was just one example, she said. Not only was the material presented in a language the students could not understand, but it also ignored their oral tradition. "Their most comfortable way of learning is from people, from interaction, not from written material, not from worksheets or even from the computer," Marshall told the court.

Marshall said English language learners are divided into six levels, beginning with *entering*, and that all of the students in the Lancaster lawsuit fell into this category. Entering students have the least English proficiency of all and are capable of stringing together only a few words to form simple sentences, she said. Their vocabulary is sparse, and when they speak, their words are often out of order. Such students need two to three hours of direct English language instruction per day to succeed. They need to be taught the new language in tandem with core subjects like math, science, and social studies.

And it's not about a math teacher teaching a little slower, Marshall said. It's about a math teacher teaching a lesson in geometry and in the English language at the same time. "It's very difficult not to dumb down the content but to make the language accessible," she told the court.

Marshall said the Lancaster district already had a successful program for these students in McCaskey's International School. Those assigned to the program learned English in their core subjects, just as she recommended. It also promised close communication with families, access to appropriate translation services, and to help students connect with community resources. It was exactly what one might expect of a successful newcomer program. The International School offered ninety-eight minutes of English instruction per day, which showed its dedication to helping students learn the language.

Marshall also liked the school's decision to group the newcomers together throughout the school day. Such a tactic made it easier for their teachers to accommodate their needs, helping them progress more quickly.

Phoenix's decision to place newcomer students alongside native English speakers didn't work, Marshall said. "It's too much of a spread." In this model, the students who did not speak English felt overwhelmed and native English speakers suffered too: Their progress slowed as their teachers focused on the needs of the newcomers, she said.

Marshall said McCaskey was the clear choice for the refugees, including students like Alembe Dunia, who had been turned away by the district. He would have benefited mightily from a year at the International School, she said.

The program would have given him a window into math, science, and social studies and would have made him literate in English. Plus, she told the judge, he was entitled to it.

O'Donnell objected, saying this was not Marshall's decision to make. "Whether or not a child is entitled to an education the way she's testified is subject to the court's discretion," the attorney said. The judge listened patiently but ultimately allowed Marshall to continue.

The professor said the refugees would have had more opportunity for meaningful interaction with their peers at McCaskey than they did at Phoenix. She cast doubt on the notion that Phoenix could somehow serve as a bridge to the mainstream campus because the students would first need a strong foundation in English, something the alternative school did not provide.

And it wasn't clear that the school or the district had fully assessed whether Phoenix's model was actually working for the refugees, she told the court.

Marshall also had problems with the alternative school's staffing. According to the records she was shown, Phoenix had only one English as a second language teacher, though it was later revealed that at least two others had ESL certification. Even then, Marshall said, it wasn't clear how much of their time was devoted to English language instruction. In most cases, the refugees had been placed in classrooms taught by instructors who did not hold ESL credentials.

The professor also took issue with how the students were assessed upon attempting to enroll in the school system. Though each was given an aptitude test, the school district, at least according to its records, did little to understand their academic ability. It should have used a more systematic analysis to identify gaps in their knowledge, Marshall said. Instead, all that was written were a few scattered notes.

"There was not a particular form that was being filled out . . . it was more of an informal understanding of their background," Marshall told the court.

She also was struck to learn that Phoenix was designed for second-chance students, kids who had already been through the system. They were quite unlike the refugees who were learning everything for the first time. "There was an underlying assumption that students who attended this school were in some way antisocial or need behavior adjustment," the professor said.

Marshall went on to say Phoenix's Handle With Care protocol, confrontational atmosphere, and dress code had converged to make the refugee students feel alienated. "What it encouraged was for them to feel marginalized in a sense," she told Judge Smith. "They already don't completely fit in." These students came from extraordinarily difficult backgrounds, she said. It was hard enough for them to adjust to a new country and a new style of learning without feeling like they'd done something wrong.

"If you feel you don't fit in from the start, it's much harder for you to focus and pay attention to your learning," she told the court.

Students who are made to feel like outsiders are forced to make a choice in order to survive: They either reject the new culture and retreat inward to a more comfortable environment, or they abandon their original culture and completely Americanize themselves, she said. But neither is the right answer. Current theory calls for students to retain their original culture while also embracing and adapting to their new country—to become, as Marshall said, bicultural. "We're not in the days of assimilation, the melting pot, where everybody's going to blend and be the same," she told the court. "This is a diverse society and we value other cultures."

But of all Phoenix Academy's shortcomings, the no-homework policy was perhaps the most harmful to the refugees, Marshall said. In order for the students to learn English, they needed maximum exposure to the language, which included the chance to study at home where they would otherwise speak in their native tongue.

She cited the school's failure to connect with families as another significant problem. The refugees' parents had little understanding of their children's educational experience. They didn't know why their children were placed at Phoenix and had no knowledge of the other programs offered by the school district, they told her. Marshall said families should be made to feel comfortable visiting the district and taking part in activities designed for English language learners. But even that, she said, is merely a start. "It's not simply a matter of visiting the school or having even a parent-teacher conference," Marshall said. "Those are two very minimal approaches."

She also believed the district was wrong to keep siblings apart. Those allowed to enroll on the same campus would have provided critical support for one other, filling in information the other had missed, she said.

As for the refugees' high grades—many scored A's on their report cards—they didn't reflect what they actually knew, Marshall told the court. Khadidja was allegedly number one out of eighty-four students, yet the teen could barely speak a full sentence in English.

And, Marshall testified, some of the refugees were not enrolled in core subjects like math and social studies, as is required by the state. All struggled mightily with listening to, speaking, reading, and writing in English, Marshall said, and some had racked up dozens of absences, making their high marks even more unlikely.

And there were other problems too. The refugees' course material was not age-appropriate: it was meant for far younger native English speakers. And many of the assignments, meant to build students' vocabulary, relied on ambiguous drawings rather than photographs, which are far more specific.

She also took a close look at the refugee students' writing samples, which seemed to indicate they had a strong grasp of the English language. In examining a passage written by Khadidja, Marshall told the court she doubted the teen understood what she wrote, that it was more likely she simply copied the material. "I've seen it in one hundred ESL classrooms," Marshall said. "They sound perfect and then you turn to them and say, 'Oh, tell us what you just read,' and the student draws a blank."

Marshall came to the same conclusion regarding one of the Burmese sisters' written work. After interviewing the girl and listening to her testimony in court, Marshall found it highly unlikely she wrote the passage on her own. Marshall spotted a similar inconsistency in her sister's grades: The girl scored lower in her English as a second language class than she did in her core subjects, where she earned A's.

"How can that be?" Marshall asked. "It doesn't make sense to me."

One of the refugees could only complete math problems on a third-grade level, yet all of these students were somehow pushed through from one grade to the next. Phoenix administrators later said these students earned their promotions and were not simply skipped ahead. While the students had not yet mastered English, they had a wide variety of other skills that lead to their success, they said.[2]

But in interviewing the refugees, Marshall made a troubling discovery: Anyemu told her that school seemed "the same every day."

The professor thought the comment odd, considering students are constantly exposed to new material, but after consideration, his remark made sense. Anyemu understood almost none of what was said in class, making each day the same as the one before, Marshall told the court.

"It's detrimental, what they're doing," she said, adding that the students, even after several months of schooling, were still only beginning to learn English.

. . . .

Marshall brimmed with information, but O'Donnell's relentless questioning wore her down. She sounded, at times, confused. A series of seemingly innocuous questions about her preparation for trial left her visibly upset. The professor couldn't name the building in which she interviewed the refugees or the organization that coordinated the meetings. Her memory, O'Donnell implied, was suspect.

"I can picture the building in my mind and I went there two days in a row and spent all day in the building interviewing these folks," Marshall said, falling into the attorney's trap.

"You just don't know what building you were in?" O'Donnell pressed.

"If I had known it was important, I would have made sure I knew it," the professor said, trying not to sound too sarcastic or vulnerable. "I was focused on my interview. I was focused on the information. I was not focused on which building I was in or the particular organization that had made the arrangement for the interviews."

Marshall could not name the order in which she spoke to the refugees, or, with certainty, how many children she interviewed each day. O'Donnell pointed out that she also did not reach out to any of the school district officials to ask about their programs. "I did not know that it was appropriate or expected for me to do that," Marshall told the court, sounding defensive.

"If you had known that it was appropriate and possible, would you have asked to interview these folks?" O'Donnell asked.

"I think so," Marshall admitted.

The professor, growing only more fatigued as the minutes wore on, was desperate to leave the stand and uttered her displeasure into a hot microphone as O'Donnell took a moment to speak directly to the judge. "I'm sick of all this," said Marshall.

Moments later, during a friendly chat between O'Donnell and the judge, Marshall chided the pair for laughing. The judge, surprised by the admonishment, told her to relax, that she had done well in what was an exhausting day. But Marshall had hit her limit. She repeatedly asked the court how much longer she would have to remain on the stand.

O'Donnell, inexhaustible, pressed on. Did Marshall know that the school district had based its instructional plan on the work of two experts in the field? No, Marshall said, but she also didn't know if those experts catered to the type of high-needs students like the refugees who filed the lawsuit.

The attorney also questioned the state's stance on the amount of English language instruction that should be made available to non-English–speaking students. Was the state's suggestion a requirement, a recommendation, or a guideline, the attorney asked. Marshall said it was somewhere in between.

"Well, stronger than a guideline, I think," the professor said. "They expect it."

But there was an even more fundamental issue in the way Marshall was assessing the school district, one that cut to the core of the case: To what degree did she take into account a student's ability to graduate in evaluating their overall educational experience, O'Donnell asked.

She didn't. Marshall instead focused on whether students could overcome language barriers because that was what was mandated for them, she told the court, adding it was more important for them to learn English than earn a diploma.

"It is my conclusion that these students have a better chance of graduating faster by going to McCaskey if we think of graduation as meaningful, not simply grades on a transcript, but really understanding the material and understanding English," she said. McCaskey's International School was so strong and powerful that students could "light the world on fire" afterward, Marshall told the court.

But what if, O'Donnell asked, school officials could convince her that all of the support at McCaskey is also offered at Phoenix Academy. Would that change her mind about the alternative school?

"Impossible," Marshall said, because Phoenix places refugees alongside native English speakers. "That's the deal-breaker."

CHAPTER 15

DISCONNECTED

I T TOOK UNTIL DAY FOUR OF THE TRIAL FOR SHARON O'DONNELL TO call her first witness. In what seemed like a surprising tactic for the defense, the lawyer did not focus on Phoenix's academic program as a means to convince the judge it was a suitable place for refugees, but rather she compared its disciplinary measures to those of the mainstream campus. The implication was clear: if the refugees were wary of the alternative school's tactics, they'd be even more appalled by what goes on at McCaskey.

Amber Hilt, coordinator of the school district's English as a second language program, said the mainstream campus was, in some ways, even stricter than Phoenix. It was patrolled by police who walked the halls with Tasers, batons, and guns.

"To your knowledge, have they ever had to use one of those weapons?" O'Donnell asked.

"Yes, they used a Taser," she said.

"How recently?" the attorney inquired.

"I believe within the last school year," the administrator said.

"Is that the same type of de-escalation techniques that are used at Phoenix Academy?" O'Donnell asked.

"No," Hilt said, because the alternative school was not patrolled by active-duty police.

While law enforcement personnel are increasingly common in schools throughout the country in the wake of devastating school shootings, their presence has always been controversial. Two weeks after the Lancaster trial began, Secretary of Education John B. King Jr. called on administrators to reconsider having them on campus, saying he was concerned about possible civil rights violations against students. He said unnecessary citations or arrests would only feed the school-to-prison pipeline, a phrase used to describe the linkage between school-related incidents and criminal records.[1] No one knows for sure how many "school resource officers" patrol the nation's 130,930 elementary, middle, and high school campuses.[2] But they remained a staple throughout the nation, including Lancaster, though some were removed in 2020 at the urging of the Black Lives Matter movement.

Moving on to the heart of the case, the district's treatment of refugees, O'Donnell focused on Mahamed Hassan, asking Hilt whether she believed he wanted to attend school. Hilt said she didn't, saying he was pushed to enroll by his mother "so she could get her benefits."

And while school officials believed his claims of bullying were unfounded, they still helped him identify several staff members he could turn to for help in the future, she said. "He told us that he could talk to anybody, that he felt comfortable," Hilt told the court.

But the claim was dubious. Mahamed felt powerless. Even if he nodded along with their plan, it didn't make him feel safer. He dropped out in part because his bullying went unaddressed.

Hilt also challenged the notion of "seat time" as it had been described earlier, saying students would not earn credit for merely being present in class but for participating. And she defended the school district's decision not to use translators: not only would it be nearly impossible to hire staff fluent in some of the more obscure languages spoken by the newcomers but translation isn't necessarily the best way to teach a child English. "You use visuals," she said. "You use gestures. You might use songs and chants. And that's the way you access the language. It's not through interpretation of exactly what's going on in the classroom throughout the whole period."

She also pushed back on the notion that Phoenix had too few English language instructors. There was one for every forty students at McCaskey as opposed to one for every thirty students at the alternative school, she said.

But at least some of Hilt's claims fell apart under cross-examination. No matter how many police officers roamed the mainstream campus, its students were not subject to daily pat-downs upon entrance, said Eric Rothschild, attorney for the refugees. Nor were they ordered to remove their shoes or empty their pockets. There were no school uniforms, no ban on books or backpacks, and the Handle with Care protocol was not demonstrated during orientation, he said.

And there were other important distinctions between the mainstream and alternative campuses, differences that had an enormous impact on students' ability to learn, Rothschild contended. Those at McCaskey's International School spent much of their class time with students at the same language level, allowing them to feel more comfortable about speaking in class. Those assigned to Phoenix were often taught alongside native English speakers, prompting them to clam up.

Their loss went well beyond academics, Rothschild told the court. Phoenix students who wished to join extracurriculars, including clubs and sports, had to be bused to McCaskey. And there was no guarantee they would be welcomed: Phoenix students were sometimes shooed away from the mainstream campus, treated by some staff as an unwanted element.

Rothschild turned the court's attention to a grant proposal written by the district describing its treatment of refugee children. The document, which Hilt helped prepare, was submitted to the Commonwealth of Pennsylvania to support a request for funding. It said that when high school refugees first arrived in the district, they were enrolled at McCaskey's International School. It made no mention of an age restriction.

It went on to say students could either continue with their studies at McCaskey or enroll in Phoenix. But that's not what happened to the plaintiffs in this case, Rothschild told the court.

"That's what should have happened, right?" the attorney asked Hilt.

"Based on that document, yes," Hilt said reluctantly.

The grant went on to say that students must be at least eighteen years old and have earned at least five credits to be enrolled in the alternative school. But students as young as seventeen were sent to Phoenix, having spent not a single day at McCaskey, Rothschild said.

The document said translators would be brought on to help with testing, but that didn't happen either, the attorney alleged. Hilt said such services were used only during statewide exams, not day-to-day testing.

The attorney went on to address Mahamed's initial rejection by the school district. Hilt reported that school administrators initially believed he was nineteen years old and that his age was a factor in their decision. They also considered his transcripts and credits. But none of this was grounds to turn him away, the attorney contended.

"Do you agree with me that regardless of whether he's age seventeen or age nineteen, that should not have been an impediment to his enrolling in the Lancaster school district and receiving his free education?" the attorney asked.

Hilt stuck to the district's original claim. "Well, I believe the Literacy Council is a robust program that supports individuals in learning English," she said. "So, depending on what his goal was then, it could have been a good option for him."

But that's not what the attorney asked, he told her. He asked whether Mahamed had a legal right to attend school.

"Yes," she said reluctantly. But she and the other school officials believed Mahamed was disinterested because of his behavior in his December 2015 meeting with enrollment gatekeeper Jacques Blackman.

"One of the reasons that Mr. Blackman refused to enroll him was because of how he was behaving, right?" Rothschild asked.

"Yes," Hilt said. "He was not sitting at the table with us and interacting."

But why would his demeanor mean so much, the attorney wondered. "Mahamed was not acting disruptively, right?" Rothschild asked.

"No," Hilt said.

"He wasn't acting out physically?" the attorney pressed.

"No," Hilt responded.

"He wasn't yelling?" the lawyer inquired.

"No."

"He was pretty silent, right?"

"He stood in the corner," Hilt replied.

"And for a student who has had Mahamed's experiences, it's not necessarily that surprising the he would act in a way that we might perceive as inappropriate, including being standoffish like that," the attorney said.

"Sure," Hilt said. "We did our best to invite him to the table and interact and engage him with the conversation."

"I mean, even some of our own teenagers might act like that, right?" Rothschild asked, referring to American-born students.

"Certainly," Hilt replied.

"And we wouldn't say they can't enroll in school for that reason, right?"

"Correct," Hilt responded.

"But that is what happened to Mahamed, right?" the lawyer asked.

Hilt repeated that it was Mahamed's mother who was pushing him to enroll.

But how could Hilt know that, the attorney wondered. "His mom was more interested in school, is that right?" Rothschild asked.

"Correct," Hilt said.

"And Mahamed was more interested in work," the attorney said.

"Uh-huh," Hilt responded.

"Even though he was silent?" Rothschild asked.

The courtroom went quiet. It was an impressive tactic, one that forced the district to come face to face with its own inconsistency. Hilt, who hesitated in answering, said that while Mahamed didn't say much, "that is what he presented."

The attorney didn't budge. "Isn't the best indication of whether a student and the student's family want that student to go to school is that he enrolled to go to school?"

"My understanding is that it's an obligation of the resettlement agency to do so with the family," Hilt replied.

"And you feel like it's within the school district's discretion to override the judgment that is reflected in that enrollment effort and make your own determinations about how he or she can best be educated?" Rothschild asked.

"I don't work in placement, but I believe that that's why we have those discussions and try to formulate a plan that the student would be successful at graduation," she said.

Rothschild went on to reveal another important discovery: the School District of Lancaster told the state and federal governments that Mahamed was enrolled in school starting in October 2015, which was when he first tried to gain admission—even though he wasn't seated until months later. Such an announcement triggered funding for the district, he said.

The attorney moved on to another critical point, one the judge latched on to. Rothschild said that if age was not a factor, Mahamed and all of the other refugees in the lawsuit would have been placed at the McCaskey's International School per the district's own standards. Judge Smith seemed to agree, marking a major victory for the refugees. "I see the law as saying twenty-one is twenty-one, that you have a right to a public education until you're twenty-one," he said.

Though he could not remember the student's name, the judge cited Anyemu's case as particularly relevant to the discussion. According to Smith's interpretation of the law, Anyemu was entitled to years of additional schooling. Instead, he was ushered out the door at age eighteen after just sixteen months. "He still could have graduated before he aged out, with the benefit of the International School as well as the accelerated credits," Smith said.

Hilt did her best to defend Phoenix, saying it routinely offered ESL training for staff and that it welcomed parental involvement. She said the district regularly evaluated its ESL program, but Rothschild contended the assessments were incomplete.

The district examined key test scores for ESL students based on grade level, not individual campus, making it impossible to compare one school to another, so the district had no way of knowing whether Phoenix's methods actually worked, Rothschild told the court.

Judge Smith pressed Hilt to explain what harm might have resulted from allowing the students in the lawsuit to have attended McCaskey's International School upon their arrival. "What would be the unintended consequences that I can't see?" he asked.

Hilt's answer was simple: They would not be able to earn a diploma before aging out.

"Bingo," the judge responded. "So, there's three real issues here. One is getting them to learn English as well as they can. Two is getting them to learn the other core subjects so they increase their education."

"Right," Hilt said.

"And three is getting the diploma," the judge continued.

But how are those goals chosen? he asked. Might the refugees be better served by learning English without earning a diploma as opposed to graduating unable to speak the language? "Isn't the diploma almost like a false diploma if you haven't truly educated them?" the judge asked.

Hilt told Smith these students would be well served by programs outside the school district, adding that many had a hard time committing to four years of high school. Plagued with money woes, some dropped out to help their families, she told him.

. . . .

It was during this fourth day of testimony that the court learned just how disconnected the School District of Lancaster was from the outsourced Phoenix Academy. Superintendent Damaris Rau, who had been in her post for only a year when the case went to court, hadn't spent much time at the alternative school.

Rau had twenty campuses to oversee and was responsible for the success or failure of some eleven thousand students. She was new to Lancaster but had much in common with its most at-risk children. A product of the foster care system, Rau started her career as a classroom teacher in the Bronx. She would go on to hold several administrative posts and earn a doctorate from Teachers College at Columbia University.

Though she was polite under questioning, she was visibly irritated about having to testify. Her programs and schools had already been assessed by the state and she did not welcome outside scrutiny.

Rau said she was hired by the district because she shared its vision that all students should graduate "college or career ready," meaning they should be capable of continuing their education or joining the workforce.

"I think that the research has demonstrated that without a high school degree, the chances of positive outcomes for students is negligible," she told the court. "We need to graduate our students so that they can have options in their life and opportunities."

And, she said, schools are judged in part on their graduation rates. Those that failed to reach certain thresholds were monitored by the state and must submit improvement plans meant to show what changes they would make to boost student performance. A half dozen schools within her district had already earned this unwanted distinction in recent years—including Mc-Caskey, Rau said.

She acknowledged during her testimony that refugees posed unique challenges. Some spoke uncommon languages and felt an obligation to work to support their families, so it could be tough to keep them in school, she said. Despite this, the district welcomed all students, including those just learning English, Rau said. It even opened a refugee center at one of its middle schools to help newcomer families access social services.

Rau said the school district had good relationships with its community partners, including the local resettlement agencies, though she chided some caseworkers for pushing too hard. Everybody who went to school thought they could be a teacher, she said, but they failed to understand the scope of the school district's responsibilities. "Sometimes the refugee agencies are very narrow-minded and don't think about all students—just about their

small, select group," she told the court. "But we think about them in rela-
tion to all of the other students as well."

High schools are notoriously inflexible. A change for one student group
might cause a change for others, the superintendent said, and the district's
problems were many: The past year was one of the worst on record in terms
of its finances. The Commonwealth of Pennsylvania had failed to pass a
budget, forcing the district to suspend key programs.

"We actually had to go into savings mode—no hiring of permanent
staff, no professional development," she said. "We just had to slash a lot
of things. No supplies were ordered after January because we didn't have a
budget . . . There is no district that has limitless funds."

Despite their financial woes, Lancaster schools worked hard to meet the
state's requirements for their students, often exceeding those standards, Rau
told the court. But that was lost on some of the refugee advocates. Resettlement caseworker Elise Chesson was particularly combative during a winter
2016 meeting, Rau said.

"She was just very rude and disrespectful and, you know, I said, 'You get
more with honey than you get with vinegar' . . . because her approach was
just so negative towards me and she continued to be very belligerent to the
point that I said, 'We need to end this meeting, because if we're not going
to collaborate, if we're not going to work together, then there's no point,'"
the superintendent said.

Rau said Chesson eventually calmed down. The superintendent listened
to her concerns and pledged to double back in a few months. She spent the
next several weeks meeting with officials at Phoenix Academy and with
members of her own staff, investigating Chesson's claims about the disciplinary nature of Phoenix's program, its English language offerings, its
homework and backpack policies. She was scheduled to meet with Chesson
and the others in the summer, but the district was sued in federal court before the meeting could take place. Rau said she felt "sort of tricked" by her.

And while the superintendent didn't admit to the court that her school
district had erred in terms of its enrollment or any other policies, she said
it could always improve. "We can do better in all areas," she said. "We are
not saying that we are perfect, but we are, I think, very willing to work with
our organizations."

Rau defended Phoenix's policies around books and backpacks, telling
the court the school stayed open until 6:00 p.m., allowing students ample

time to finish their coursework on-site after school closed around 3:00 p.m. But how could a child who stayed late at Phoenix participate in the district's after-school programs, including clubs and sports, Rothschild asked.

"Well, that's a choice every high-schooler makes," Rau answered. "Do I go to a tutor or do I go play athletics?"

Rothschild's question was a simple one, but it tugged at the heart of the case. How could Phoenix's students have the same educational opportunities as those at McCaskey if their experience was so different?

The attorney went on to ask if the superintendent had taken a look at any student files during the course of her investigation. She hadn't—nor had she talked with the students or their parents or teachers.

"And you're aware that Pennsylvania law actually requires that students begin school within five days of enrollment?" Rothschild asked.

"Yes," the superintendent said, but she did not know just how badly her own staff had violated this requirement. "I trusted that it was happening within five days."

Asked how long Mahamed waited to be placed in the school district, Rau said she had no knowledge of such minor details. "I am not involved in that level of the weeds, so it's very difficult for me to be able to confirm what you're saying," she told Rothschild coolly.

And even as she acknowledged the district's enrollment foibles, Rau seemed to support the idea that one administrator, Jacques Blackman, should determine where each child should be placed. As for Mahamed, Rau said she did not know caseworkers were advocating for his enrollment. All she knew was that he did not wish to attend.

"What I remember was that he didn't want to come to school," she told the court.

"And the source of your information for that is what?" Rothschild asked.

"I believe that was Jacques," she said.

"Would you agree with me, Dr. Rau, that if a student's mother has enrolled that student in school and has expressed to Mr. Blackman at a meeting, 'I want my son to attend school,' that he should enroll him in school?" the attorney asked.

Rau conceded, but only in part. The mother's wish should be granted unless her child expresses a desire to go to work instead. "What we don't want is to enroll a child who's not going to come to school," she told the court.

Rothschild went on to point out that the district had misrepresented the start dates for several students, telling state and federal officials they were enrolled months before they were seated. "No organization is perfect and things do slip through the cracks," the superintendent said. "We have over 700 refugees which we serve in our community each year, and it's unfortunate if anyone falls through the cracks, whether you're a refugee or not a refugee."

But had she heard of any other student, any non-refugees, who waited months to be seated? the attorney asked.

No, the superintendent said.

Rothschild went on to address the importance of enrolling older students as soon as possible so they could take full advantage of their time in the classroom before aging out. "If we're talking about students seventeen at the youngest and some as old as twenty, every day that they can go to school is important to them, right?" Rothschild asked the superintendent.

"I would have to ask them, yes," she said.

"Huh?" the attorney replied.

"Yes," she said, reluctantly. "If you ask them, they would say yes."

"Every day that they could get an education is important?" the attorney clarified.

"Every day that we all can get an education is important, absolutely," the superintendent said.

"Good," the attorney said. "And that's true for all students, right?"

"Yes," Rau said.

Rothschild, in pivoting back to enrollment, used his toughest language yet. "If the school district was regularly making immigrant and refugee students wait weeks or even months from the date they enrolled to the date they could start school, you would agree that's basically deliberate indifference to the right of those students?" he asked.

Rau's eyes narrowed, but before she could respond, her attorney objected. Rothschild tried to approach the subject from a different angle, asking the superintendent if she knew that state regulations allowed students to stay in school through the semester in which they turned twenty-one.

"Yes, I understand we should, must educate students up to the age of twenty-one or until they graduate from high school," the superintendent said.

"And are you aware that the district doesn't follow that policy for refugee students?" Rothschild asked.

Rau didn't agree with his assessment, insisting, against all of the evidence presented, that the district does follow the appropriate protocols.

Rothschild persisted, using Alembe's story as a model.

"If he had gone to school but didn't graduate . . . he would be recorded as a dropout according to the statistics that the school district has to report to the state," Rothschild said. "And that affects the district's graduation rates, right?"

"Yes," the superintendent said.

"That's not actually a legal reason to bar a student who wants to enroll in a school from enrolling, right?" he asked.

O'Donnell objected before her client could answer. Judge Smith intervened, agreeing with Rothschild's assertion. "I believe you are correct," he told the attorney. "I'm almost certain that the school district cannot do this. . . . You cannot say, 'I don't want my dropout rate to get worse, so I'm going to deliberately not enroll somebody that I know the only way they can end their career at my school is as a dropout.'"

The ACLU attorneys beamed. Rothschild pressed on, asking the superintendent if Alembe Dunia would have been well served by a year of public schooling, an opportunity he was denied when he was turned away from the district.

"I don't know, because I don't know him," Rau said. "He may have wanted to go to work. He may have wanted to just learn enough English to get a job, so I would need to know much more about this young person."

But Rothschild told the court Alembe's motive for enrolling shouldn't matter.

"If he came to the school to learn enough English to get a job, that's pretty good for him, right?" Rothschild asked.

"But that is not the mission of our schools," Rau said. "Our mission is to educate you so you can graduate, so you can have opportunities in your life."

She said a high school diploma carries weight not only with colleges but also with potential employers. "If we want our students to be able to make a living wage, they need to have a high school diploma," she said.

Rau said she did not want the school to become a dropout factory. Instead, the refugees and their attorneys argued, it had become a diploma mill.

Rothschild said students who graduated unable to speak English were unprepared for college or the workforce, but the superintendent disagreed, saying the local community college offered English language courses to non-native speakers—though she conceded that students must pay to attend. And they can't be admitted without a high school diploma or a GED.

Rothschild told the court that McCaskey's International School would have been a better choice for the refugees. Not only did it offer the academic support they needed, but it also was free.

Rau downplayed the merits of the program. She also questioned its decision to separate non-English speakers from their peers. "I do have a concern about segregating students because I think children learn more English by being in the general population," she said.

Rau admitted the school district made no judgment regarding the language proficiency of the students it sent to Phoenix, nor did it consider whether they had missed years of schooling. The district also did not factor in whether the students were academically equipped to handle Phoenix's accelerated model.

In fact, Rothschild said, the district never really considered whether the alternative school was a good fit for the refugees at all. Instead, he told the court, their focus was solely on a student's perceived ability to graduate.

Rau agreed, saying students are placed at McCaskey only if the district has confidence they will earn their diploma before aging out. "We do not want them to fail," the superintendent said.

And she said something else too, something that some might consider unusual. Rau said she had different—and far lower—educational expectations for students like the ones involved in the lawsuit. "We cannot expect a student who has never been to school or had very limited education who is eighteen to come to us and learn the depth of knowledge that a native speaker would learn in four years of high school," she said.

Rau told the court she visited Phoenix three times in her brief tenure as school superintendent. And, as the trial went on, she had listened to nearly a dozen other witnesses, including teachers, refugee advocates, and students, discuss its disciplinary policies. But it was clear from her statements in court that she still did not know the full extent of Phoenix's infamous pat-downs. "I do not believe that they were patting down every child every day," she told the court, to the puzzlement of the ACLU and Education Law Center.

Rothschild reminded the superintendent of Mahamed's testimony about how the pat-down made him feel like a bad person. And he recounted Jandy Rivera's account that some female refugees, when patted down by strangers, would stiffen in response. "You could see why that would really make school an unwelcoming place for them," Rothschild said.

Rau agreed, saying she had asked the alternative school to stop the practice for the coming school year. She told the court she demanded another critical change: Camelot must also allow students to bring books home from school. While she understood the company's concern about the texts becoming lost in transit, such a worry could not override their need to learn at home.

Still, the Handle With Care policy would stay in place. Rau said she agreed it left an "ugly taste in the mouths" of parents and students who were made to witness the hold during orientation, so it would not be demonstrated unless students and parents asked for it. Rothschild couldn't help but laugh, further irking the already irritated superintendent.

Rau also pushed back against criticism of the alternative school's dress code. While the refugees said the policy led to a dystopian hierarchy among students, Rau said they and their advocates had it all wrong. "The agencies thought it was a punishment system, but in fact it was the opposite," she said. "It gives children something to attain."

One thing was clear from Rau's testimony: She was not accustomed to her judgment being challenged. Judge Smith was gentlemanly as always but did not hold back when he questioned her about the district's practices. Evidence suggested some eligible students were turned away by school administrators, he said, and one child who was admitted completed his entire high school career in just sixteen months, leaving at age eighteen. And, Judge Smith said, enrollment was delayed in many cases. "I think there's a little bit of a theme suggesting that this was all done to manipulate dropout rates," he said.

There was no manipulation, Rau countered. It was just that the school district did not see the point of enrolling a student who had no plans to graduate. Students must earn their high school diploma, Rau said, adding, "I just believe that with all my heart." That was why the district placed older refugees in Phoenix's accelerated setting, to increase the likelihood that they would reach this important benchmark.

But Judge Smith challenged the idea that non-English–speaking refugees would be best served in such an environment. Typically, he said, accelerated programs are designed for advanced students. "I would never have thought of it as being someone who can't even speak English, who comes from another culture and has asylum in this country, sitting in a classroom being taught in a language other than the language they speak," and graduating from such a program in as little as sixteen months, he said. "And that's without ever having gone through kindergarten, elementary school, middle school, et cetera."

Rau contested the notion that Phoenix moved at a faster pace, saying that it had longer class periods, allowing teachers to cover more material in one sitting. "We're enabling students to learn more, faster," she told the court.

Smith, winding down his questioning, told the superintendent that the ACLU and Education Law Center were asking for four key measures on behalf of their clients. The first was for the district to allow all refugees aged seventeen to twenty-one to attend the main high school. The second was for the district to properly assess all newcomer students for language proficiency, and the third was for the district to ensure that the refugees and all similar students had full access to the after-school and extracurricular activities afforded to their peers.

Finally, the judge said, the plaintiffs, Khadidja and Mahamed among them, wanted the district to stop automatically enrolling older refugees at Phoenix. And the reason for this, Smith told Rau, was to honor the Equal Education Opportunities Act and other related rights with respect to English language learners.

The judge asked the superintendent what bothered her most about the proposals. Rau turned her body to address Smith face to face and was unapologetic in tone.

"One of our biggest concerns is that the school code gives authority to the board of directors to place students in a school," she said. "And there's a real concern of taking away that authority of the school board in making those decisions."

The ACLU was stunned by Rau's frankness. Another attorney, a friend of Vic Walczak's who had come to court that day to show his support, encapsulated the feeling in the courtroom in one quick quip.

"Did the superintendent of the Lancaster school district just tell Judge Smith to fuck off?" he whispered in Walczak's ear.

"Seems like that to me," the attorney replied.

CHAPTER 16

A MISSED OPPORTUNITY

O F ALL THE ADMINISTRATORS AT THE SCHOOL DISTRICT OF LAN-
caster, Jacques Blackman, coordinator of counseling and dropout pre-
vention, was by far the most feared by older refugees.

Those who were required to meet with him as a condition of their enrollment called Blackman snide and disdainful. Even more troubling, he
seemed to make admissions decisions on a whim, not on any set guidelines,
allowing his mood or perception of the students themselves to steer his
decision.

Blackman's testimony on this last day of the pretrial hearing would
mark the first time the administrator was forced to explain his rationale to
the public. Not all of the students in the case were able to attend court on
the day he took the stand—nor could they understand him because of the
language barrier—but all were eager to see him held accountable.

Blackman walked to the witness stand stone-faced, barely acknowledg-
ing the small crowd that had gathered to see him. He told the court the
refugees and their advocates were mistaken in thinking McCaskey's International School was somehow superior to Phoenix.

The International School, he said, was at its best in the early 2000s
when it was flush with funding from the Gates Foundation. But that money
had long ago dried up. And even at its most robust, when students celebrated various cultures through food, music, and dancing, the program was
academically weak.

The current pared-down version mirrored what was offered at Phoenix, so students assigned to the alternative school were not missing out, he said. This sentiment extended to the mainstream campus's sports programs: The Pennsylvania Interscholastic Athletic Association prohibited nineteen-year-olds from participating, Blackman told the court, effectively banning many of the refugees who had filed the lawsuit.

Asked about the district's enrollment policies, the administrator said there was, in fact, some degree of uniformity in its approach. Students who came to the district at age seventeen with no credits were automatically placed in the ninth grade at the Phoenix Academy, he said, adding they did not have a choice in the matter. "We assign them there," Blackman told the court. "We tell them that is the best academic placement for them."

The administrator admitted that some students resisted their assignment to the alternative school. His response depended on their age, Blackman said. Students sixteen and under were mandated by the state to attend school. If they objected to their placement at Phoenix, Blackman would discuss the issue with their parents. But older children were treated differently. "The older they are, the more we talk with the student and not the parent because when you turn eighteen, you're legally making decisions for yourself," he told Judge Smith.

Sharon O'Donnell, the school district's attorney, reminded the court that older students were not required by the state to continue their education. "So, the kids in this lawsuit, ages seventeen to twenty-one, would be outside the scope of compulsory attendance?" she asked.

"That is correct," Blackman replied.

The assertion was an odd one, with the subtle implication that the district was not compelled to serve any child seventeen and older. But a quick glance around any of its high schools showed they appeared in numbers: Blackman himself testified that eighteen-year-olds made up 87 percent of the district's graduates just three years earlier.

Rothschild immediately picked apart Blackman's testimony. While it may be true that students nineteen and older could not play sports, there were no similar age restrictions regarding other school clubs like theater, newspaper, or yearbook, he told the court. And while Blackman said twice earlier in his testimony that the English language offerings at both Phoenix and McCaskey were the same, Rothschild reminded the court that English language instruction was not the administrator's area of expertise.

Blackman testified that roughly 85 percent of students assigned to Phoenix attended McCaskey first and that many had requested the switch so they could earn credits faster.

"Not true for immigrant and refugee students who come to the school district age seventeen or older, right?" Rothschild asked.

"Not true for seventeen and older students, refugee or not," Blackman said.

"For those, you make the decision for them," Rothschild continued.

"Correct," the administrator said.

Blackman conceded that students have the right to a free public education until age twenty-one. And he admitted that the refugees at the heart of the lawsuit were required to meet with him before they could start school, even if they had completed all other enrollment requirements and paperwork. "I wouldn't necessarily call it policy," he said of the requirement. "I would say practice."

Blackman also recalled his fateful meeting with Mahamed, saying the district decided against enrolling the teen because he failed to partake in the discussion about his academic future.

But that wasn't true, Rothschild told the court. It was Mahamed's perceived demeanor that kept him off the roster.

"That really was the main reason, wasn't it?" the attorney asked.

The administrator said it was a combination of factors.

"And you recognized that this young man was not an English language speaker at all, right?" the attorney asked.

"I would say yes, but he didn't try to communicate, so I don't know—but I would say yes," he said.

Rothschild wondered why Blackman was so offended by Mahamed's disposition. Didn't he have years of experience with students who had faced severe trauma in their lives? Didn't he expect that a young man who had witnessed horrible atrocities and who came from another culture might behave differently from a typical student? And how, the attorney wondered, could Blackman make such a critical decision about Mahamed's fate in such a short time?

"It's not like you talked with his family for an hour and got to know them," the attorney said. "This was a few minutes' meeting, right?"

"It was about fifteen, I'd say," Blackman said.

But the meeting wasn't just about Mahamed, Rothschild told the court. His other siblings also had to be enrolled as well. The conversation that cost Mahamed a year of schooling took not much longer than a commercial break.

As for the email Blackman had mistakenly sent to a refugee caseworker, the one in which he wrote, "This guy is nuts," and "Makes me say no all the time," he denied it had anything to do with enrollment.

"This was no evil plot to keep people out of the school or any of that sort of thing," he said, adding that the district was looking for ways to speed up the enrollment process for all students.

Like the other school administrators who testified before him, Blackman spoke with passion about the value of a high school diploma. It was a necessary precursor for college and a requirement for joining the military or for securing a job, he told the court. There was no reason for a child to be enrolled in high school if he or she did not intend to graduate. "So, for people to be in school and leave without a diploma, it's a failure for us as a system," he said. "It's a failure for the district. It's a failure for the school."

He added that there is a "maturity disparity" between older and younger students, saying it was academically and socially unwise to, for example, place a seventeen-year-old student in the ninth grade alongside thirteen- and fourteen-year-old peers.

"High schools aren't really designed for older students," Blackman said, adding that they had a level of sophistication that might help them take advantage of their younger classmates. While younger students might flirt with one another innocently, he said, older boys are far more advanced. "So, when you're thirteen and fourteen and you like a girl, you kind of push her in the back, play with her hair," he said. "They're afraid to say, 'I like you,' where an eighteen-year-old, they know what to say."

· · · · · · · · · ·

Next to the stand was Aura Heisey, former principal at Phoenix Academy. By the time she delivered her testimony, she was just weeks away from starting a new job as assistant principal at McCaskey.

Heisey, in defending the district's decision to send the refugees to Phoenix, told the court the two schools were essentially the same. They shared the same curriculum and even read the same books in many cases, she said.

Heisey knew some of the students who filed the lawsuit, though she had no idea they were unhappy with Phoenix. She told the court she spoke with Anyemu on several occasions, adding, "We had the kind of relationship where I feel like we could openly talk about his experiences in school."

As for Khadidja, Heisey blamed the student for her own lack of progress learning English, saying she was not advancing as fast as some of the other refugees. The administrator acknowledged the teen appeared to rate high among her peers—she was ranked number one in her class—but said this was more a reflection of the school's complicated grading system than of Khadidja's academic ability. The ranking system, Heisey said, included factors such as class participation, attendance, and completion of in-class assignments. "It's not the same as what you would think it would mean in a traditional high school," she told the court.

But her explanation didn't make sense: how could Khadidja rank so high in these categories if her effort was so lacking?

ACLU attorney Vic Walczak hammered Heisey on the notion that the two schools were the same. Like Blackman before her, Heisey also was not qualified to compare the two. She had no ESL credentials and played no role in designing either school's curriculum.

Walczak also noted that Phoenix awarded course credits far faster than the mainstream campus: Students could earn up to twenty-two credits in a single year at the alternative school compared to just seven at McCaskey.

While one might think this would require students at Phoenix to spend more time learning the material, Walczak said this wasn't the case. It was true that Phoenix's class periods were longer, coming in at eighty minutes versus forty-eight minutes at McCaskey. But in reality, its students had twenty-four fewer hours of instruction per course: Phoenix awarded students a full course credit in only a single semester while those assigned to the mainstream campus were given a full year.

The attorney then moved on to question Heisey about Anyemu, the student who had graduated from Phoenix just days earlier. Anyemu didn't know he was in the twelfth grade and said he was unprepared for life after high school. "In any of those meetings that you had with him, did you have an interpreter?" Walczak asked.

"No," Heisey said. "I never needed an interpreter to communicate with him."

"You had no problem communicating with him?" Walczak asked, incredulous.

"No, I did not," Heisey said, to the surprise of the courtroom.

Anyemu was barely able to utter a few words in English. He was also extraordinarily shy around adults, even those assigned to help him. So it was hard for the court to imagine he would be brimming with information for school staff.

Walczak then moved on to Phoenix's goals for students: to help them recover credits needed toward graduation, to change their behavior from "anti-social" to "pro-social," and to help them develop the life skills necessary to sustain this change. The school was clearly meant for students who had behavioral issues, he said. So what made it an appropriate setting for refugees?

"Are you aware of any antisocial behavior by any of the five refugee plaintiffs who attended Phoenix?" Walczak asked.

"No," Heisey said.

"Is there any antisocial behavior that needs to be changed in them?" he asked.

"No," she admitted.

Phoenix had no advanced placement (college-level) courses while McCaskey had ten. The mainstream campus was also an International Baccalaureate school, meaning it offered a rigorous, world-renowned academic program that required students to dive deep into their coursework. McCaskey also boasted robust vocational training in a diverse array of fields. Its School of Health Sciences, for example, gave students a chance to study nursing, radiology, and operating room technology at Lancaster General Hospital, among other health-care centers. Khadidja, who dreamed of becoming a nurse, would have given just about anything to enroll there. None of this was available at Phoenix.

"Sounds like a terrific program to help students actually get gainful employment once they graduate from high school, correct?" Walczak asked Heisey.

"Yes," she said.

And as for the notion that Phoenix students could join McCaskey's sports teams, Walczak found no evidence that it actually happened. Records showed no sports participation from students at the alternative high school.

But sports were not the attorney's primary focus. Walczak was far more concerned about the amount of time Phoenix's students spent learning English: They sat for just one ESL class compared to two at the mainstream campus, he found.

Walczak then turned his attention to the English language instructors themselves. Heisey testified that there were three ESL teachers at Phoenix in the 2015–2016 school year. But the attorney pointed out that only one actually taught the subject: The others taught communication arts or social studies.

"So, in terms of teachers at Phoenix who actually teach just direct ESL, there's only one, correct?" he asked.

"Yes," she conceded.

The attorney moved on to discuss the data that the district reported to the state each year, information that made up its performance profile, a sort of report card on the district itself, focusing on the 2014–2015 school year. Phoenix's dropout rate was 12.5 percent compared to McCaskey's 1.22 percent, the attorney told the court. Just more than 28 percent of its students were English language learners, about 9 percent higher than the mainstream campus.

More concerning, the alternative school had just a 53.75 percent cohort graduation rate compared to 86.51 percent at McCaskey. Phoenix officials would later defend the figure, calling it "a feat to be celebrated," given that none of the students at the alternative school were on track to graduate on time with their four-year cohort when they first enrolled at the campus. "The intensity of the program and the individualized attention and support offered by Phoenix Academy are what enables these students to catch up to their grade-level peers at McCaskey and graduate on-time," they later said.[1]

Overall, Walczak argued, McCaskey's students were better prepared for college or to enter the workforce: Records showed not a single student at Phoenix had taken the PSATs, the practice exam for the all-important SATs, arguably the most critical college entrance exam in the country. District officials later took issue with the statistic, saying PSAT participation is not something the school tracked.

Walczak went on to talk about Anyemu Dunia, who graduated high school after just sixteen months. Anyemu, who was enrolled at age seventeen, could have continued his education for another three years, Walczak said, a point Heisey could not deny. In fact, she discussed this option with him around the time he enrolled at the district, she testified.

"Did you have a translator at that meeting?" Walczak asked.

"No, because I speak to him in English frequently," Heisey said.

"And do you know that he understands what you're saying?" the attorney asked.

"I would say he does," she replied.

"You would say?" the attorney shot back. "Do you know that he understands?"

"Yes, I do know that he understands," Heisey said.

· · · · · · · · · ·

It was up to Megan Misnik, executive director of Phoenix Academy, in charge of the day-to-day activities at the school, to bolster its reputation in front of the court.

Phoenix took great pride in its close relationship with students, she said. Staff took note of each child's needs and challenges, information they used to help explain and improve student grades, behavior, and attendance.

Misnik, who greeted every child who entered the building with a fist bump, handshake, or wave at the start of the school day, had at least a cursory knowledge of every student's academic standing, she told the court. "I'm able to look at them and know what's going on at home," she said.

Misnik went on to defend the school's use of so-called behavioral specialists. While former teacher Jandy Rivera called them disruptive, saying they undermined her credibility in front of her students, Misnik insisted they supported classroom instruction. "Sometimes, they join in the lesson," she said. Other times, they pulled students aside to see why they were not participating or why they weren't on task with their peers, she told Judge Smith.

Misnik also insisted Phoenix made regular use of translation devices and services, including Language Line, but admitted she kept no logs to support the assertion. "It's not that we would ever leave someone in the dark," she said.

Most important, she told the court, Phoenix wasn't created to warehouse troubled youth. Instead, it was built to help students earn the credits they needed to graduate.

But even that wasn't the school's end point. "You need that diploma, but we want you to be successful, productive citizens," she said. "We're going to make sure that you're prepared to go on to live life after high school."

As for the notion that students were encouraged by the school to confront one another—a practice that confused and alarmed the refugees—Misnik said it was not as aggressive as it sounded. It was all part of the school's greater mission to teach children life skills, including how to deal with minor irritations, she told the court.

"I don't care where you come from, what your background is, whether you've been at McCaskey and come to Phoenix, whether you've been a refugee, you're going to get frustrated as an individual, and we're going to teach you how to handle those behaviors," she said. Non-English–speaking students might not understand these confrontational interactions at first, but they came around, she said, adding, "We witness it."

But not everything Misnik said added up. Despite her close connection with students, she was unaware of the refugees' deep frustrations with the school. No one told her about Mahamed's bullying until he essentially dropped out and none of the other refugees told her they wanted to be transferred, she said.

"You didn't know that they wanted to go to McCaskey over Phoenix?" the refugees' attorney Maura McInerney asked.

"It was never brought to my attention, so I can't know things that no one tells me," Misnik said.

McInerney, homing in on the issue of translation, said key documents, including report cards, were delivered in English. Misnik justified the school's position by saying that student grades are easy to understand, even for people who do not speak the language. "I mean, we could translate it, but an A is . . . a grade that you can pretty easily determine," she said.

"And are interpreters provided during Townhouse for the students who are English language learners?" McInerney asked.

"No," Misnik said. "I would have a ton of translators in my Townhouse if that was the case."

As for the color-coded shirts that reflected students' standing at Phoenix, McInerney told Misnik that whatever message the district was trying to send was lost on the refugees. "Would it surprise you to learn that the students that are named plaintiffs in this case did not understand the different colors of the shirts and didn't understand how it correlated to behavior?" the lawyer asked.

It would, Misnik said, adding that one of the plaintiffs, Anyemu, had actually attained Firebird status, a boost in ranking based on his good behavior.

As for the daily pat-downs, Misnik said she thought the refugees would be grateful for the policy because it helped ensure their safety. "I personally feel that, you know, students coming in from war-torn countries would appreciate the fact that there's no weapons or drugs in their school—that they're able to, again, focus solely on academics and not have to worry about that other component that potentially comes up in public high schools," she told the court.

As for the no-homework policy, Misnik was of two minds on the issue. She denied there was such a hard-and-fast rule, but added, "It's not fair to send work home with a student that they're not going to be able to feasibly do on their own."

. . . .

Arthur Abrom, director of student services at the School District of Lancaster since 2011, oversaw more than a dozen administrators, including Jacques Blackman. He confirmed that the district allowed Blackman to decide whether to accept older students based on a review of their transcripts.

Blackman also determined where to place them, Abrom told the court, adding that the district had since committed itself to crafting better enrollment policies.

Judge Smith cut into Abrom's testimony with comments of his own, saying, essentially, that it was understandable for refugee advocates to be sensitive to anything that might appear to discriminate against their clients, children whom the United States had accepted for asylum.

The students in question, the judge said, had not been enrolled in accordance with state law, had experienced months-long delays, and were ultimately sent to an outsourced school that specialized in children with challenges—just not the same challenges as the refugees. Walczak and Rothschild smiled in unison; Judge Smith was doing their work for them.

Abrom admitted the school's enrollment procedures needed to be improved. "I learned a lot," he said after listening to other testimony. "I need to be down a little more in some of the decision-making in those issues. That's my mistake and my lesson."

But he insisted it was wrong for the court or anyone else to assume the alternative school was not a good place for refugees. "I wouldn't characterize Phoenix as a school for the maladjusted . . . That's not what they exist to do," he said. The real problem kids, the ones who brought weapons and drugs to school, who were violent or made terroristic threats, were assigned to Buehrle Academy, the district's other outsourced campus, he told the court.

Abrom's testimony ended with a back and forth with the judge.

"Now, the plaintiffs have introduced evidence to suggest that the opportunities available at McCaskey are significantly greater than the opportunities available at Phoenix—or at least, even if they're available at Phoenix, they're really unattainable because of the difficulties involved taking advantage of them," the judge said, to the delight of the refugees' attorneys. "And I think the response from the defense has been, yes, but they don't have the time to take advantage of all those opportunities because we have to get them these accelerated credits to get them this diploma so that they can move on with their life."

Abrom agreed, saying late-arriving students had difficult choices to make in how to spend the limited time they had in the public school system but that it would be wise to focus on graduation. It was the perfect setup. Judge Smith moved in for what should have been the ACLU and Education Law Center's kill. "But wouldn't your goal in achieving that be a lot easier if you weren't so concerned that they graduate when they're seventeen or eighteen with their [same age] peers—and were willing to use the state law maximum of twenty-one?" the judge asked.

On this point, Abrom would not bend. "The question is, will a twenty-year-old or a twenty-one-year-old want to go to high school every day when they're working, they're taking care of babies, and they're in class with a thirteen- or fourteen-year old," Abrom said. "It's too much of an age disparity."

O'Donnell, reinforcing the notion, reminded the court that eighteen-year-olds are old enough to die for the country or cast a ballot, and that twenty-one-year-olds can buy alcohol. They're so old that the school is not obliged to send grades home to parents.

But something about what was being said didn't appear to sit well with Judge Smith, though he remained uncharacteristically quiet.

. . . .

Marianne Ortiz, who taught English as a second language at Phoenix for six years, held a unique position at the trial. Beloved by staff and students, she bolstered Phoenix's reputation while at the same time tearing it down.

Ortiz challenged the district's assertion that Phoenix's and McCaskey's English language learner programs were essentially the same. Mc-Caskey had far greater resources—more and better qualified teachers as well as updated equipment—though she admitted to never having taught at the school.

Ortiz said she was the only ESL-certified teacher at the alternative school for years until two others earned the certification. But even then, the ratio of ESL teachers to ESL students was not one to thirty as Hilt testified. Since one of the teachers didn't actually teach the subject, it was more like one to fifty, Ortiz said, making it substantially worse than at McCaskey.

Asked if she was surprised to hear the refugees in the case contend their teachers made little effort to help them understand their course material, the teacher said it would be hard for noncertified ESL teachers to remember to make accommodations for them, especially in Phoenix's sped-up model. "I think they need more assistance, more time to learn things," she said of the students, adding that they might benefit from having more than one teacher in the classroom.

Ortiz said she could not possibly provide all the help that newcomer students needed. She taught only two classes, what she called direct ESL instruction, though she opened her door during a third period for non-English-speaking students to ask questions about their coursework. She did not coordinate with other teachers, so there was no greater planning, strategy, or protocol involved, she said.

And although non-English–speaking students were entitled to accommodations surrounding testing, this wasn't always possible: Ortiz offered help in this area only when a teacher had asked—and when her own schedule would allow. She also said that in her six years at the school, her classroom had been observed by an administrator only once.

Ortiz was not surprised to hear the refugees claim to have learned virtually nothing outside their ESL classes. The twenty-to-thirty-minute training sessions she led for non-ESL teachers wasn't nearly enough to make the practices stick, she said, confirming Jandy Rivera's earlier testimony. She also confirmed the ACLU and Education Law Center's assertion that non-English–speaking students were essentially kept apart from the mainstream high school's sports and extracurricular programs.

"I don't think that they knew that they could possibly participate in any activity," she told the court, adding she could recall only one such student at Phoenix having played baseball at McCaskey. But, unlike the refugees in this case, he had formerly been enrolled at the mainstream campus before transferring to Phoenix. "So, he already knew the system," she said.

CHAPTER 17

GRANTED

N EITHER THE REFUGEES NOR THEIR ATTORNEYS COULD PREDICT
when Judge Smith would render his decision—or what he might say
in his opinion—but the clock was ticking. The new school year was just
days away.

Khadidja and Mahamed believed there was only one possible outcome:
he simply had to decide in their favor. Neither could endure another year at
Phoenix Academy. It might be better, they reasoned, to join the workforce
and help their families if they couldn't learn anything in the classroom.

The six young refugees felt their argument was sound and their stories
persuasive. The judge was clearly moved by their perseverance, as was revealed in the pretrial hearing. But Smith's compassion in the courtroom
was no indicator of how he might rule. In the end, as a conservative, his
findings were influenced only by the letter of the law, not by the students'
tragic backstories or their shared wish to attend a quality school.

The judge's opinion was announced by an email blast to the attorneys
who'd argued the case before him. Just days before fall semester was to begin, he handed the refugees the win they'd prayed for, ruling that Khadidja,
Mahamed, and the other plaintiffs must be sent to the district's main high
school, McCaskey, as the case made its way through the courts.

Smith didn't adjudicate the entire case. By the time he rendered his
opinion, he was tasked only with deciding whether the refugees should be
sent to the mainstream high school, not whether the district had violated
their civil rights as the ACLU and Education Law Center claimed. But, he

wrote, the refugees were likely to win such an argument if the case went to a full trial. Evidence showed the school district had violated the Equal Educational Opportunities Act by requiring newly arrived immigrants to be relegated to Phoenix. His decision served as a sort of warning to the school district that if it pressed on, it would likely be defeated.

Smith said the refugees' attorneys fought the case on many fronts, but the issue boiled down to just two key questions. The first centered on whether a school district could deny an eligible child's enrollment because it believed he or she was unlikely to graduate before age twenty-one. The second hinged on whether the district had taken appropriate action to overcome the students' language barriers by diverting them to an alternative school where nearly all of their courses were taught in a language they couldn't understand.

The answer to both was no, the judge wrote, before unpacking his response.

Smith started by assessing the two schools at the heart of the case, the mainstream campus and the alternative program. "McCaskey is a credit to the state," he wrote, noting it had all the standard academic and extracurricular programs one might expect, plus an International School for older students just learning English. "Phoenix," he said, "is a little different."

Enrollment at the for-profit campus is generally a choice offered to students and their families, he said, but there was one group of prospective enrollees who were not offered an alternative: new arrivals to the district age seventeen and older who were under-credited. This rule of sending such students to the alternative campus applied even to those who did not speak English, meaning young immigrants were regularly placed in a program that covered material at twice the speed of the regular campus and almost always in a language they couldn't comprehend, Smith wrote. "On its face, this practice appears to be counterintuitive," he said. "Expert testimony confirmed that the practice was unsound."

Many such students graduated unable to speak English and, as a result, were unprepared for whatever might come next, he said. And the alternative school did not examine whether its practices were effective as they related to students like Khadidja and Mahamed. Although the raw data were available, the school district did not separate the test scores of the students assigned to the alternative campus so they could be compared to those at McCaskey, making it difficult to discern which served these students better. And none of the refugees were enrolled within five days of submitting their completed application as is mandated by state law, the judge said.

Smith went on to address what was once a concern of the greater Lancaster refugee community, whose elders feared that by filing the lawsuit, the students would appear to be asking for special treatment. "Before going any further, it is useful to identify what this case is not about," Smith wrote. "The plaintiffs are not seeking the creation of a new entitlement, or new and better schools."

What they're asking for, he said, is to be enrolled into a program that already exists, "and that is specifically designed for students with their unique language needs." And while Smith agreed with Superintendent Rau that federal judges should not design school curriculum, public education was bound by law, and it was the court's responsibility to decide whether the law was being followed, he wrote.

But perhaps the most profound of his conclusions came toward the end of his opinion when he said, "Denial of a free public education, either by refusing or delaying enrollment, is irreparable harm," meaning it was a type of damage that could not be undone by monetary compensation. The refugees had been denied a meaningful education, he wrote. Not even a later reinstatement in school could make up for the loss. And their placement at a campus that failed to overcome their language barriers was likely a violation of the Equal Education Opportunities Act, Smith found.

The students who testified in the case didn't immediately learn of the judge's ruling. Unable to be reached by phone, the two Burmese sisters had no idea they had won and showed up at Phoenix Academy on opening day. When they finally did hear of the decision, the refugees marveled at their own accomplishment.

· · · · · · · · · ·

But Smith's ruling marked only a limited victory. The ACLU and Education Law Center wanted a much broader group of students to be included under the umbrella of his decision: any immigrant within the district's boundaries who was between the ages of seventeen and twenty-one and who spoke limited English. But the judge's opinion was narrow in scope and applied only to the six refugees who filed the claim. He never decided on the class element of the case.

Smith suggested that all similar students be sent to McCaskey, but he didn't mandate the change. It was because of this that the district continued to send older, non-English-speaking students to Phoenix in the new school year, which began just days after he rendered his decision.

Nineteen-year-old Handja Elice, assigned to the campus after Smith's August ruling, was so ashamed to attend the alternative school she would rip off her school-issued shirt as soon as she left the grounds. Though she described Phoenix's teachers as friendly and accommodating, she quickly grew fearful of her fellow students. Just days into the new school year, after she accidentally sat in another girl's chair, Handja said the teen called her a "friggin' bitch" in a move that left her speechless. It was just not in her nature to push back, no matter how badly she was treated by her peers. "I'll never say anything," she said, sitting on her living room couch, eyes cast down at the floor.

Handja also was frustrated by the school's ban on backpacks and its no-homework policy—like the refugees who filed the lawsuit, she wanted to continue learning at home. She said, too, the food in the cafeteria sometimes made her sick, and that she wished she could bring lunch from home. But that was not permitted.

Handja said Phoenix's numerous rules made her feel as though the school didn't trust her. She was desperate to go to McCaskey and was confident she could graduate before aging out at twenty-one. "I need to get my diploma," she said. "I want to go to college next year."

The school district's decision to continue sending older immigrants to the alternative campus infuriated the refugees' attorneys. It was not in the spirit of the judge's opinion, they contended.

The district was equally incensed: The federal court had no right to override their judgment about where students should be placed, administrators believed. They filed an appeal almost immediately.

By that point, the case had cost the refugees' legal team more than $2 million. They simply had to win.

. . . .

Khadidja and Mahamed relished the opportunity for a fresh start at McCaskey. No longer subject to daily pat-downs, both felt far more at ease at their new campus. Mahamed described his teachers as welcoming and accessible. And his fellow students were far better behaved. "McCaskey is a good place to be," he said, a few weeks into the new school year. "They treat you like a human being. They respect you. If you don't understand, they'll help you."

Judge Smith's decision to allow the refugees to attend the mainstream campus had both practical and intangible benefits: Not only did it give Mahamed the education he felt he deserved, but it also helped him let go of the bitterness sparked by his initial rejection by the school district and his time at Phoenix. Finally, for the first time in months, and with his family's encouragement, he was optimistic, both about his future and about the nature of the place he now called home.

"This country stands for freedom," Mahamed said, sitting in his mother's living room one afternoon in the fall of 2016. "No one can tell me that I don't have the right to go to school. I do have that right."

Mahamed, who had essentially dropped out of Phoenix because of ongoing harassment and because he had trouble learning the curriculum, pledged to attend McCaskey until graduation. His attendance, though, was spotty. Mahamed was a looker who had no trouble attracting attention from the opposite sex. He sometimes found it difficult to peel himself away from his girlfriend long enough to attend school.

Khadidja was more focused. Though she had met many other refugees in Lancaster, including a handsome suitor a few years her senior who showed interest by helping her family with sundry tasks in an effort to win their favor, she had eyes for only her schoolwork. Love would have to wait. "I don't have time for anything like that," she said, waving her arms in front of her face and laughing away an inquiry about her dating life.

Khadidja's view on romance had changed dramatically since she arrived in the States. She was neutral on the topic of teen marriage when she first landed on American soil and remained so longer than any of her sisters. When Nouracham railed against the notion in an animated rant one fall afternoon about a year after the family's resettlement—"It's craaaazy!" she said, drawing out the word—Khadidja sat in an awkward silence. To condemn the practice was to condemn her mother, Mariam, the woman she loved and admired more than anyone. Mariam was married at age fourteen. Had her children remained in Sudan, they would likely have followed the same path.

It took Khadidja several months longer than her younger sisters, but she eventually came to see teen marriage as a tool of oppression against women and girls, one that quashed their ambitions and left them needlessly vulnerable. "This is America," Khadidja said one afternoon, more than a year after her arrival. "This is not Sudan. People don't do that here. Here, you go to college."

No matter the refugees' devotion to their education, both Khadidja and Mahamed struggled academically. By the time they were enrolled in Mc-Caskey, they had missed almost a full year of schooling because of delays followed by their months at Phoenix. And, like many young immigrants who come to the States unable to speak English, they rarely spoke up in class, self-conscious about how they might sound. A so-called silent year is common for students in their situation, but unfortunately, it would be extra costly for them: it took up much of their remaining time in the public school system and left them feeling uncertain about the future.

Khadidja had a tough time committing to summer school after her junior year, wondering if she should instead become a hotel maid so she could give her mother the money she needed to move the family to a better apartment in a safer part of town. Mahamed wrestled with similar problems. He worried not only about his family's immediate needs but also about his own life as he headed into adulthood. As a young man, he worried about his prospects. With little chance for a solid income, what could he offer a wife? "In the future, I will be single because I don't have money," he wrote in an end-of-year essay for school.

· · · · · · · · · ·

While the School District of Lancaster was at least partially, through Judge Smith's order, recommitting itself to young refugees, the Commonwealth of Pennsylvania and the nation as a whole were headed in the opposite direction.

Progressive hearts sank when the Keystone State's ballots were counted on the night of the 2016 presidential election, with Donald Trump receiving 44,292 more votes than Hillary Clinton, turning the recently blue state red.[1]

The nation, split in its ideology, refused the chance to elect its first female leader, a longtime public servant and former US senator who had recently come off a successful stint as secretary of state, in favor of a draft-dodging businessman and reality television star who had never held public office. Insecure about his victory because Clinton won the popular vote and angry at the lack of adulation from mainstream media, Trump spent the weeks after his election assailing news outlets and singling out individual reporters.

His hostility was boundless and soon focused on the American people themselves. When thousands of protesters gathered around the nation to show their disappointment with his election, he questioned the authenticity of their demonstrations, implying they'd been paid for their efforts.[2]

"Just had a very open and successful presidential election," he wrote on the social network Twitter on November 10. "Now professional protesters, incited by the media, are protesting. Very unfair!"[3]

Trump made headlines again on November 29 when he remarked on the long-settled issue of flag burning. The US Supreme Court ruled the practice "symbolic speech" protected by the First Amendment back in 1989, but the president-elect somehow wanted to undo the decision.[4] "Nobody should be allowed to burn the American flag—if they do, there must be consequences—perhaps loss of citizenship or year in jail."[5]

The idea of a president somehow upending the law was alarming to those who feared he'd do just that once in office, perhaps around other far more pressing issues like immigration. One of Trump's most ominous comments on the topic came a day earlier, after a vehicle-ramming and stabbing attack at Ohio State University in Columbus. The perpetrator in that case, Abdul Razak Ali Artan, was an eighteen-year-old transfer student whose family hailed from Somalia.[6] He, his mother, and several siblings arrived in the States as refugees in 2014.[7]

Authorities say Artan, who had frequently complained on social media about the mistreatment of Muslims around the world, might have been inspired by ISIS.[8] He was shot dead within minutes of the attack.

Trump, condemning the incident, wrote on social media that Artan should never have been admitted to the United States. "ISIS is taking credit for the terrible stabbing attack at Ohio State University by a Somali refugee who should not have been in our country," he wrote, seizing on the tragedy as a means to once again stoke fear of those seeking asylum here.[9] It seemed Muslim Americans would know no rest during his presidency.

CHAPTER 18

HIGHER GROUND

A TTORNEYS ON BOTH SIDES OF THE REFUGEE STUDENTS' LAWSUIT took a pummeling in front of the US Court of Appeals for the Third Circuit in Philadelphia on December 5, 2016.[1]

Sharon O'Donnell had stepped away from the suit as it moved through the appeals process. Thomas Specht, another lawyer from O'Donnell's firm, took her place. Specht graduated *magna cum laude* from the University of Scranton in 1993 and had been practicing law for twenty years when he was called upon to represent the school district in court. His tactic, it seemed, was to relitigate the case. Firmly but gently, he argued that the refugees received an adequate education at the alternative school.

But the three-judge panel was skeptical based on Judge Smith's earlier findings. Its questions flew through the air like BB pellets: Would Lancaster have treated English-speaking students the same way? What was the purpose of obtaining a degree if a student couldn't speak English? What was so magical about the age of seventeen, the school district's seemingly arbitrary cutoff age?

The panel told Specht he had a heavy burden in attempting to contradict evidence revealed at trial. The attorney conceded the point but insisted the district was working in the refugees' best interest in sending them to Phoenix Academy. The school board had already considered the issue, he said, implying it was its decision, not the court's, that mattered most.

Judge D. Michael Fisher agreed, but it didn't stop him from further examining the case. "I'm not unsympathetic to you being in front of us and saying the federal courts shouldn't be running the Lancaster school district," Fisher said, but the fact remained the court did not understand why Khadidja, Mahamed, and the others had been singled out.

Vic Walczak, representing the refugees, told the court Specht's job wasn't to reargue the case. Judge Smith had already decided the matter after five long days of trial, considering the testimony of more than a dozen witnesses and wading through more than two thousand pages of records in crafting his opinion.

Judge Cheryl Ann Krause didn't disagree but said it also wasn't the court's job to "second guess school districts' budgetary or educational policy decisions."

The hearing ended in less than an hour with no clear victor. Walczak worried about what he heard. "There were things they should easily have gotten that they didn't," he said of the panel.

. . . .

While the Lancaster case was at a standstill, the rest of the nation was moving forward under a new leader. Just days after taking office, Trump made good on his campaign promises to curtail legal and illegal immigration by signing a series of executive orders taking aim at refugees and the undocumented. Two such presidential decrees, signed by Trump on January 25, 2017, were said to be an effective means of curtailing immigrants' purported threat to national security.

"Transnational criminal organizations operate sophisticated drug- and human-trafficking networks and smuggling operations on both sides of the southern border, contributing to a significant increase in violent crime and United States deaths from dangerous drugs," read the document on border security and immigration enforcement. "Among those who illegally enter are those who seek to harm Americans through acts of terror or criminal conduct."[2]

The other order, focused on public safety, was even more direct in its demonization of the undocumented. "Many of these aliens are criminals who have served time in our Federal, State, and local jails," it read. "The presence of such individuals in the United States, and the practices of foreign nations that refuse the repatriation of their nationals, are contrary to the national interest."[3]

Taken together, the orders directed the secretary of Homeland Security to plan and erect a wall along the nation's southern border, build detention facilities to house the undocumented, hire thousands of additional Border Patrol agents, empower state and local law enforcement to act as immigration officers, punish sanctuary cities by withholding federal funds, and create and update a list of crimes committed by undocumented immigrants in sanctuary jurisdictions.

Within a month, children were being separated from their families at the border, though the public was not made aware of the practice until it was announced more than a year later. Even then, the start and end dates were unclear as officials issued contradictory statements on the matter. Secretary of Homeland Security John Kelly said in March 2017 his department was "considering" the practice, implying that it had not yet been implemented.[4] But Commander Jonathan White, who oversaw the care of minors for the Department of Health and Human Services, first noticed the phenomenon in February 2017, shortly after Trump took office.

White told Congress two years later that as soon as he learned of it, he warned his superiors about the psychological trauma it would cause children and about the strain it would put on the Office of Refugee Resettlement (ORR).[5] "Neither I nor any career person in ORR would ever have supported such a policy proposal," he said. Despite his warnings, the practice continued.[6] According to an announcement from the ACLU in October 2019, the Trump administration had taken some 5,500 migrant children from their families through the years, far more than officials had initially admitted.[7]

But the numbers were not reliable. The federal government, by its own admission, kept only scattered and incomplete records of the removals. The Department of Homeland Security "was not fully prepared to implement the Administration's Zero Tolerance Policy or to deal with some of its after-effects," according to a September 27, 2018, report from the Office of Inspector General. It also "struggled to identify, track, and reunify families" because of "limitations with its information technology systems."[8] According to the report, some parents didn't understand they would be separated from their children and were unable to communicate with them once they were taken.

The public also was not properly informed. It wasn't until May of 2018 that Attorney General Jeff Sessions announced the initiative, which many believed to be a new approach. "If you are smuggling a child then we will prosecute you, and that child will be separated from you as required by law," Sessions said at a law enforcement conference in Scottsdale, Arizona. "If you don't like that, then don't smuggle children over our border." Strangely, a month later, Homeland Security Secretary Kirstjen Nielsen contradicted him, writing on social media, "We do not have a policy of separating families at the border. Period."[9]

Prior to the policy's enactment, border patrol agents typically placed adult undocumented migrants in civil immigration proceedings without referring them for criminal prosecution. Children were removed only when their parent had a criminal history, outstanding warrant, or if authorities could not confirm their guardianship, according to the Office of Inspector General.[10] As a result, in most cases, families either remained together in detention centers while their civil immigration cases were pending or were released into the States with an order to appear in immigration court at a specified date.[11]

As stringent as Trump's executive orders seemed to immigration advocates, it was the next decree, issued January 27, 2017, that spawned protests across the country. The "Executive Order Protecting the Nation from Foreign Terrorist Entry into the United States" halted the admission of all refugees to the country for 120 days. It banned foreign nationals from seven predominantly Muslim countries—Iran, Iraq, Libya, Somalia, Sudan, Syria, and Yemen—from the States for ninety days and barred Syrian refugees from entering the country indefinitely. It portrayed legal immigrants as enemies of the state.

"Numerous foreign-born individuals have been convicted or implicated in terrorism-related crimes since September 11, 2001, including foreign nationals who entered the United States after receiving visitor, student, or employment visas, or who entered through the United States refugee resettlement program," it read, adding that deteriorating conditions in their home countries will only "increase the likelihood that terrorists will use any means possible to enter the United States."

The order didn't mention Sharia Law, but easily could have. "The United States cannot, and should not, admit those who do not support the Constitution, or those who would place violent ideologies over American law," it read. "In addition, the United States should not admit those who engage in acts of bigotry or hatred (including 'honor' killings, other forms of violence against women, or the persecution of those who practice religions different from their own) or those who would oppress Americans of any race, gender, or sexual orientation."[12]

The order left the nation in chaos as immigration attorneys scrambled to make sense of what it meant for the refugees already en route to the States, including those waiting inside the nation's airports.

The president did little to address their concerns. Trump defended the policy on social media, writing days later, "Everybody is arguing whether or not it is a BAN. Call it what you want, it is about keeping bad people (with bad intentions) out of country!"[13]

Anxiety had already permeated every facet of immigrant life in the run-up to the election. The orders made it worse. Fear ripped through the nation's public school system as foreign-born students worried what might happen to them or their families. "Some of the students are assuming that they're just going to be deported anyway and started to talk about how there's really no point in coming to school anymore," said a school principal from Brooklyn, New York. "It's a lot of lost potential."[14]

. . . .

The so-called Muslim ban sent shock waves throughout Lancaster. Immigrant advocates, including many former refugees, held an emergency meeting in a local church days after it was signed. Mustafa Nuur, the Somali refugee and activist who spent his spare time sharing his story with members of his community in effort to bridge the gap between the newcomers and their neighbors, helped organize the gathering. The first to arrive, he explained the order to heartsick friends.

"The whole refugee program is suspended," he told a man who inquired about the decree.

"Is that what they said?" he asked.

"The whole thing," Mustafa confirmed, shaking his head.

The attendees' worries were varied. What would happen to green card holders? What about those who had already been granted permission to come but had not yet arrived? Could the list of seven countries be expanded to include others? Perhaps their most pressing worry centered on the refugees who, like themselves, already lived in America. Could President Trump take his executive order a step further and call for their removal? Even after they won citizenship? The answers were unclear.

Advocates warned the decree might mean additional screening for refugees already in America, and no one knew what that might mean. Though they took comfort in one another's presence, the meeting did little to dispel the refugees' concerns.

"People don't know what to do," said a Sudanese refugee and community organizer who attended the gathering. But, the woman added, Americans' show of support through the airport protests were extraordinarily meaningful. "The people are feeling they are not alone," she said, pushing her headscarf away from her forehead. "They feel they are not strangers, that they are part of this country. It is very emotional for them to see other people fighting for them. This unity gives us hope that things will be better."

But the mood inside Khadidja's home was less optimistic. Her stepfather was still living in Sudan and it was unclear when he would be able to join the family. A paperwork glitch had kept him from accompanying them back in 2015 and the ban meant only more delays, more time for Khadidja's mother, Mariam, to fend for the family on her own.

The couple's separation tore at their relationship. "How can we stay together if he's not here?" Mariam wondered aloud at her kitchen table as she struggled to raise her family and pay her bills. "How long can I wait?"

. . . .

Sheila Mastropietro, head of Lancaster's own Church World Service, was sickened by the order. Tears don't come easily to her but the news kept her up at night. She worried about the refugees caught in limbo, including an elderly Russian couple whose trip to Lancaster was canceled because of the ban, and about the welfare of a newly arrived twenty-three-year-old Somali refugee who had cried continually upon learning her family would not be joining her. The young woman, who had never before lived alone, said she wanted to go back to Africa.

Mastropietro also was anxious about her office's finances. Church World Service and other organizations just like it are funded based on the number of newcomers they settle each year. A sharp drop meant her staff of thirty-eight was about to shrink for the first time. In the end, the United States would admit just 53,691 refugees in fiscal year 2017.[15] The figure was down significantly from 2016, when it hit nearly 85,000.[16]

Sitting at her desk in early 2017, Mastropietro pored over her expenses, trying to spare as many jobs as she could. "They're all good and well-trained people who want to be here," she said of her staff. But it was no matter. The cuts meant she would lose some of her most beloved employees, including a former refugee from Somalia. He'd lived in the States for nearly a decade. "He has six children," Mastropietro said wistfully. "Oh my gosh, he's such a good dad."

. . . .

Between the signing of the executive orders, the resulting decrease in new refugees admitted to the country, and the confusion sown in the United States and abroad regarding the status of asylum seekers, there seemed to be no good news for immigrants in the weeks after Trump took office.

Trump's top aides even searched for a means to give states authority to keep undocumented children from enrolling in the public school system. According to *Bloomberg News*, Stephen Miller, a senior adviser to the president, "had been a driving force behind the effort as early as 2017, pressing cabinet officials and members of the White House Domestic Policy Council repeatedly to devise a way to limit enrollment." Miller eventually gave up on the idea, believing it ran counter to the 1982 Supreme Court decision that granted these students access.[17]

Khadidja and Mahamed were slowly starting to understand the drama that had been unfolding in their new country for months. But they had an even more pressing concern: wondering whether they'd have a chance to pursue their education at McCaskey or if they would be yanked back to Phoenix.

Finally, on January 30, 2017, they had their answer: The appellate court stood firmly on their side. The three-judge panel agreed with the ACLU and the Education Law Center that the Lancaster students were denied equal educational opportunities. It was as validating a decision as they could have hoped for. The judges appreciated the immediacy of their situation and didn't want the refugees' education to be frittered away. "Time is of the essence: Their eligibility to attend public school in Pennsylvania is dwindling," they said, adding, "We recognize that a sound educational program has the power to 'change the trajectory of a child's life.'"

Khadidja, Mahamed, and the other plaintiffs learned of the decision through their attorneys and were elated by the ruling, though they did not fully understand its scope. They had no idea their case might one day serve as an example for others. "Finally, we did it," Khadidja said.

As for the school district, administrators vowed to take the case to a full trial, saying the courts had no right to interfere in their educational program. But after what amounted to two losses—one in Judge Smith's courtroom and another on appeal—its resolve was waning. Negotiations stalled at first, but in the end, the district settled.

According to the terms of the March 2017 agreement, the school district would no longer place new immigrants age seventeen to twenty with little to no English skills at the alternative campus. Instead, these students would be assigned to a Newcomer Program housed inside the district's main high school, McCaskey. The program would be a new and updated version of the International School and would separate the older students from their younger peers. While there, students would receive extensive language training, and only after becoming proficient in English would they be given the option to enroll in Phoenix. The settlement also meant that all immigrant students assigned to the alternative campus since Judge Smith's opinion was rendered in August 2016 would be offered the opportunity to transfer to McCaskey.

The district also agreed to pay $66,500 toward a fund that would be used to supplement the educational costs of refugees who were placed at the alternative campus in recent years—and to allow the ACLU and Education Law Center to monitor the district's compliance with the judges' orders.

Kristina Moon of the Education Law Center called the win a major coup. There are very few cases fought under the Equal Education Opportunities Act, she said, making the victory even more remarkable. "Having such a clear decision is a big win," she said. "And that win belongs to the students who were so resolute in their desire and passion to learn . . . and their bravery to stand up and say, 'I have this right also.'"

CHAPTER 19

A ROOM OF HER OWN

M ARIAM BASKED IN HER DAUGHTER'S VICTORY FOR MONTHS. BUT with the win behind them, it was once again time to search for a better place for the family to live. What she wanted more than anything was a well-kept three- or four-bedroom apartment with at least one and a half bathrooms. She prayed for rent lower than the $792 she was currently paying but knew it was impossible: That type of unit cost at least $1,000 a month. With just a few hundred dollars in savings, Mariam had no idea where she'd come up with the first month's rent, let alone the security deposit or moving costs.

Christine Baer, who had come to be the family's de facto case manager at Church World Service, told Mariam to lower her expectations. [1] "The second bathroom is not going to happen," said the normally exuberant Baer. But Mariam was undeterred and told friends she was looking. Finally, in the summer of 2017, an Iraqi refugee with whom she worked told her of a three-story apartment on a picturesque block in a far safer neighborhood that had just become available. It might even be within the family's price range, she said. Mariam could barely fathom the possibility but decided to visit the property anyway.

It was even better than she hoped. The block was beautiful; every unit had a small front garden full of colorful flowers. The front porches were neatly kept. The doors all bore welcome signs of one shape or another and neighbors seemed to know each other.

But it was the apartment itself that made Mariam gasp with delight. The front door opened to a spacious, well-kept living room that led to a similarly large dining area. The kitchen was nearly twice as big as the one in her current apartment and the landlord promised to install new cabinets for the next renters. The walls were recently painted, not spotless, but nearly so. The floors had no jagged edges and managed to meet the walls at every point.

Mariam couldn't help but picture how she and her family would make the apartment their own. She envisioned her two eldest daughters, Khadidja and Nouracham, sharing the cavernous, sun-drenched bedroom on the top floor. She imagined herself and her two youngest children, Rania and Howa, occupying the large master bedroom on the second floor. Her sons Ibrahim and Jalal would each have a room to themselves down the hall from their mother.

The apartment had an additional surprise, a tiny half bathroom on the first floor just off the kitchen. Mariam couldn't believe it. But she was even more taken aback when she heard what the landlord was asking: just $600 a month. Elated, she told Baer about the apartment right away. "Please tell me you didn't give them any money," Baer said, worried it was a scam. Mariam hadn't but was eager to sign the lease.

Mariam was so impressed with the unit's owner that she took a picture of him, just as she had come to do with all of the volunteers, caseworkers, and others who helped her and her family. She shared the photo with Baer and the caseworker was immediately relieved: She knew him. Though he was a web designer by trade, he was devoutly religious and bought the property not to turn a profit, but to help those in need. He reduced Mariam's rent to just $300 for the first month and required no security deposit.

Mustafa Nuur, the Somali refugee and activist, knew the property well. It was the first home he and his family shared when they moved to Lancaster. The owner was Mustafa's boss and had become a close friend. Mustafa and his family left the house only after they outgrew it and moved less than a block away. Several other refugee families also lived in the neighborhood, giving Mariam a built-in network. The apartment felt like an enormous gift.

Mariam woke up early on the morning of August 30, 2017, to stuff the last of her children's belongings into mismatched luggage and oversized black garbage bags. With no car or driver's license of her own, she relied on a friend to transport the family's belongings in his minivan. Though they had lived in the States for fewer than two years, Mariam and her children had amassed a trove of used clothing and furniture, enough to open a tiny secondhand store their friend teased.

The move was a success, but Mariam miscalculated her eldest daughters' interest in the top floor. It was hot and had no door, they said. Khadidja asked to move with Nouracham to the second floor and her mother agreed. But even that plan would change: Nouracham, who had reservations about living with her bossy older sister, moved to the attic with the rambunctious Rania. Finally, in her eighteenth year of life, Khadidja had a room of her own.

She would celebrate yet another milestone less than a year later when she and Mahamed graduated from McCaskey. The event was so momentous that Khadidja's mother bought her an ankle-length gown for the occasion and one for herself too, which she cinched with an elegant rhinestone belt, the kind a bride might wear on her wedding day.

Khadidja tucked her headscarf under her cap, adjusted the red and black tassel that hung at the right side of her face, and smiled graciously throughout the ceremony, even as the school superintendent, who fought hard against her in court, handed her her diploma. "I have waited so long for this day," Khadidja said minutes after she walked across the stage. "Now, it's finally here."

· · · · · · · · · ·

Much had changed since Khadidja and Mahamed left Phoenix Academy. Jacques Blackman, once Lancaster's gatekeeper of admissions for older immigrant students, retired in the summer of 2017. And just as district officials promised Judge Smith, pat-downs were discontinued at the alternative school. Students are permitted to bring backpacks to school; they are collected and stored during the day and returned at dismissal.

But not every vestige of the earlier era had been erased. Despite the claims made against Camelot Education in court, the school district renewed its contract with the for-profit at $4.4 million annually through June 2021. The partnership saves the district roughly $1 million per year and school officials say they are happy with the results. More than a thousand students have graduated from Phoenix under Camelot's stewardship, district officials said.

And some newcomer students, including refugees, have been placed at Phoenix. "Helping students earn a high school diploma is *the* core mission of any school district, including the School District of Lancaster," district administrators said. And the Handle With Care protocol also has remained in place, though Camelot officials say it is rarely used, implemented just a half a dozen times at Phoenix Academy since the 2015–2016 school year.

· · · · · · · · · ·

Sheila Mastropietro, head of Church World Service, saw her staff shrink from thirty-eight to thirty in Trump's first years in office. Her organization's annual funding was bound to shrivel under his immigration crackdown: it resettled just 160 refugees in 2018, down from 407 the year before. "It's been terrible," Mastropietro said. "Trump has meant only bad news." As she neared retirement, she worried the president was aiming to destroy the program entirely.

Mastropietro said her organization's relationship with the local school district had suffered as well. "They don't like us at all," she said. Teachers eager to bring Church World Service into their schools to talk about its work and outreach efforts are routinely rebuffed by district leadership, she said.

But, Mastropietro added, there was something to celebrate in Lancaster's new mayor, Danene Sorace, elected in 2018. Sorace, considered a friend to the immigrant community, prioritized the lifting up of one of the city's most impoverished regions that is home to many refugees and has partnered with Church World Service to provide translation services to newcomer families. The mayor also helped create a class for recent arrivals to learn how the city works and about their rights and responsibilities.

· · · · · · · · · ·

As for the attorneys who argued the Lancaster case, each has gone on to score subsequent victories. Vic Walczak of the ACLU reached a critical settlement with Pennsylvania's Department of Corrections in 2019, one that would drastically improve the lives of more than 130 people on death row. Eric Rothschild left Pepper Hamilton LLC in 2016 for Americans United for Separation of Church and State before moving on to the National Student Legal Defense Network, where he spends much of his time taking aim at for-profit colleges. He took a stunning pay cut to switch gears. "I miss having more money than less, but we are still among the lucky ones," he said of his family.

Attorneys with the Education Law Center, including Maura McInerney and Kristina Moon, made considerable progress in their yearslong battle for adequate and equitable school funding: They won a major victory in 2017 when Pennsylvania's Supreme Court ordered the Commonwealth Court to hold a trial to determine whether state officials violated the state's constitution by failing to supply poor communities with the money they needed. It was a big win for economically disadvantaged districts, including Lancaster's.

Sharon O'Donnell, who represented the district in court, successfully defended a Pennsylvania school district accused of discriminating against two Black female employees based on race and gender. "In my closing argument, I asked them [the jury] to send a message to the plaintiffs that only merit, and not entitlement, wins leadership positions," she said. "And they did."

Judge Smith continued to surprise those who believe they know how a staunch conservative might decide a controversial case. When three Boyertown, Pennsylvania, high school students and a recent graduate sought to challenge their local school district's policy of allowing transgender students to use the bathroom, locker room, and shower of their choice, Smith came down on the side of transgender youth. The plaintiffs had claimed their presence in these facilities caused "confusion, embarrassment, humiliation, and loss of dignity."[2] But Smith didn't buy it, saying they failed to make their case at every level.

· · · · · · · · · ·

On the national stage, Trump used his first pardon in office to keep former Maricopa County Sheriff Joe Arpaio out of prison.[3] Weeks later, on September 5, 2017, he announced he was "rescinding" DACA, the Obama-era Deferred Action for Childhood Arrivals program that shielded from deportation some eight hundred thousand people brought to the United States as children.[4] The Supreme Court ruled against the move in the summer of 2020 but the program's fate was not sealed in either direction.[5]

Betsy DeVos took her seat as the nation's new education secretary and stayed mostly silent on issues of immigration until May 2018, when she said schools and local communities could decide whether to alert authorities to undocumented students.[6] The deeply unpopular DeVos later attempted to walk back the comments but her intentions were clear. Two years later, when the COVID-19 pandemic rocked the globe, she exempted Dreamers from $6 billion in emergency relief funds for college students devastated by the economic impact of the virus.[7] More than 450,000 undocumented students were enrolled in the nation's colleges and universities at the time.[8]

In fiscal year 2017, which ended September 30, 2017, roughly 53,700 refugees were resettled in the United States, according to the Pew Research Center.[9] The number reflected the temporary freeze on admissions that so shook the nation, sparking pro-immigrant and refugee rallies around the country. Trump set a new limit of 45,000 refugees for the following year, though the US only admitted about 22,500, with stunning cuts in the admission of Muslim and Latin American people.[10] The figure included just 62 Syrians, despite their country's ongoing humanitarian crisis.

The president set the refugee ceiling at thirty thousand for the fiscal year that ended September 30, 2019, and refugee admissions reached this cap, Pew found.[11] Still the figure was minuscule compared to the need: Some 79.5 million people were forcibly displaced from their homes by the end of 2019. Forty percent were children.[12] Experts predict the need will only grow in the coming years. Latin America, sub-Saharan Africa, and South Asia are expected to generate up to 143 million more climate migrants by 2050, according to the World Bank.[13]

With the political turmoil in the United States, it's unclear to what extent the nation will help those most in need. The refugee cap reached the stunning low of eighteen thousand in 2020. Increased vetting and the global pandemic brought the number down further still: only about half that amount were admitted to the country by September 2020.[14] At the same time, the United States started turning minors away at the border, deporting those who already made it to the States, and pressuring families to give up their dreams of living in America or risk losing their children.[15] Months later, Trump announced the country would accept only fifteen thousand refugees for fiscal year 2021.[16]

The outlook was equally bleak for those seeking entry to America from the nation's southern border. The United States started turning away asylum seekers in 2018, forcing families to wait for admission in dangerous border towns, often on the bridges linking the two nations.[17] US Customs and Border Protection officials said their agency was at capacity and didn't have the personnel to manage the claims, "but given the empty waiting rooms we've routinely seen, this is difficult to believe," observed the ACLU.[18]

It was around this time that hate crime data showed a disturbing trend: according to the FBI, personal attacks motivated by bias or prejudice reached a sixteen-year high in 2018 and reflected a sharp uptick in violence against Latinos.[19]

The United States held nearly seventy thousand migrant children, including infants and toddlers, in government custody in 2019; that's more children detained away from their parents than in any other country, the UN found.[20] Six children died in Border Patrol care between September 2018 and May 2019, marking the first such deaths in a decade.[21] The migration crisis only worsened when Trump's "Remain in Mexico" policy took effect, stranding some sixty thousand asylum seekers on the Mexican side of the border.[22] Their condition has become so permanent, with many living in squalid refugee camps for more than a year, that schools have cropped up to serve children who would otherwise have nothing to fill their days and would fall only further behind educationally.[23]

· · · · · · · · · ·

Khadidja and Mahamed are glad to have made it to the United States before the door closed. Life for them has not always been easy: Not only did they have to fight for a chance to attend a high school that served their academic needs, but their paths to college also would prove circuitous. Still, as they and their families know, there is far more opportunity in America than in their home countries. And while each of them would love to return and throw their arms around the grandparents, aunts, uncles, and cousins they left behind, they are thankful for the life they've crafted in America.

"Here, it's much better than where we were living," Khadidja said, referring to both Sudan and Chad. It is easier to find work, she said, schooling is free, and families, no matter their wealth, have at least some access to health care. "There is no help over there," she said. "Life is very hard."

Mahamed and his family moved to Minnesota in the fall of 2019, and he soon began working full time at an Amazon processing center near Minneapolis. He was thrilled to bring home a steady paycheck. "It's a very good job," he said. "They treat me well."

Unfortunately, he said, college would have to wait. "Right now, I can't because we rent a house and rent is high," at $1,500 a month, he said. While he was still interested in becoming a mechanic and perhaps one day owning his own car repair shop, it just wasn't the time, he said.

Khadidja enrolled part time in community college after high school and also worked, first as a cook in a local retirement home. The job came with an unexpected benefit: it forced her to enunciate and project her voice for those who were hard of hearing, greatly improving her language skills.

She later served as a home health aide but dropped the work during the COVID-19 pandemic, fearful of contracting the illness. In the summer of 2020, when she was twenty-two, she married the man who had looked after her family since they arrived in the States. Loyal and loving, he reminded her of her father, Adam. "He cares for my family so much," she said. "He's very kind to my brothers and sisters."

Just as important, he supports her studies and looks forward to the day she becomes a nurse. Khadidja wouldn't have married him if he didn't. "Nothing will get in the way of my dreams," she said.

ACKNOWLEDGMENTS

S PECIAL THANKS TO KHADIDJA ISSA, MAHAMED HASSAN, AND THEIR families, who tolerated my constant prodding, and to Theodore "Teddy" and Brandy Griffiths, who gave me more than shelter in their friendship. Credit must also be given to Christopher Mele for his invaluable fact-checking and to Raquel Pidal for her outstanding copyediting. Hats off to Katy Nishimoto, who sold this book with her heart and soul, and to Beacon Press, who bought and nurtured it. Rachael Marks, you knew exactly when to rein me in and when to let me fly. I so appreciate your wonderful editing and positive spirit. Susan Lumenello, you made my work shine. Thanks, too, to the Spencer Foundation for investing in this project and to Columbia University for giving me the tools and knowledge to see it through. I'm forever indebted to professors LynNell Hancock, Dale Maharidge, and Samuel Freedman, who answered my book-related questions with remarkable speed even years after my fellowship ended. Thanks also to the Fund for Investigative Journalism, which awarded me a generous grant to help see this project through, and to Emily Richmond of the Education Writers Association, who helped with important ethical decisions about how the story should be told. And of course, I could not have done this without the support of many friends and mentors, including the phenom that is Dana Canedy and my beloved L. Renée, whose faith helped bring this work to fruition. Special credit goes to Orencu Liberman, for showing me all that is so beautiful in this world. And thanks to my mother, the unstoppable Mom Napolitano, who passed on to me her strong work ethic and passion for social justice—and who never failed to ask when the hell I would finish this book. My love to you all.

NOTES

INTRODUCTION

1. OECD, *A Broken Social Elevator? How to Promote Social Mobility* (Paris: OECD Publishing, 2018), https://doi.org/10.1787/9789264301085-en.

CHAPTER 1: THE LONGEST GOODBYES

1. *Trends in High School Dropout and Completion Rates in the United States: 2018: Compendium Report* (Washington, DC: National Center for Education Statistics, US Department of Education).

2. Jason M. Breslow, "By the Numbers: Dropping Out of High School," *Frontline*, September 21, 2012; Kayla Fontenot, Jessica Semega, and Melissa Kollar, "Income and Poverty in the United States: 2017," Table 3, US Department of Commerce, Economics and Statistics Administration, US Census Bureau, September 12, 2018; Bureau of Labor Statistics, US Department of Labor, *Economics Daily*, "Unemployment Rate 2.5 Percent for College Grads, 7.7 Percent for High School Dropouts," January 2017.

3. Andrew Sum, Ishwar Khatiwada, and Joseph McLaughlin, with Sheila Palma, *The Consequences of Dropping Out of High School: Joblessness and Jailing for High School Dropouts and the High Cost for Taxpayers* (Boston: Center for Labor Market Studies, Northeastern University, October 2009); Michael G. Vaughn, Christopher P. Salas-Wright, and Brandy R. Maynard, "Dropping Out of School and Chronic Disease in the United States," *Journal of Public Health* 22 (2014): 265–70.

4. Robert A. Hummer and Elaine M. Hernandez, "The Effect of Educational Attainment on Adult Mortality in the United States," *Population Reference Bureau* 68, no. 1 (June 2013).

5. Phoenix Academy, Home of the Firebirds, *2015–2016 Student Handbook*, Camelot Education, Exhibit 2 during the pre-trial hearing for *Issa v. School District of Lancaster*, trial dates August 16–22, 2016.

CHAPTER 2: A NEW WORLD

1. "Global Trends: Forced Displacement in 2015," UNHCR: The UN Refugee Agency, June 20, 2016.

2. "With 1 Human in Every 113 Affected, Forced Displacement Hits Record High," UNHCR: The UN Refugee Agency, June 20, 2016.

3. Jens Manuel Krogstad and Jynnah Radford, "Key Facts About Refugees to the U.S.," Fact Tank, Pew Research Center, January 30, 2017.

4. "Refugee Arrivals: Fiscal Years 1980 to 2015," US Department of Homeland Security, December 15, 2016.

5. Krogstad and Radford, "Key Facts About Refugees to the U.S."

6. "Refugee Arrivals: Fiscal Years 1980 to 2015."

7. Gardiner Harris, David E. Sanger, and David M. Herszenhorn, "Obama Increases Number of Syrian Refugees for U.S. Resettlement to 10,000," *New York Times*, September 10, 2015.

8. Arnie Seipel, "30 Governors Call for Halt to U.S. Resettlement of Syrian Refugees," NPR, November 17, 2015.

9. Manny Fernandez, "Federal Judge Tosses Texas' Lawsuit to Bar Syrian Refugees," *New York Times*, June 16, 2016.

10. Hannah Dreier, "A Betrayal: A Teenager Told Police All About His Gang, MS-13. In Return, He Was Slated for Deportation and Marked for Death," ProPublica, co-published with *New York Magazine*, April 2, 2018.

11. CNN Staff, "Which Countries Have the World's Highest Murder Rates? Honduras Tops the List," April 11, 2014.

12. Jacqueline Bhabha, "Opinion: We Can Do Better," *Harvard Magazine*, July 24, 2014.

13. "Fact Sheet: 27 Million Children out of School in Conflict Zones," UNICEF, April 24, 2017.

14. "Over 3.5 Million Refugee Children Miss Out on School, Report Finds," UNHCR: The UN Refugee Agency, September 12, 2017.

15. "Over 3.5 Million Refugee Children Miss Out on School, Report Finds."

16. Jo Napolitano, "Border School for Asylum Seekers Goes Virtual," The 74 Million, June 17, 2020.

17. "News Note: 25 Million Children out of School in Conflict Zones," UNICEF, April 24, 2017.

18. "Somalia Famine Killed Nearly 260,000 People, Half of Them Children," UN News Centre, May 2, 2013.

19. "NYCLU, LSCNY Sue Utica School District for Illegally Denying Refugee Youth an Education," ACLU, April 23, 2015.

20. "A.G. Schneiderman Files Civil Rights Lawsuit Against Utica City School District Regarding Enrollment Barriers Faced by Immigrant and Refugee Students," New York State Office of the Attorney General, November 18, 2015.

21. Hansi Lo Wong, "Refugees Say N.Y. School District Blocked Them from Going to High School," NPR, March 1, 2016.

22. Jeff Hawkes, "White House Honors Pedro Rivera, Lancaster School Superintendent," *Lancaster Online*, September 22, 2014.

CHAPTER 3: BEYOND THE HORSES

1. "Statistics: Tourism Works for Lancaster County," Discover Lancaster, n.d., https://www.discoverlancaster.com/advocacy/statistics.

2. John Hinshaw, "Dutchirican: The Growing Puerto Rican Presence in the Pennsylvania Dutch Country," *Pennsylvania Magazine of History and Biography* 140, no. 3 (2016): 365–92.

3. Laurence R. Stains, "The Latinization of Allentown, Pa.," *New York Times Magazine*, May 15, 1994.

4. Stains, "The Latinization of Allentown, Pa."

5. Hinshaw, "Dutchirican."

6. Tim Stuhldreher and Susan Baldrige, "Sanctuary City? No, but Lancaster Doesn't Actively Pursue the Undocumented, Either," *Lancaster Online*, November 28, 2016.

7. Rick Gray, author interview, December 7, 2016.

8. John Luciew, "KKK Flags Fly on Pa. Capitol Steps as Neo-Nazi Group Rallies and Counter-Protesters Rage," Pennsylvania Real-Time News, November 5, 2016; Peter Hall, "Feds: White Supremacist Group Discussed Bombing Pa. Capitol Rally," *Morning Call*, March 16, 2018.

9. "Five Men Associated with the Aryan Brotherhood Indicted for Illegal Possession and Transfer of Firearms and Conspiracy to Distribute Methamphetamine," Department of Justice, US Attorney's Office, Middle District of Pennsylvania, April 28, 2017.

10. "Harrisburg School District Used Illegal Admissions Policy to Deny Enrollment of Refugee Students," ACLU Pennsylvania, August 3, 2017.

11. Jack Brubaker, *Massacre of the Conestogas, On the Trail of the Paxton Boys in Lancaster County* (Charleston, SC: History Press, 2010), 19.

12. Jack Brubaker, author interview, February 26, 2019.

13. K. Scott Kreider, "New Historical Marker Honors Native Americans Massacred by Vigilante Group in Lancaster," *Lancaster Online*, September 22, 2015.

14. Lancaster Mayoral Forum, April 7, 2017.

15. Sheila Mastropietro, author interview, August 30, 2016.

CHAPTER 4: THE UNINVITED

1. Barack Obama, "Barack Obama's Remarks to the Democratic National Convention," *New York Times*, July 27, 2004.

2. Marie A. Failinger, "Islam in the Mind of American Courts: 1800 to 1960," *Boston College Journal of Law & Social Justice* 32, no. 1 (January 2012); Khaled A. Beydoun, "Viewpoint: Islamophobia Has a Long History in the U.S.," *BBC News Magazine*, September 29, 2015.

3. Swathi Shanmugasundaram, "Anti-Sharia Law Bills in the United States," Hatewatch, Southern Poverty Law Center, February 5, 2018.

4. "ACT for America," Southern Poverty Law Center, n.d.; Elsadig Elsheikh, Basima Sisemore, and Natalia Ramirez Lee, "Legalizing Othering: The United States of Islamophobia," Haas Institute for a Fair and Inclusive Society at UC Berkeley, September 2017.

5. George W. Bush, "Remarks by the President at Islamic Center of Washington D.C.," White House, online archives, September 17, 2001.

6. Brian H. Levin, "Responses to the Increase in Religious Hate Crimes," US Senate: Committee on the Judiciary, Center for the Study of Hate and Extremism, Department of Criminal Justice, California State University, San Bernardino, Washington, DC, May 2, 2017.

7. Greg Miller, "Senate's Iraq Probe to Include Bush, Aides," *Los Angeles Times*, February 13, 2004.

8. Glenn Kessler, "Trump's Repeated Claim That Obama Is Accepting 200,000 Syrian Refugees," *Washington Post*, October 8, 2015.

9. Jenna Johnson, "Donald Trump: Syrian Refugees Might Be a Terrorist Army in Disguise," *Washington Post*, September 30, 2015; Patrick Temple-West, "Trump Calls German Chancellor's Immigration Moves 'Insane,'" *Politico*, October 11, 2015.

10. "Donald Trump: I Would Send Syrian Refugees Home," BBC News, US & Canada, October 1, 2015.

11. Besheer Mohamed, "A New Estimate of the U.S. Muslim Population," Fact Tank, Pew Research Center, January 6, 2016.

12. Patrick Healy and Michael Barbaro, "Donald Trump Calls for Barring Muslims from Entering U.S.," *New York Times*, December 7, 2015.

13. Levin, "Responses to the Increase in Religious Hate Crimes."

14. Nick Gass, "Trump: 'Absolutely No Choice' but to Close Mosques," *Politico*, November 18, 2015; Trip Gabriel, "Donald Trump Says He'd 'Absolutely' Require Muslims to Register," *New York Times*, November 20, 2015; Ben Jacobs, "Donald Trump on Waterboarding: 'Even If It Doesn't Work They Deserve It,'" *Guardian*, November 23, 2015; David Mark and Jeremy Diamond, "Trump: 'I Want Surveillance of Certain Mosques,'" CNN, November 21, 2015; Healy and Barbaro, "Donald Trump Calls for Barring Muslims from Entering U.S."

15. "U.S. Resettles Fewer Refugees, Even as Global Number of Displaced People Grows," Pew Research Center, Global Attitudes & Trends, October 12, 2017.

16. "Children in U.S. Immigrant Families (By Age Group and State, 1990 versus 2019), Migration Policy Institute, n.d.

17. *English Language Learners in Public Schools* (Washington, DC: National Center for Education Statistics, May 2020).

18. *Washington Post* Staff, "Full Text: Donald Trump Announces a Presidential Bid," *Washington Post*, June 16, 2015.

19. "Rising Child Migration to the United States," Migration Policy Institute, n.d.; US Customs and Border Protection, "Southwest Border Unaccompanied Alien Children FY 2014," Department of Homeland Security, November 24, 2015.

20. Michael Martinez and Holly Yan, "Showdown: California Town Turns Away Buses of Detained Immigrants," CNN, July 3, 2014.

21. Matt Hansen and Mark Boster, "Protesters in Murrieta Block Detainees' Buses in Tense Standoff," *Los Angeles Times*, July 1, 2014.

22. John Blackstone, CBS Evening News, July 1, 2014.

23. "PV Schools Demographic Breakdown and Interesting Stats," Paradise Valley Unified School District website, 2019–20 demographics.

24. Louis Sahagun, "A Maverick Lays Down the Law," *Los Angeles Times*, August 9, 1994.

25. Arizona Senate Bill 1070, State of Arizona Senate, Forty-Ninth Legislature, Arizona State Legislature website (passed April 23, 2010).

26. Nicholas Riccardi, "Arizona Passes Strict Illegal Immigration Act," *Los Angeles Times*, April 13, 2010.

27. Beason-Hammon Alabama Taxpayer and Citizen Protection Act, Alabama House Bill 56, Alabama State Legislature, Legiscan (passed June 2, 2011).

28. "Preliminary Analysis of HB 56 'Alabama Taxpayer and Citizen Protection Act,'" ACLU, n.d.

29. Arizona Senate Bill 1070.

30. Stacy Teicher Khadaroo, "Alabama Immigration Law Leaves Schools Gripped by Uncertainty," *Christian Science Monitor*, September 30, 2011.

31. "Regents Adopt New Policies on Undocumented Students," University System of Georgia, October 13, 2010.

32. "Preliminary Analysis of South Carolina's Senate Bill 20," ACLU, n.d.

33. Jeremy Redmon, "Georgia Lawmakers Pass Illegal Immigration Crackdown," *Atlanta Journal Constitution*, April 15, 2011; Michael Puente, "Latino Group Joins Lawsuits against Indiana over Immigration Law," WBEZ News, December 22, 2011.

34. Tom Baxter, "Alabama's Immigration Disaster," Center for American Progress, February 15, 2012.

35. Daniel Trotta and Tom Bassing, "In Alabama, Strict Immigration Law Sows Discord," Reuters, May 30, 2012.

36. Ed Pilkington, "Alabama Immigration: Crops Rot as Workers Vanish to Avoid Crackdown," *Guardian*, October 14, 2011.

37. Samuel Addy and Ahmad Ijaz, "Preliminary Economic and Fiscal Impacts of the April 27, 2011 Tornadoes on Alabama," Culverhouse College of Commerce and Business Administration Center for Business and Economic Research, June 2011; Paul Reyes, "'It's Just Not Right': The Failures of Alabama's Self-Deportation Experiment," *Mother Jones*, March/April 2012.

38. Kent Faulk, "Alabama Church Leaders Filed Lawsuit to Stop State's New Immigration Law," AL.com, August 1, 2011.

39. Benjy Sarlin, "How America's Harshest Immigration Law Failed," MSNBC, December 16, 2013.

40. Crystal Bonvillian, "More Than 200 Hispanic Students Absent in Huntsville Following Immigration Law Ruling," AL.com, October 1, 2011.

41. Bonvillian, "More Than 200 Hispanic Students Absent in Huntsville Following Immigration Law Ruling."

42. Adam Liptak, "Blocking Parts of Arizona Law, Justices Allow Its Centerpiece," *New York Times*, June 25, 2012.

43. Jennifer Stults, author interview, July 13, 2019.

44. "Department of Justice Files Lawsuit in Arizona Against Maricopa County, Maricopa County Sheriff's Office, and Sheriff Joseph Arpaio," US Department of Justice, Office of Public Affairs, May 10, 2012.

45. Fernanda Santos, "Judge Finds Violations of Rights By Sheriff," *New York Times*, May 24, 2013.

46. Steve Almasy and Artemis Moshtaghian, "Sheriff Joe Arpaio, Three Others Found in Civil Contempt," CNN, May 15, 2016.

47. Jim Lee, author interview, May 29, 2020.

48. Rita Tantillo, author interview, June 25, 2019.

CHAPTER 5: HANDLE WITH CARE

1. Brian Wallace, "School District of Lancaster to Outsource Buehrle School," *Lancaster Online*, July 22, 2009.

2. Brian Wallace, "School District of Lancaster Cuts Proposed Tax Hike," *Lancaster Online*, February 17, 2010; Brian Wallace, "School District of Lancaster

Lays off 77 Employees as It Tries to Make up for Funding Cuts," *Lancaster Online,* June 13, 2011.

3. William Penn School District et al. v. Pennsylvania Department of Education et al., Pennsylvania Commonwealth Court, April 21, 2015.

4. "Analysis: Pennsylvania's 2011–12 Budget," Pennsylvania Budget and Policy Center, July 13, 2011.

5. Larry Cuban, "The Failures of For-Profit K–12 Schools," *Washington Post,* October 4, 2013.

6. Gary Miron and Charisse Gulosino, "Profiles of For-Profit and Nonprofit Education Management Organizations: Fourteenth Edition—2011–2012," National Education Policy Center, November 26, 2013.

7. "Our Schools: Overview," Camelot Education, n.d.

8. Brian Wallace, "School District of Lancaster to Vote Tuesday on Outsourcing Schools," *Lancaster Online,* May 16, 2011.

9. Jandy Rivera, author interview, July 17, 2019.

10. "Camelot Awarded Contract to Operate Alternative Education Programs for Lancaster School District," *Camelot News,* May 17, 2011.

11. Thomas C. Boysen Sr., *The Camelot Experience: Learning in a Safe Environment at Accelerated and Transitional Schools* (Camelot Board of Directors' Safety and Security Committee, August 22, 2017).

12. Phoenix Academy statement, September 1, 2020.

13. Lisa Gartner, "Pennsylvania Closes the Glen Mills Schools amid Child-Abuse Investigation," *Philadelphia Inquirer,* April 8, 2019.

14. Sarah Carr, Francesca Berardi, Zoe Kirsch, and Stephen Smiley, "That Place Was Like a Prison," *Slate,* March 8, 2017.

15. Carr, Berardi, Kirsch, and Smiley, "That Place Was Like a Prison."

16. Interviews and observations by author, August 29, 2016.

17. Arthur Abrom, email to Elise Chesson, April 15, 2016.

CHAPTER 6: NOT ON MY WATCH

1. Lorraine Fontaine, author interview, October 28, 2017.

2. Elise Chesson, author interview, April 8, 2017.

CHAPTER 7: BIG LEAGUES

1. Vic Walczak, author interview, March 24, 2017.

2. Eric Rothschild, author interview, April 30, 2017.

3. School officials later claimed the number of refugees they turned away or sent to Phoenix was fewer than fifty between 2013 and 2016.

4. Phillip Inman, "Social Mobility in Richest Countries 'Has Stalled Since 1990s,'" *Guardian,* June 15, 2018.

5. Class Action Complaint filed on behalf of six refugees against the School District of Lancaster, July 19, 2016.

6. Sharon O'Donnell, author interview, April 16, 2017.

7. Southern Poverty Law Center, "Florida County Denies Education to Immigrant Kids, Sparks SPLC Lawsuit," May 18, 2016, https://www.splcenter.org/news/2016/05/18/florida-county-denies-education-immigrant-kids-sparks-splc-lawsuit.

8. Maria Perez, "Lawsuit: Collier Schools Illegally Deny Immigrant Students Access to Education," *Naples Daily News*, May 18, 2016.

CHAPTER 8: NOT IN OUR NAMES

1. *Face the Nation* transcripts, December 6, 2015: Trump, Christie, Sanders.

2. Lauren Carroll and Louis Jacobson, "Trump Cites Shaky Survey in Call to Ban Muslims from Entering US," PolitiFact, December 9, 2015.

3. Dan Friedman, "Trump Cites 'Sickness' in Defense of Muslim Immigration Ban Proposal," *Washington Examiner*, December 13, 2015.

4. Theodore Schleifer, "Donald Trump: 'I Think Islam Hates Us,'" CNN, March 10, 2016.

5. Scott Stump, "Donald Trump: Brussels Is 'Catastrophic,' Waterboarding Paris Suspect 'Would Be Fine,'" *Today*, March 22, 2016.

6. Mustafa Nuur, author interview, January 31, 2017.

7. LNP + LancasterOnline, "Six refugees filed a class action lawsuit . . .," Facebook, July 19, 2016, https://www.facebook.com/LancasterOnline/posts /10153802306016395.

8. "Dadaab—World's Biggest Refugee Camp 20 Years Old," UNHRC: The UN Refugee Agency, February 21, 2012.

CHAPTER 9: THIS LAND IS YOUR LAND

1. "U.S. Immigrant Population and Share over Time, 1850–Present," Migration Policy Institute, n.d.

2. Jie Zong, Jeanne Batalova, and Jeffrey Hallock, "Frequently Requested Statistics on Immigrants and Immigration in the United States in 2016," Migration Policy Institute, February 8, 2018.

3. "Refugee Trauma," National Child Traumatic Stress Network, n.d.

4. Amelia Hererra, author interview, September 4, 2019.

5. Michael M. Grynbaum and Sharon Otterman, "New York City Adds 2 Muslim Holy Days to Public School Calendar," *New York Times*, March 4, 2015.

6. Barbara Marler, author interview, September 10, 2019.

7. Office of Refugee Resettlement, "Unaccompanied Alien Children Frequently Asked Questions," US Department of Health and Human Services, July 9, 2018.

8. Author interview with middle school English teacher, Brownsville, Texas, June 29, 2018.

9. Veronica Calderon Speed, author interview, September 7, 2019.

10. Catherine E. Shoichet and Dr. Edith Bracho-Sanchez, "These Doctors Risked Their Careers to Expose the Dangers Children Face in Immigrant Family Detention," CNN, May 23, 2019.

11. Matthew Haag, "Thousands of Immigrant Children Said They Were Sexually Abused in U.S. Detention Centers, Report Says," *New York Times*, February 27, 2019.

12. Caitlin Owens, Stef W. Kight, and Harry Stevens, "Thousands of Migrant Youth Allegedly Suffered Sexual Abuse in U.S. Custody," *Axios*, February 26, 2019.

13. Samantha Schmidt, "Trump Administration Must Stop Giving Psychotropic Drugs to Migrant Children Without Consent, Judge Rules," *Washington Post*,

July 31, 2018; Garance Burke and Martha Mendoza, "AP Investigation: Deported Parents May Lose Kids to Adoption," Associated Press, October 9, 2018.

14. Transactional Records Access Clearinghouse, "Representation for Unaccompanied Children in Immigration Court," TRAC Immigration, October 31, 2014.

15. Christina Jewett and Shefali Luthra, "Immigrant Toddlers Ordered to Appear in Court Alone," *Texas Tribune*, June 27, 2018.

16. Transactional Records Access Clearinghouse, "Representation for Unaccompanied Children in Immigration Court."

17. Jerry Markon, "Can a 3-Year-Old Represent Herself in Immigration Court? This Judge Thinks So," *Washington Post*, March 5, 2016.

18. Letter by child and immigration advocates to Attorney General Loretta E. Lynch, April 29, 2016, https://ylc.org/wp-content/uploads/2018/11/Letter-to-AG-Lynch-re-counsel-for-immigrant-youth-4.29.16.pdf.

19. Human Rights Watch, "US: Surge in Detention of Child Migrants," HRW.org, June 25, 2014.

20. Nicole Austin-Hillery and Clara Long, "We Went to a US Border Detention Center for Children. What We Saw Was Awful," Human Rights Watch, January 24, 2019.

21. Staff Report, *Protecting Unaccompanied Alien Children from Trafficking and Other Abuses: The Role of the Office of Refugee Resettlement* (Washington, DC: US Senate Permanent Subcommittee on Investigations, Committee on Homeland Security and Government Affairs, 2016), 25.

22. "Leader of Human Trafficking Organization Sentenced to over 15 Years for Exploiting Guatemalan Migrants at Ohio Egg Farms," US Department of Justice, Office of Public Affairs, June 27, 2016.

23. Molly Hennessy-Fiske, "Is Ohio Case of Migrant Youth Trafficking Evidence of a 'Systemic Problem'?," *Los Angeles Times*, November 15, 2015.

24. Associated Press, "Haphazard Government Care Left Migrant Children Vulnerable to Human Trafficking, Senators Say," *Los Angeles Times*, January 28, 2016.

25. Emmarie Huetteman, "U.S. Placed Immigrant Children with Traffickers, Report Says," *New York Times*, January 28, 2016.

26. John Portman, "Adequacy of Department of Health and Human Services' Efforts to Protect Unaccompanied Alien Children From Human Trafficking," US Senate Permanent Subcommittee on Investigations, Committee of Homeland Security and Governmental Affairs, January 28, 2016.

27. Staff Report, *Protecting Unaccompanied Alien Children from Trafficking and Other Abuses*, 32.

28. Mary Clare Jalonick and Garance Burke, "U.S. Placement Program Failed to Protect Child Migrants from Trafficking, Senate Panel Says," *NewsHour*, PBS, January 29, 2016.

29. Kiara Alvarez and Margarita Alegría, "Understanding and Addressing the Needs of Unaccompanied Immigrant Minors," CYF News, American Psychological Association, June 2016.

30. Lorna Collier, "Helping Immigrant Children Heal," *Monitor on Psychology* 46, no. 3 (March 2015): 58.

31. Jerome J. Schultz, author interview, September 24, 2019.

CHAPTER 10: UNDACAMENTED

1. Jeffrey S. Passel and D'Vera Cohn, "Children of Unauthorized Immigrants Represent Rising Share of K–12 Students," Pew Research Center, November 17, 2016.

2. Herlinda, author interview, October 9, 2019.

3. Tal Kopan, "Trump Ends DACA but Gives Congress Window to Save It," CNN, September 5, 2017.

4. Author interview with former Bronx middle school principal, September 8, 2019.

5. Julie Ball, "Buncombe Schools' Newcomer Center to Close," *Citizen Times*, April 30, 2015.

6. Julie Lutz, author interview, September 16, 2019.

7. "Unaccompanied Alien Children Released to Sponsors By State," Department of Health and Human Services, September 27, 2019.

8. Victor Manuel Ramos, "Unaccompanied Minors on Long Island: Everything You Need to Know," *Newsday*, September 15, 2017.

9. "Hempstead High School Graduation Rate 4-Year Outcome as of June," New York State Education Department, n.d.

10. Jo Napolitano, "Hempstead on Deadline," *Newsday*, November 12, 2014.

11. Napolitano, "Hempstead on Deadline."

12. US Department of Education, "Resource Guide: Supporting Undocumented Youth," October 20, 2015.

13. Robert T. Teranishi, Carola Suárez-Orozco, and Marcelo Suárez-Orozco, "In the Shadows of the Ivory Tower: Undocumented Undergraduates and the Liminal State of Immigration Reform," UndocuScholars Project, Institute for Immigration, Globalization, and Education, University of California, Los Angeles, 2015.

14. Teranishi et al., "In the Shadows of the Ivory Tower."

15. Teranishi et al., "In the Shadows of the Ivory Tower."

16. Jeffrey S. Passel and D'Vera Cohn, "Children of Unauthorized Immigrants Represent Rising Share of K–12 Students."

17. Sunil Samuel, author interview, October 17, 2019.

18. Marisa, author interview, October 10, 2019; Teranishi et al., "In the Shadows of the Ivory Tower."

19. Nate Cohn, "The State of the Clinton-Trump Race: Is It Over?" *New York Times*, August 15, 2016.

20. Donald Trump, "Full Text: Donald Trump's Speech on Fighting Terrorism," *Politico*, August 15, 2016.

21. Donald J. Trump (@realDonaldTrump), "CLINTON REFUGEE PLAN . . .," Twitter, August 15, 2016, 4:26 p.m., https://twitter.com/realdonaldtrump/status /765283490887790592?lang=en.

22. Julie Hirschfeld Davis and Somini Sengupta, "Trump Administration Rejects Study Showing Positive Impact of Refugees," *New York Times*, September 18, 2017.

CHAPTER 11: OPENING ARGUMENTS

1. All the material for the case quoted in chapters 11 through 17 comes from court transcripts and direct observation from inside the courtroom for both the federal pretrial hearing and the appellate court hearing. Khadidja Issa; Q.M.H.,

a minor, individually, by and through his parent, Faisa Ahmed Abdalla; Alembe Dunia; Anyemu Dunia; V.N.L., a minor, individually, by and through her parent, Mar Ki; Sui Hnem Sung; and all others similarly situated v. The School District of Lancaster, 5:16-cv-03881-EGS (filed in the US District Court for the Eastern District of Pennsylvania, July 19, 2016).

2. Phoenix Academy administrators said in a statement issued September 1, 2020, that they resented comparisons that likened their school's appearance to that of a prison, saying the building previously housed a Boys and Girls Club. "We take offense to the implication that Phoenix Academy is anything other than an accredited, respectable education institution," they wrote.

3. Wayne E. Wright, "Landmark Court Rulings Regarding English Language Learners," Colorín Colorado, n.d.

CHAPTER 14: TOUGH CROWD
    1. Phoenix Academy statement, September 1, 2020.
    2. Phoenix Academy statement, September 1, 2020.

CHAPTER 15: DISCONNECTED
    1. John B. King Jr., "Letter to Chief State School Officers and Superintendents about School Resource Officers and School Discipline," US Department of Education, September 8, 2016.
    2. Maya Riser-Kositsky, "Education Statistics: Facts About American Schools," *Education Week*, January 3, 2019; "Frequently Asked Questions," National Association of School Resource Officers, n.d.

CHAPTER 16: A MISSED OPPORTUNITY
    1. Phoenix Academy statement, September 1, 2020.

CHAPTER 17: GRANTED
    1. Staff, "Pennsylvania Presidential Race Results: Donald J. Trump Wins," *New York Times*, August 1, 2017 (Pennsylvania voted Democrat in the six presidential elections leading up to 2016).
    2. Reuters/AP, "Protests Across US After Donald Trump Elected President—Video," *Guardian*, November 10, 2016.
    3. Donald J. Trump (@realDonaldTrump), "Just had a very open . . .," Twitter, November 10, 2016, https://twitter.com/realdonaldtrump/status/796900183955095552?lang=en.
    4. "Facts and Case Summary: Texas v. Johnson," United States Courts website, n.d.
    5. Donald J. Trump (@realDonaldTrump), "Nobody should be allowed. . .," Twitter, November 29, 2016, 6:55 a.m., https://twitter.com/realDonaldTrump/status/803567993036754944.
    6. Darran Simon, "Ohio State Attacker Said He Was 'Scared' to Pray in Public," CNN, November 29, 2016.
    7. Pete Williams, Tom Winter, Andrew Blankstein, and Tracy Connor, "Suspect Identified in Ohio State Attack as Abdul Razak Ali Artan," CNN, November 28, 2016.

8. Max Blau, Emanuella Grinberg, and Shimon Prokupecz, "Investigators Believe Ohio State Attacker Was Inspired by ISIS," CNN, November 29, 2016.

9. Donald J. Trump (@realDonaldTrump), "ISIS is taking credit . . .," Twitter, November 30, 2016, 6:20 a.m., https://twitter.com/realDonaldTrump/status /803921522784092160.

CHAPTER 18: HIGHER GROUND

1. All the material for the case quoted in chapter 18 comes from court transcripts and direct observation from inside the courtroom for the appellate court hearing. Khadidja Issa, et al. v. School District of Lancaster, 5-16-cv-03881, US Court of Appeals for the Third Circuit (argued December 5, 2016).

2. Donald J. Trump, "Executive Order: Border Security and Immigration Enforcement Improvements," White House website, January 25, 2017.

3. Donald J. Trump, "Executive Order: Enhancing Public Safety in the Interior of the United States," White House website, January 25, 2017.

4. Daniella Diaz, "Kelly: DHS Is Considering Separating Undocumented Children from Their Parents at the Border," CNN, March 7, 2017.

5. Alan Gomez, "Democrats Grill Trump Administration Officials over Family Separation Policy on the Border," USA Today, February 7, 2019.

6. John Washington, "The Government Has Taken at Least 1,100 Children from Their Parents Since Family Separations Officially Ended," Intercept, December 9, 2019.

7. Jasmine Aguilera, "Here's What to Know About the Status of Family Separation at the U.S. Border, Which Isn't Nearly Over," Time, October 25, 2019.

8. Office of Inspector General, "Special Review—Initial Observations Regarding Family Separation Issues Under the Zero Tolerance Policy," US Department of Homeland Security, September 27, 2018.

9. Kirstjen M. Nielsen (@secNielsen), "We do not have a policy . . .," Twitter, June 17, 2018, 5:52 p.m., https://twitter.com/SecNielsen/status/1008467414235992069.

10. Office of Inspector General, "Special Review—Initial Observations Regarding Family Separation Issues Under the Zero Tolerance Policy."

11. Office of Inspector General, "Special Review—Initial Observations Regarding Family Separation Issues Under the Zero Tolerance Policy."

12. "Executive Order Protecting the Nation from Foreign Terrorist Entry into the United States," Whitehouse.gov, January 27, 2017.

13. Donald J. Trump (@realDonaldTrump), "Everybody is arguing . . .," Twitter, February 1, 2017, 7:50 a.m., https://twitter.com/realDonaldTrump/status /826774668245946368.

14. Corey Mitchell and Francisco Vara-Orta, "Trump Orders on Immigration Rattle Some Educators," Education Week, February 3, 2017.

15. "Table 13. Refugee Arrivals: Fiscal Years 1980 to 2017," US Department of Homeland Security, April 1, 2019.

16. Nadwa Mossad and Ryan Baugh, Refugees and Asylees: 2016; Annual Flow Report (Washington, DC: Office of Immigration Statistics, US Department of Homeland Security, January 2018).

17. Jennifer Jacobs and Justin Sink, "White House Looked into Ways to Block Migrant Children from Going to School," Bloomberg, August 17, 2019.

CHAPTER 19: A ROOM OF HER OWN

1. Christine Baer, author interview, August 30, 2017.

2. Judge Edward G. Smith, memorandum opinion, August 25, 2017, Joel Doe, a minor, by and through his guardians, John Doe and Jane Doe; Mary Smith; Jack Jones, a minor, by and through his parents, John Jones and Jane Jones; and Macy Roe vs. Boyertown Area School District; Dr. Richard Faidley, in his official capacity as superintendent of the Boyertown Area School District; Dr. Brett Cooper, in his official capacity as principal; and Dr. E. Wayne Foley, in his official capacity as assistant principal and Pennsylvania Youth Congress Foundation, Intervenor-Defendant, 5:17-cv-01249-EGS (US District Court for the Eastern District of Pennsylvania).

3. Kevin Liptak, Daniella Diaz, and Sophie Tatum, "Trump Pardons Former Sheriff Joe Arpaio," CNN, August 27, 2017.

4. Michael D. Shear and Julie Hirschfeld Davis, "Trump Moves to End DACA and Calls on Congress to Act," *New York Times*, September 5, 2017.

5. Robert Barnes, "Supreme Court Blocks Trump's Bid to End DACA, a Win for Undocumented 'Dreamers,'" *Washington Post*, June 18, 2020.

6. Maureen Downey, "Betsy DeVos: Up to Schools Whether to Report Undocumented Students," *Atlanta Journal Constitution*, May 23, 2018.

7. Erica L. Green, "DeVos Excludes 'Dreamers' From Coronavirus College Relief," *New York Times*, April 22, 2020.

8. "New Report: More Than 450,000 Undocumented Students Enrolled in Colleges & Universities in United States," Presidents' Alliance on Higher Education and Immigration, April 15, 2020.

9. Jens Manuel Krogstad, "Key Facts About Refugees to the U.S.," Fact Tank, Pew Research Center, October 7, 2019.

10. Deborah Amos, "2018 Was a Year of Drastic Cuts to U.S. Refugee Admissions," NPR, December 27, 2018.

11. Krogstad, "Key Facts About Refugees to the U.S."

12. "Figures at a Glance," UNHCR: The UN Refugee Agency, June 18, 2020.

13. Kanta Kumari Rigaud, Alex de Sherbinin, Bryan Jones, Jonas Bergmann, Viviane Clement, Kayly Ober, Jacob Schewe, Susana Adamo, Brent McCusker, Silke Heuser, and Amelia Midgley, "Groundswell: Preparing for Internal Climate Migration," World Bank, 2018.

14. Ted Hesson and Mica Rosenberg, "Exclusive: Trump Administration Considers Postponing Refugee Admissions, U.S. Official Says," Reuters, September 10, 2020.

15. Lauren Villagran, "Despite Coronavirus, Children Are Still Arriving at the Border. They're Being Turned Away," *El Paso Times*, June 10, 2020; Caitlin Dickerson, "10 Years Old, Tearful and Confused After a Sudden Deportation," *New York Times*, May 21, 2020; Molly O'Toole, "Family Separation Returns Under Cover of the Coronavirus," *Los Angeles Times*, May 27, 2020.

16. Zolan Kanno-Youngs and Michael D. Shear, "Trump Virtually Cuts Off Refugees as He Unleashes a Tirade on Immigrants," *New York Times*, October 1, 2020.

17. Neena Satija, "The Trump Administration Is Not Keeping Its Promises to Asylum Seekers Who Come to Ports of Entry," *Texas Tribune and Reveal*, July 5,

2018; Shaw Drake and Edgar Saldivar, "Trump Administration Is Illegally Turn-ing Away Asylum Seekers," ACLU.org, October 30, 2018.

18. Shaw Drake, policy counsel, ACLU Border Rights Center, and Edgar Saldivar, senior staff attorney, ACLU of Texas, "Trump Administration Is Illegally Turning Away Asylum Seekers," ACLU, October 30, 2018.

19. Adeel Hassan, "Hate-Crime Violence Hits 16-Year High, F.B.I. Reports," *New York Times*, November 12, 2019.

20. Christopher Sherman, Martha Mendoza, and Garance Burke, "US Held Nearly 70,000 Migrant Kids in Custody in 2019," Associated Press, November 12, 2019.

21. Robert Moore, "Six Children Died in Border Patrol Care. Democrats in Congress Want to Know Why," ProPublica, January 13, 2020.

22. Adam Liptak and Zolan Kanno-Youngs, "Supreme Court Revives 'Remain in Mexico' Policy for Asylum Seekers," *New York Times*, March 11, 2020.

23. Jo Napolitano, "A Border School for Asylum Seekers Goes Virtual," The 74 Million, June 17, 2020.